In Between Worlds

Ayda Önder

In Between Worlds

Memory, Belonging and Quest for the Self in Contemporary Black British Women's Autofiction

Berlin · Bruxelles · Chennai · Lausanne · New York · Oxford

Library of Congress Cataloging-in-Publication
A CIP catalog record for this book has been
applied for at the Library of Congress.

Bibliographic Information published by the Deutsche Nationalbibliothek
The Deutsche Nationalbibliothek lists this publication in
the Deutsche Nationalbibliografie; detailed bibliographic
data is available in the internet at http://dnb.d-nb.de.

Cover image © Shutterstock

ISBN 978-3-631-91585-1 (Print)
E-ISBN 978-3-631-93137-0 (E-PDF)
E-ISBN 978-3-631-93138-7 (E-PUB)
DOI 10.3726/b22595

© 2025 Peter Lang Group AG, Lausanne
Published by Peter Lang GmbH, Berlin, Germany

info@peterlang.com - www.peterlang.com

All rights reserved.

All parts of this publication are protected by copyright.
Any utilization outside the strict limits of the copyright law, without the
permission of the publisher, is forbidden and liable to prosecution.
This applies in particular to reproductions, translations, microfilming,
and storage and processing in electronic retrieval systems.

This publication has been peer reviewed.

Table of Contents

Preface 7

Acknowledgements 9

Introduction 11

Chapter 1 Development of Autofiction as an In-between Genre 17
           Historical Overview of Autofiction in the Continent 17
           Autofiction in the Anglophone Context 41

Chapter 2 Theoretical Contexts 55
           Autofiction within Literary Theory 55
           Conceptual Framework 71
           Autoethnography and Postcolonial Theory 81

Chapter 3 Multiethnicity as an In-between Cultural Position 87
           Conceptualisation of Multiethnicity 87
           Autotheory and Multiethnicity 97
           Autofiction/Autoethnography by Multi-ethnic Black British
           Women Authors 110

Chapter 4 Charlotte Williams's *Sugar and Slate* (2002) 117
           Entwinement of Individual and Collective Memories 119
           "Travelling Across Worlds of Thinking" 128
           Blurring of the Borders Around Britishness, Welshness and
           Blackness 132
           "Sugar and Slate": Entangled Histories of the West Indies and
           Wales 137

Chapter 5 Jackie Kay's *Red Dust Road* (2010) 143
   Story of Adoption and Dual Heritage Interwoven with Fantasy .. 146
   "Red Dust Road": Journey to the Interior 151
   Dislocation from Personal and National Home 154
   "Nature or Nurture": Possibility of an Afro-Scottish Identity 160

Chapter 6 Bernardine Evaristo's *Lara* (1997/2009) 165
   History of the Self Knitted with "Untold" Stories of Ancestors .. 169
   "Family Is Like Water": Crossing the Waters 174
   "Where Are You from Originally?": Myth of "Purity" 177
   Transnational/Transcultural Reformulation of Cultural Identity ... 182

Conclusion 189

References 197

Preface

This book is based on the author's doctoral dissertation of the same title. It examines the development of autofiction along with the other directions it has led to such as autoethnography and autotheory, and explores their textual potentialities to reproduce the underrepresented realities of multi-ethnicity. In contradistinction to the white heterosexual male subject of traditional autobiography, the project is concerned with the ways in which these mixed literary novelties permit racialised and gendered individuals to resist the dominant systems of representation and to depict their multi-layered subjectivities and existence outside normative definitions. Although the book claims to focus specifically on works by the authors who are grouped under the label "Black British women", it seeks to demonstrate ineffectiveness of homogenising categories of identification by offering a comparative analysis of Welsh-Guyanese Charlotte Williams's *Sugar and Slate* (2002), Scottish-Nigerian Jackie Kay's *Red Dust Road* (2010), and English-Nigerian Bernardine Evaristo's *Lara* (1997/2009). These mixed-descent authors' portrayals of the diversity of their ethnic backgrounds and uniqueness of their life journeys evidence that there is not a single way of being "British", "black" or "woman". The contention of the book is that hybridity and in-betweenness of autofiction mirror the multi-ethnic feeling of being caught between different cultural worlds, and its ambivalence within literary categorisation provides spaces of inclusion for individuals whose multiple ethnicities transcend the strict borders of pre-existing racial, national, ethnic and cultural classifications. It is further argued that autoethnography enables these authors to imagine their personal worlds as intricately connected to multiple collective worlds, and to assert interconnectivity of cultures and societies, which disrupts the hegemonic divisions between Europeanness and Africanness. The book is structured around the contemporary perspectives on the concepts of memory, belonging and subjectivity, which are argued to be relevant to the main assumptions of both autofiction and multiethnicity.

Acknowledgements

This book is a revised version of my doctoral dissertation. In this regard, I am deeply grateful to my Ph.D. supervising committee for their invaluable guidance. I owe a special debt to my chair, Prof. Dr. Charles Daniel Sabatos, whose course on autofiction provided the initial inspiration for this work. His expertise, mentorship, and unwavering support have been instrumental in shaping its arguments and sustaining my motivation throughout the process.

I also extend my sincere appreciation to Assoc. Prof. Dr. Catherine MacMillan and Assoc. Prof. Dr. Sercan Hamza Bağlama for their insightful feedback, which has significantly enriched the depth and scope of this book. Working with them has been both a privilege and a source of immense professional growth.

I am further indebted to Prof. Dr. Adriana Luminita Raducanu, Prof. Dr. Mehmet Oğuz Cebeci, and Asst. Prof. Dr. Nina Cemiloğlu of Yeditepe University for equipping me with the academic foundation necessary for this research. My colleagues at Istanbul Arel University have also been a source of support and encouragement, for which I am sincerely thankful.

Finally, my deepest gratitude goes to my family and friends. Their unwavering love and support have been my greatest strength.

Introduction

One of the most remarkable trends in contemporary literature is the merging of fiction with autobiography. In today's cultural world, the truth claims of nonfiction are seen as based on the misconception that the reality can be unproblematically represented in an objective way. Identically, fiction appears to have lost its appeal among many writers and readers due to its perceived disconnectedness from reality and artificiality. As a result, the traditional distinction between fact and fiction loses its significance and functionality, giving rise to tendencies to experiment with the possibilities that emerge from amalgamation of factual and fictional forms and elements. In this cultural context, autofiction originates as a mode of self-narration that deliberately blurs the boundaries between referentiality of embodied experience and imagination. It is a hybrid genre which combines components of autobiography and fiction. Autofiction's positioning between these two traditional genres is both a response and reaction to the assumptions of recent literary theories. In line with poststructuralist thinking, autofiction acknowledges the incompetence of language to represent the reality and constructedness of any narrative, and yet it is not so distrustful of the possibility of "truth". Grounded on the psychoanalytic approaches, autofiction claims that using language to engage with the unconscious contents and mysteries of mind can yield valuable and highly subjective meanings of self and life. Autofiction proposes that generic undecidability provides an opportunity to create a more credible representation of reality and existence with all their complexities and ambiguities. As postmodernist approaches offer pluralistic perspectives on subjectivity, space and literature, autofiction claims to embody multiplicities and to occupy a plural position between factual and fictional realms, which can be reconsidered in relation to the postulations of contemporary theories of multiethnicity.

This book aims to investigate the development of autofiction along with the other directions it has led to such as autoethnography and autotheory, and its relevance to the concepts of memory, belonging and subjectivity in general, and particularly in the selected works of contemporary multi-ethnic Black British women authors: Charlotte Williams' *Sugar and Slate* (2002), Jackie Kay's *Red Dust Road* (2010) and Bernardine Evaristo's *Lara* (1997/2009). Despite their cultural, ethnic and stylistic differences, these writers are united in their desire to experiment with the boundaries between fact and fiction, and their use of the motif of a literal and metaphorical journey in search of a sense of belonging to a space and identity. In accordance with poststructuralist, postmodernist, and postcolonial theories of memory, space and selfhood, these authors' individual journeys reveal vague and fragmented nature of memory, a multi-layered understanding of places, and a plural and shifting conception of subjectivity, which correspond to the ambiguity and plurality that autofiction contains. Therefore, the book attempts to explore autofiction as a mode of communicating multi-ethnic experiences of the authors' sense of uprootedness, in-betweenness and disorientation across transcultural living spaces. It is argued that autofictional text provides a platform for exploration and inscription of multi-ethnic identities of mixed-race authors, where narrative of autofictional self creates a space for assertion of subjectivities that do not fit in pre-existing racial and ethnic categories. The main questions the book seeks to answer are as follows: How do authors of mixed descent employ autofiction to explore their experience of multiethnicity? How can multi-ethnic identities impact on and are connected to autofictional texts? Can transgression and instability of autofiction as a genre be stretched to ethnic classifications? Can autofiction reveal new insights into discussions of multiethnicity? Can autofictional playfulness create negotiations for multiple and often contradictory subject positions adopted by individuals of dual heritage? Can autofiction contribute to production of new ethnicities through poststructuralist discussions of fragmented memory, multifaceted spaces and plurality of the self?

Because the typical autobiographical subject that is identified as white heterosexual man excludes black women from writing autobiography due to their race and gender, this project is concerned particularly with the ways in which autofictional strategies permit racialised and gendered authors to represent their selfhood and life experiences. Considering that little research has been carried out on life writing of mixed-decent authors in Britain, the book focuses on autofictional works by authors of dual heritage. It is proposed that autofiction offers black British multi-ethnic female authors an opportunity to challenge the dominant monolithic discourses of race, gender and cultural identity, and to reimagine and re-assert their manifold subjectivities in society and history. The three authors who are examined in the book resist the homogeneous group identity "black British woman" that is imposed on them, and they promote their own individual subjectivities. The authors' exploration of diversities within the normative categories of "black", "British", and "woman" problematise their assumed uniformity and coherence just as autofiction destabilizes the classifications of "fact" and "fiction" by suggesting that both are inseparable from each other. Charlotte Williams' Welsh and Guyanese, Jackie Kay's Scottish and Nigerian, Bernardine Evaristo's English and Nigerian ethnic heritages evidence that not only black identity but also British nationality are composed of internal differences, which casts doubt on functionality of singular perceptions of race, nation, ethnicity, culture as well as gender since the analysis of these authors' works shows that they experience femaleness in diverse ways.

One of the main challenges in this project is setting boundaries around the definition of autofiction, considering the fact that it is still a developing genre and lacking in an established canon for the time being. Hence, Chapter 1 aims to investigate the origins of autofiction, retracing various definitions that have been provided by authors and critics of both European and Anglophone Literatures. For this purpose, the project probes Serge Doubrovsky's views on autofiction as the point of departure in that the term was coined by him in 1977 upon realisation that his books defied Philip Lejeune's formulation of autobiographical pact, which raises another crucial question which needs to be addressed, that is, in what aspects autofiction is distinguished from autobiography. Many authors and critics such as Serge Doubrovsky, Philippe Gasparini, Vincent Colonna and Gerard Genette have built their definitions around this taxonomical debate. Furthermore, the question of proportions of weight that must be given to the elements of "auto" and "fiction" in the term has caused a great deal of disagreement among the theorists of autofiction, leading to emergence of three main fractions in treatment of autofiction. Giving consideration to disputes on characteristic principles of autofiction, the chapter examines formulations of other prominent names who have attempted to define the genre, such as Marie Darrieussecq, Jacques Lecarme, Philippe Forest, Régine Robin, Madeleine Ouellette-Michalska, Arnaud Schmitt, Catherine Cusset, Isabelle Grell, Arnaud Genon in France, Frank Zipfel, Karen Ferreira-Meyers, Martina Wagner-Egelhaaf in other European countries. Then the chapter focuses on the ways in which the debates on autofiction have been taken up by Anglophone critics like Elizabeth H. Jones, Jonathan Sturgeon, Marjorie Worthington, Hywel Dix, Christian Lorentzen, and Mary Bloom. It investigates the aspects in which their views of autofiction are similar to and different from the European approaches. Finally, the chapter examines the ways in which works of Anglophone authors such as Juliet Jacques, Tim Parks, David Shields, Sheila Heti, Chris Kraus, Rachel Cusk, Ben Lerner, Jessica Winter, and Tope Folarin have helped to define autofiction in Anglophone Literature. Following the research on the origins and development of autofiction, the boundaries of the term will be established for the aims of the book.

With the goal of contextualizing autofiction within literary criticism, Chapter 2 investigates the critical catalysts that have led to the emergence of autofictional mode of writing. It is contended that autofiction has a dialectical relationship with the twentieth century critical theories. Autofiction both affirms and questions the poststructuralist dismantling of the traditional perspectives on the concepts of authority, authenticity and truth by bringing the authorial presence back to the text but fictionalising it to some extent, committing to narrate the truth but creating an ambivalence around it. Autofiction is seen as engaging with both the possibilities and limits of language in representing the referential world. Autofiction accepts that language fails to portray the reality truthfully; however, at the same time, it holds what language creates to be still connected to the reality of the author. Autofiction's contention of the possibility of truth depends heavily on psychoanalytic theories of Sigmund Freud and Jacque Lacan. It is observed that although autofiction assumes the subject to be fractured by the unconscious and denied access to the whole picture of the self's reality, little pieces of information that are recovered through psychoanalytic processes in autofictional narration provide truthful insights into their beings and create opportunities to conceive subjective versions of reality. The postmodernist presumption of collapse of grand narratives is argued to pave way to autofiction's preoccupation with subjective histories. Having scrutinised the ways in which autofiction conjoins with the assumptions of poststructuralism, psychoanalysis and postmodernism, and breaks away from them, the chapter proceeds to examine how contemporary perceptions of memory, belonging and subjectivity contribute to development of autofiction, and vice versa, how autofiction yields new insights into these topics, which sets ground for the conceptual framework of this book. Next, the chapter proposes that the realisation of constructed nature of knowledge and plurality of the self has led to emergence of autoethnography which breaks down the conventional distinction between autobiography and ethnography. Autoethnography seeks to locate the subject in a social context, enabling the writer to recount his/her life story in relation to the social circumstances in which it has been lived. Considering that autoethnography allows the writer to engage with diverse subject positions ascribed by different communities, and to explore multi-layered connections between people and places, it is suggested that autoethnography can be a useful tool to represent cultural hybridity of individuals and societies which postcolonial theorists have often pointed out. Hence, the chapter discusses autoethnography as an effective means of resisting stereotypical representations of marginalised people by the West and disrupting its regimes of truth and identity. Autoethnography is considered as providing a "third space" where authors can renegotiate their multiple identities resulting from their links to diverse places. The book argues that hybridity and in-betweenness of autofiction and autoethnography reflect multi-ethnic individuals' feeling of being caught between different cultural worlds, and therefore, these literary forms and the state of multiethnicity can help illuminate each other.

Chapter 3 aims to create a bridge between autofiction/autoethnography and multiethnicity, depicting diverse ways in which they criss-cross. After conceptualisation with a brief historical overview of approaches to ethnicity and its engagement with multiplicity, in comparison to autofiction/autoethnography, multiethnicity is defined as an ambivalent cultural condition that constantly evolves, embodies varieties and disrupts hegemonic discourses of cultural identity. Because the book is restricted to the context of Britain, the theoretical framework for the discussions of multiethnicity is built on the views of Black British critical figures, Stuart Hall, Hanif Kureishi and Paul Gilroy, who have offered non-essentialist and pluralist perspectives on ethnicity. Stuart Hall's declaration of "the end of the notion of the essential black subject", promotion of thinking about new ethnicities that engage differences, and suggestion of at least two constituents, collective and individual, of cultural identity, Hanif Kureishi's appeal for recognition of different ways of being British, and Paul Gilroy's accentuation of cultural hybridity through movement, like the Black Atlantic journey, help us to understand the examined authors' expressions of their multi-ethnic experiences and to evaluate autofiction/autoethnography's potentials in narrativization of multi-ethnic realities. Autofiction/autoethnography's aptness for narration of multi-ethnic authors' life stories is asserted through the fact that Stuart Hall and Hanif Kureishi have published works in which they at once recount their life experiences and theorise multi-ethnic identity drawing on autofictional/autoethnographic strategies, and contributing to development of a new direction that is autotheory. Autotheory as a means of decolonising the field of literary theory enables theorists to ground their ideas on their life experiences. Having elaborated on assumptions of autotheory, the chapter examines how autofiction, autoethnography and autotheory become instrumental for Hanif Kureishi's exploration of his relationship with his Pakistani father in *My Heart at His Heart* and Stuart Hall's establishment of inseparable links between his life and his ideas in *Familiar Stranger: A Life Between Two Islands*. Because the book intends to focus on the works by black British female authors, the chapter concludes with an overview of the theorists of black British feminism who call attention to the double marginalisation of black women in Britain because of their race and gender, define the label "black woman" as a site of heterogeneity, contradictions and ambivalence, and express black women's desire to be freed from categorisation. Then the book moves on to investigate how autofictional/autoethnographic strategies permit the examined authors to represent the ways in which they experience their multi-ethnicity and femaleness.

In Chapter 4, it is argued that autofiction/ autoethnography enables Charlotte Williams to invent for herself a black Welsh historical heritage by virtue of the fact that she has had to grow up in a small Welsh town as a "historyless" person away from her Guyanese father and without the knowledge of Africa and her African ancestors. By blurring the lines between embodied experience and imagination, the individual and social worlds, the author both discovers and imagines her ties to multiple cultures. She establishes connections between Wales, Africa and the West Indies by portraying her highly individualised travels to Sudan and Guyana from Wales in relation to the historical movements of her ancestors within the same trajectories, which results in entangled histories and help Williams reclaim her belonging to the countries of "sugar" and "slate". In Chapter 5, it is asserted that Jackie Kay uses autofiction/ autoethnography in order to invent a story of origins for herself as a result of her adoption. The author's fantasies about her natural parents, their pasts, other futures that she could have had all become a part of her reality about her self and life. The ambivalence of autofiction/ autoethnography enables Kay to articulate her feeling of a double dislocation from personal and national home, which she succeeds to overcome through her awakening to shared experiences in the histories of Scotland and Nigeria, and the role of both "nature" (genetic relations) and "nourish" (cultural environment) in identity formation. Chapter 6 proposes that Bernardine Evaristo employs autofiction/ autoethnography to reconstruct ancestral pasts that have not been transferred to her on intention by her parents because of the traumatic experiences in them. In this regard, her dreams and visions prove to be revelatory, attesting her unconscious connectedness to the untold lives of her ancestors. The author's physical and symbolic journeys to the places where her forebears once lived and into their pasts end in the discovery of cultural and racial hybridity on both English maternal and Nigerian paternal sides. Moreover, they reveal to the author shared experiences of dislocation and discrimination in the histories of both her African and European ancestors. Through autofiction/ autoethnography's plurality and hybridity, Evaristo is able to explore and express the possibilities of multiplicity and interconnectivity of cultures and places. In all three autofictional/autoethnographic narratives, the authors disavow homogeneity of cultural identity and are reconciled to their supposedly conflicting ethnic heritages. In addition to similarities in their experiences, the conclusion part calls attention to differences between their unique journeys of life. It also offers discussions of how these narratives can contribute to debates around formulation of autofiction, and of autofiction/ autoethnography's potentials for enabling a broader comprehension and representation of multi-ethnic identities.

Chapter 1 Development of Autofiction as an In-between Genre

Historical Overview of Autofiction in the Continent

Defining autofiction is a literary conundrum. Many authors and critics have attempted to establish its fundamental principles and delineate its boundaries, as any traditionally designated literary classification requires, yet their endeavours have served only to complicate the term to a further extent. As such, the word autofiction signifies diverse realities according to various critics and authors. It has been discrepantly defined from a minimalist form in which the inevitability of fictionalisation in any textual reconstruction of life is accentuated, to a more far-reaching version where lived experiences provide a mere basis for deliberately invented characters and scenes that diverge explicitly from the referentiality of author's life. Vincent Colonna encapsulates the phenomenon of ever-growing dissension over the conception as follows:

> Since there is neither a codified genre, nor a simple form, but a sheaf of joined and joining practices, a complex shape, nobody is altogether wrong: each grabbed a "piece" of autofiction, a blow of the great whirlwind that inspires him or her. (2004, as cited in Ferreira-Meyers, 2015)

Since autofiction as a genre is in a flux and still to be developed fully, its current lack of generic classification permits authors and theoreticians to engage with what might be possible rather than confining them to a clearly defined literary position. Given the fact that there are no agreed precepts for what should constitute autofiction, it oscillates playfully between autobiography and fiction, assuming the status of neither but occupying a grey area on borderlines (Burgelin, 2008/2010, as cited in Fraser, 2015). This in-betweenness characterising autofiction becomes relevant particularly to the autobiographical narratives of mixed-descent authors, as this book aims to discuss.

The neologism "autofiction" stems from the blurb on the back cover of Serge Doubrovsky's novel *Fils* ['Threads'/'Son'] (1977), where he defined it as "Fiction, of strictly real events and facts: autofiction, if you like" (as cited in Gronemann, 2019). Doubrovsky uses the term to describe narratives which have autobiographical contents certified by the nominal shared identity between author, narrator and protagonist, while the narrative organisation and stylistic features are identical to those of novels. He defies conventional literary classifications by paradoxically bringing together the seemingly exclusive genres of autobiography and fiction, assumedly based on facticity and invention respectively. Doubrovsky does not perceive the resulting amalgamation as a contradiction because, for him, autofiction arises from a growing recognition by authors and theorists of autobiography that autobiography always involves an element of fiction (Gronemann, 2019, p. 77).[1]

As the well-known story recounts, Doubrovsky's coinage of the term autofiction was a response to the publication of Philip Lejeune's essay "The Autobiographical Pact" (1975/1989), in which Lejeune specified different forms of autobiographical writing that he could envisage as theoretically possible. In his taxonomical table that classifies works either as autobiography or novel based on the relationship between the protagonist's name and the kind of pact made with readers, the combination of the equality between the names of author, narrator and character with a novelistic pact is left empty. Lejeune does not leave out the possibility that such a combination could exist but maintains that, if it were the case, an internal contradiction would emerge, which would relegate the work to the order of lie, not of fiction or of autobiography (p. 16–17). Accordingly, Lejeune proceeds to define the relationship between the writer of autobiography and his or her reader as a contract, whereby the correspondence between the identity of the author, narrator and protagonist is asserted and the author's commitment to the divulgence of truth is reaffirmed. This unspoken agreement, "autobiographical pact" as Lejeune names, entitles the reader to assume that the author of the work is identical to the "I" narrator and the principal character, and that the text provides a veracious representation of the author's life (p. 22).

With his work *Fils* (1977), Doubrovsky attempts to demonstrate the flawed nature of Lejeune's formulation. Notwithstanding the established correspondence between the names of the author, narrator and protagonist, and the narration of real events, Doubrovsky does not purport to present a factual account of his life as in autobiography. Rather, he intends to explore the possibilities of the borderline position between autobiography and autobiographical novel, where he places autofiction, filling the gap in Lejeune's typology. When Lejeune's taxonomical categorisation is considered, autofiction differs from autobiographical novel by using the author's name and from autobiography by the implication of a fictional representation. On the other hand, Doubrovsky's understanding of the

---

1 Roland Barthes and others in France in the 1970s postulate that no precise truth about the past self is accessible; the referential "real" cannot be represented; the subject is ineluctably an inconstant fiction; and the boundary between autobiography and fiction remains illusory (Smith & Watson, 2002, p. 186).

term proposes that autofictional texts belong at once to domains of both the referential and the fictional by virtue of that they intend to inscribe not the veracity of a life but a self with all its accompanying ambiguity (O'Byrne, 2019, p. 10). That way, autofiction refutes Lejeune's contention that the onomastic connection between author, narrator and protagonist qualifies an autobiographical text only as referential, and never fictional.

In "Autobiographie/ vérité/ psychanalyse" (1988), where he attempts to theorise his works, Doubrovsky describes the practice of autofiction as a "strategy of genres" (as cited in de Bloois, 2007). The tension that arises from the apparently unachievable reconciliation of autobiography and novel fulfils certain critical functions (de Bloois, 2007, p. 21). According to Elizabeth H. Jones (2009), the incorporation of fictional elements into autobiographical accounts and thus the transgression of the boundaries between fact and fiction are the chief constituents of Doubrovsky's writing. She ascribes this blurring of the lines to his sense of cultural dispossession and divided identity (p. 3). As a consequence of his Jewish heritage, Doubrovsky suffered from persecution even though he never considered himself as religious. He led his life in two continents, languages and professions as a professor and a writer. Furthermore, he often felt torn between his family and female companions (Gronemann, 2019, p. 1977). This doubleness of his life generates a split of the personality and a feeling of alienation in him. As a result, Doubrovsky attempts to write his "self" through a middle term which would provide a truer representation of his subjectivity with its in-betweenness. The sense of duality of his selfhood is mirrored in the narrating "I" of autofiction who is real but also problematic and elusive. As Marjorie Worthington (2018) puts it, the autofictional "I" does and does not refer to the author at the same time (p. 16), which problematises the idea of a unified and coherent self that is typically found in autobiography. As such, the ambivalence of "I" in autofiction provides authors who inhabit multiple spaces with the means for exploring and inscribing the plurality of their subjectivity and life.

The indeterminacy of autofiction as an in-between narrative form is furthered as Serge Doubrovsky continues to update and amend the definition and use of autofiction during his career. Hywel Dix (2018) points out that there are at least three different ways in which Doubrovsky employs the term. On the stylistic basis, Doubrovsky associates the practice of writing autofiction with readjustment of narrative time (p. 2). His experimentation with temporal order, deterring from a linear, sequential and chronological progression, brings together empirical life experiences of autobiography and literary narrative techniques of novel. In line with the fragmented and elusive quality of the autofictional "I", radical shifts in time frame, loose causality between factual events and fictional intrusions reflect the fissures and fractures of Doubrovsky's real life (Gronemann, 2019, p. 1978). Moreover, the chaotic representation of autobiographical reality rendered by fragmentation strategies such as stream of consciousness imitates the workings of memory that is understood as imperfect and filled with gaps. In contrast to autobiography's contention of recounting the truth straightforwardly, autofiction in the Doubrovskian sense foregrounds the role of memory, with its pitfalls and shortcomings, in the composition of referential narratives (Dix, 2018, p. 5). As Doubrovsky puts it, "meanings of life escape us" due to the failings of memory, which consequently requires the author of autobiographical texts to reinvent them (Célestin, 1997, p. 400). Chronological displacement is one way in which authors of autofiction counter drawbacks of memory, as they reproduce events from streams of consciousness, rather than attempting to impose an artificial order on the text. As a consequence, the process of transcribing scattered episodes from the vagueness of memory with a fragmentary narrative technique inevitably results in the blending of strictly referential facts and literary inventions. However, Doubrovsky contends that the liberty afforded to the author of autofiction to rearrange or alter factual events serves to represent the identity of the protagonist/author more "truthfully" (Worthington, 2018, p. 14).

Doubrovsky's formulation of writing autofiction is closely linked to the talking cure of psychoanalysis that seeks to dig into the hidden realities of the unconscious mind.[2] As in psychoanalytic therapy sessions, while the author translates his/her memories into words, the stories that he/she tells about himself/herself evoke a new awareness of self (Célestin, 1997, p. 401). For Doubrovsky, the self is largely inaccessible due to the splitting of the ego; therefore, he approaches his own life through "fils des mots" ["threads of words"] (Gronemann, 2019, p. 241). The interweaving of subjectivity and language is of fundamental importance to the Doubrovskian autofiction, by means of which the author discovers something "true" about himself/herself. Doubrovsky expounds,

> Autofiction represents the fiction that I have decided, as a writer, to make of myself and for myself, incorporating therein, in the fullest sense of the term, the experience of analysis, not just thematically but in the very production of the text. (1993, as cited in Worthington)

Unlike autobiography that retraces life chronologically, autofiction presents a self that is fragmented, unstable and coalesced by memory. For Doubrovsky,

---

2 In *Fils*, Doubrovsky not only includes the transcription of an analytical session (the "Rêves" ['Dreams'] chapter, which covers about 60 pages), but also transforms the first-person narrator/protagonist into a self-analyst (Gronemann, 2019, p. 242).

autofiction helps the author make sense of the self in disarray, and represent its "truth" which is different from historical or biological understandings of factuality (Worthington, 2018, p. 17). The author comes to the knowledge of the truth about the self as a result of psychotherapeutic process that autofiction provides an occasion for. Accordingly, Doubrovsky attempts to define autofiction, on a sociological basis, as a form of autobiographical narrative that is written by people who are neither well known to the public at large, nor aim to reinforce their audience's a priori knowledge of a subject matter with their own life experiences (Dix, 2018, p. 3). Doubrovsky regards classical autobiography as an elitist occupation creating a hierarchical order that permits only those who are perceived as holding a high social standing to write it (p. 3).[3] In contrast to the autobiographical "I" of an eminent status, Doubrovsky views himself as being "nobody" and naturally excluded from the sphere of autobiography. He declares the insignificance of his material existence, when compared to his textual being, with words: "I hardly exist, I am a fictive being" (as cited in Dix, 2018). Doubrovsky feels most authentic when he depicts himself as a fictional character in his autofictional works where psychoanalytic observation of the self uncovers facts that are otherwise inaccessible.

Doubrovsky develops his conception of autofiction partly so as to dismantle the hierarchy that autobiography imposes, and partly to experiment with different ways of representing subjectivity. In this sense, autofiction is an enterprise for exploring the self on the part of author who lacks the knowledge of it before writing (Dix, 2018, p. 4). The author of autofiction is aware that he or she cannot uphold the autobiographical principle of presenting a truthful account of the self because he or she does not have an access to the truth of the self. It is through the medium of language that the author gains insight into realities that shape his/her subjectivity. Therefore, Doubrovsky defines autofiction as an autobiographical form in which "language of adventure" is entrusted to "the adventure of language in liberty, outside of the wisdom and the syntax of the novel" (as cited in Ferreira-Meyers, 2015). Unlike the autobiographical "I" that purports to be in control of language and his/her thoughts, the autofictional "I" is subjected to language that leads the author to unmapped realms of the ego. As opposed to the authors of autobiography who sign a pact with readers to attest their commitment to facticity, Doubrovsky asserts that one can never know oneself

---

3 On the back cover of *Fils*, Doubrovsky declares: "Autobiography? No, that is a privilege reserved for the important people of this world, at the end of their lives, in a refined style" (Doubrovsky, 1977 as cited in Ferreira-Meyers, 2015).

totally (Célestin, 1997, p. 404). Although writing helps one discover previously unknown realities about one's subjectivity, it is not possible to grasp fully the facts entailed by the self. In Doubrovsky's words, "even after writing hundreds of pages about yourself, you're still an unknown quantity to yourself" (Célestin, 1997, p. 404). While Doubrovsky adopts autobiography's nominal identification of author, narrator and central character, he refutes its claims to truth. Thus, autofiction foregrounds a distance between the remembering "I" and the remembered "I", giving an emphasis to the splitting of the self. The author of autofiction who remembers the fragments of his/her life at the moment of writing portrays an author-character who proves to be a richer version of himself/herself for the reason that the character is embellished with psychic realities. The autofictional "I" is ultimately identical to the author on the account of shared biographical facts, but also distinct in that the author-character is a different version of the real author who is not capable of being aware of all the elements that constitute his/her subjectivity.

Furthermore, Serge Doubrovsky points to the distance between the author and the author-character on the grounds of his philosophical stance that maintains as soon as one puts his/her existence into words, it becomes fiction (Gronemann, 2019, p. 242). He conceives that the process of writing necessarily detaches narratives from referentiality. According to his formulation of autofiction on a historical basis, it is no longer possible today to write autobiography, like the kinds that Rousseau wrote, because historical conditions have changed since the time of classical autobiography (Dix, 2018, p. 5). The developments such as psychoanalysis, surrealism and poststructuralism have questioned, in diverse ways, the ability of a person to narrate his/her life story truthfully, and called into doubt the classical autobiography's pretensions to straightforward representation of personal experiences and subjectivity (p. 5). Accordingly, Doubrovsky defines autofiction as referring to autobiographical texts that involves verifiably referential information about the author and his life yet engages in rearrangements and alterations as a consequence of the process of rendering events into language. Doubrovsky's various attempts to define autofiction illustrates the difficulty of setting definite boundaries to his conception. Being already an unstable genre at its early development, autofiction has been further destabilised by the interpretations of other theorists and authors who have eventually contributed to the extension of its scope. According to Dix (2017), however, autofiction in Doubrovskian sense is distinguished by four elements that she identifies as an onomastic relationship between author, narrator and protagonist; narration of real events; designation of works as novels; and chronological displacement of events (p. 160). By the same token, Jones (2009) considers the most distinctive quality of Doubrovskian practice of autofiction to be a persistent pursuit of stripping away conventions and assumptions in order to redefine truth and forge new ground (p. 6), which is aligned with the multi-ethnic authors' endeavours to achieve new ways of understanding ethnicity as will be discussed in the following chapters.

Doubrovsky's description of the distinctions between autobiography and autofiction, mainly in respect of their stylistic strategies, has incited debates among critics and authors in France over the last decades. As such, the succeeding theorists have interrogated the relationship between the two genres which were previously thought to be separate literary areas. They have asked the questions: Is it possible to distinguish autobiography and autofiction? Should a difference be made between the two? What does the difference serve? According to Marie Darrieussecq (1996), a significant peculiarity distinguishes autofiction from autobiography:

> The fundamental difference between autobiography and autofiction is just that the latter will voluntarily assume that the reduction of autobiography to a statement of fact, to a biographical statement, a scientific, historical, clinical, in short, "objective" statement, is impossible; autofiction will voluntarily – hence structurally – assume this impossible sincerity and objectivity, and integrate blurring and fiction in particular due to unconsciousness. (as cited in Ferreira-Meyers, 2015)

Like Doubrovsky, Darrieussecq contends that despite seeking to represent the truth, autobiography inescapably fails to do so due to the fallibility of memory. The author cannot rely on memory to present an accurate portray of the past because any attempt to recollect will be interfered with the deficiencies of his/her mnemonic capacity. The autobiographer, hence, often overlooks the gaps in remembered instances when he/she purports to recount the facts of his/her life. Darrieussecq concludes that it is not possible to draw a straightforward distinction between classical autobiography and autofiction when considered that there has not been any period of time in which autobiography could be written in an unproblematic and objective way, without the impingement of disfiguring effects of memory (Dix, 2017, p. 164).[4] Therefore, she considers the attempts of defining autofiction through contradistinction to autobiography as misleading. For her, autofiction is a story narrated in the first person where the author appears under his/her own name and where some degree of semblance of his/

---

4   In her postulation, Darrieussecq is aligned with Burton Pike (1976) who remarked, "not all fiction is autobiographical, but on this deeper level, all autobiography is fiction" (p. 337).

her life is maintained through the agency of references to a set of verifiable facts about him/her, yet the experiences narrated are inevitably fictive, or even deliberately fantastic (p. 165). In other words, autofiction is situated between the two narrative forms of autobiography and fiction. Within a single text, the author professes his/her narration of facts, but shortly after it, he/she cautions the reader against such an avowal (Ferreira-Meyers, 2015, p. 215). As a consequence, factual and fictional elements of the story are juxtaposed in a way that they become indiscernible from each other, creating an ambiguity around generic status of narrated events.

Like Darrieussecq who questions the truth claims of autobiography, Jacques Lacarme (1993) not only calls into doubt the assumption that autobiography can recount faithfully events or experiences of the past, but also distrusts the notion of a straightforward identification between the author, narrator and character. Therefore, as opposed to Lejeune's autobiographical pact, Lacarme proposes an autofictional pact, in which the assumptions of autobiography are acknowledged as essentially contradictory (Dix, 2017, p. 165). In like manner, Darrieussecq (2007) mentions a contract that evades assuring confidence with the following words: "Reader, do not believe me. Do not be naive enough to adhere to the narrative, do not be fooled. Writing is not real life" (as cited in Ferreira-Meyers, 2015). In the autofictional pact, as suggested by these theorists, the author intends to recount the truth, but he/she is never able to accomplish it. For Lacarme and Darrieussecq, there is a dialectical relationship between autofiction and autobiography, that is, an unresolved tension between the impulse to tell the truth and the revelation of the truths in homodiegetic narratives that are ultimately fictive (Dix, 2017, p. 165). Along these lines, Sébastian Hubier (2003) writes that in autofiction, telling the truth is "always an intention, never a reality" (as cited in Ferreira-Meyers, 2015). As soon as the author of autofiction embarks on a quest for truth, life comes out as indescribable and elusive. Therefore, he concludes that autofiction's emphasis on truth is based on the authorial construction of truth rather than on a factual one (Fraser, 2015, p. 20). Similarly, Philippe Forest (2007) expounds that autofiction arises from the imperative to represent and the inability to do so. Narratives are not reflections of reality, but responses to it (as cited in Ferreira-Meyers, 2015). Autofiction, hence, violates the autobiographical pact by problematising the notion of giving a faithful representation of a referential object through narrative, and it raises the prospect of a nonreferential form of autobiographical writing. Conforming neither to autobiography nor to fiction, autofiction with its contradictions remains as "an undecided, hybrid, simultaneously self-referential and fictional genre" (Hubier, as cited in Ferreira-Meyers, 2015).

Lacarme distinguishes between two types of autofiction. In the strict sense, autofiction refers to a narrative that recounts strictly real events and experiences, yet includes fictional elements through the way of telling them. In the more general sense of the term, the facts of life are liable to the distorting effects of the imagination, and the act of fictionalisation deforms the content of the memories (Dix, 2017, p. 166). Lacarme's distinction of the strict and the general senses of autofiction points to a division within the field into separate approaches. Doubrovsky and his followers use the term to refer to the texts that establish a tripartite onomastic correspondence, that are written in a fragmented literary form, and that engage in psychoanalytical processes. Lacarme joins Doubrovsky in the use of psychoanalysis in autofiction as part of writing "cure", but he foregrounds particularly the late twentieth and early twenty-first centuries cultural assumption that fiction is not capable of representing the world in a mimetic way. Fictional signifiers are simply tokens for the entities of the objective world, rather than their full replicates (p. 166). Similarly, Régine Robin (1997) considers psychoanalysis as a significant strand within autofiction, yet maintains that autofiction cannot be differentiated from other forms of self-writing by the presence of psychoanalysis on its own (Fraser, 2015, p. 26). The second approach, represented by Philippe Gasparini, departs from the Doubrovskian formulation with a hybrid viewpoint on autofiction, adopted also by Régine Robin and Madeleine Ouellette-Michalska. According to this approach, there are constant shifts between facts and fiction that readers accommodate through a process of simultaneity. The author does not confine the incidents of plot to strictly real events, but incorporates invented episodes reflecting a potential identity that is never confirmed. Accordingly, Régine Robin (1997) defines autofiction as "a border area, where fantasies, illusions, aspirations, cultural imagery rooted in the writer takes form and content" (as cited in Ferreira-Meyers, 2015). The third approach, as suggested by Gerard Genette, favours the fictional part of autofiction over the referential. In his formulation, autofictional texts narrate events that are completely non-referential. By extension, Genette differentiates between "true autofictions", which are purely fictional in narrative content, and "false autofictions", which he considers as veiled autobiographies in the sense that they involve fiction for legal purposes (Worthington, 2018, p. 19).

As Marjorie Worthington (2018) points out, Serge Doubrovsky focuses mainly on the "auto" part of the term, and views autofiction as a means of arriving at a deeper understanding of the self. Philippe Gasparini, on the other hand, expands Doubrovsky's definition, classifying autofiction as a "hybrid" genre that continuously vacillates between the referential and the fictional (p. 18). As distinct from Doubrovsky, Gasparini emphasises the fictional in autofiction. For him, autofiction needs to aim for vraisemblance by pressing the fictional elements to its furthest bounds and maintaining a discrepancy between the author's life and her/his narrative of it (Edwards, 2015, p. 3). Autofiction is, therefore, not concerned with telling a true story, but with creating multiple stories about the author, which qualifies it as a novel. Gasparini conceives a dialectical relationship between autofiction and autobiography, in which the author of the former problematises the latter narrative form and develops its possibilities, rather than opposing to the genre as a whole. As a consequence, the "I" of the autofiction does not serve as the starting point of the narrative, as it is in autobiography, but appears to be the point of arrival in that rather than reproducing the self textually, autofiction explores its potentials in a nonreferential manner (Snauwaert, 2020, p. 2). Importantly, in *Est-il je? Roman autobiographique et autofiction*, Philippe Gasparini (2004) argues that the identification of the author in autofiction is not exclusively connected to his/her proper name. Instead, he suggests that there are a number of ways in which the relationship between author and character can be established, such as age, socio-cultural background, occupations or aspirations (Schmitt, 2020, p. 9). While the Doubrovskian autofiction is predicated upon the nominal identification of author, narrator and character in line with the terms of Lejeune's pact, for Gasparini, the referential part of an autofictional text is constructed through personal and sociocultural references to the author. In his formulation, therefore, the author and protagonist are allowed to bear different names as long as there is an identitarian relationship created between them by means of other shared characteristics (O'Byrne, 2019, p. 11).

According to Gasparini, a significant part of fictionalisation in autofiction draws upon the appropriation of documentary evidence that includes not only textual records but also photography, objects and drawings, oral testimonies. Nevertheless, the author, narrator and the protagonist remain as the same person, whether the identification is established through a pseudonym or exact replica of the name (Fraser, 2015, p. 27). Similarly, Lecarme argues that the main identity of the autofictional persona must be preserved, or the narrative will come out as purely fictional (p. 25). Lecarme and Gasparini use this axiom to distinguish between autofiction and autobiographical novel. Although both of the narrative forms make use of paratextual indicators as distinguishing markers, they differ in the kinds of pact that are established. While containing some biographical information about the author, the autobiographical novel is meant to be read unambiguously as a fiction; therefore, it establishes a fictional pact. In contrast, autofiction uses an ambiguous pact, refusing to be entirely fictional or referential (p. 27). As a result, before attempting to give a definition of autofiction, Gasparini stresses the ambiguity surrounding the term with the disclaimer, "This is not a definitive theory in any way because the lines move, the published texts put certainties into question, the phenomenon is far from controlled" (2008, as cited in Pitcher McDonough, 2011). Despite seeing autofiction as a complex form of narrative that is difficult define, Gasparini suggests the following definition:

> Autobiographical and literary text that features numerous oral qualities, formal innovation, narrative complexity, fragmentation, separation from the self, disparateness and auto-commentary, which tends to problematize the relationship between writing and experience. (2008, as cited in Pitcher McDonough, 2011)

After listing the stylistic traits characterising autofiction, Gasparini points to the discrepancy between the referential and its translation into textuality, which distinguishes the genre from classical autobiography, yet does not rank it with autobiographical novel. Gasparini's work aspires to delineate the boundaries of autofiction, and to place it in the conventional system of literary classifications; however, one of the most remarkable characteristics of autofiction proves to be its resistant nature against definition and categorisation, remaining "far from being controlled". This quality of autofiction renders it a useful narrative tool for recounting the multi-ethnic experiences of Black British authors who do not feel themselves fitting in the traditional categories of race and ethnicity. The literary ambiguity and in-betweenness of autofiction figuratively correspond to the social exclusion and unbelonging of the individuals with dual heritage. In a similar vein, Madeleine Ouellette-Michalska (2007) sees autofiction as a tool functional to narration of the multiplicity of fragmented identity of the female subject who was excluded from the public world of male domination and confined to the domestic sphere during the past centuries (Cominetti, 2018, p. 19). In her book *Autofiction et dévoilement de soi: Essai*, Ouellette-Michalska posits that since women were forced into the role of "angel in the house", they had access to the cultural domain only indirectly, through activities such as taking care of the education of children. While they were in charge of securing the link between nature and culture, women developed a taste for being concealed and exposed concurrently (p. 19). Accordingly, they produced autofictional texts in the forms of diary, letters, poetry where they could articulate the "I" in a tactful way. Ouellette-Michalska, hence, considers autofiction as an effective instrument particularly for the recounting of the female experience of being "a figure between two worlds" (p. 19), that is, the experience of occupying a liminal position in society, shared also by the multi-ethnic authors discussed in this book.

Gasparini's non-homonymic and non-referential approach is enhanced further by Vincent Colonna, who was formerly a doctoral student of Gerard

Genette.[5] Like Gasparini, Colonna departs from the Doubrovskian assumption that autofiction needs to narrate strictly real events. However, despite treating differently, he preserves the self-fictionalisation criterion of Doubrovsky's original definition of autofiction, that is, the central character having the same name as the author. In *Autofiction et autres mythomanies littéraries* (2004), Colonna defines autofiction as a literary work in which the author conjures up a personality and existence while keeping his personal identity and real name intact (Snauwaert, 2020, p. 1).[6] In his formulation, autofiction is centred around the writer's fictionalisation of his/her own persona. He views the term as encompassing all the processes of self-fictionalisation, and applies it to the works in which authors are engaged in inventing a personality and a literary existence for themselves (Worthington, 2018, p. 18). According to his conception of autofiction, authors write the self as they fantasise it without a concern for what they perceive it to be (Boyle, 2007, p. 18). In this approach, autofiction is concerned with the narrative construction of a self, as in Doubrovsky's definition, yet it is free to make use of any fictional elements that are necessary to do so (Worthington, 2018, p. 19). As a result, autofictional texts are, in Colonna's view, classified as both fictional and referential, with little attention given to distinction between fact and fiction (p. 19).[7] One distinctive feature of Colonna's formulation of autofiction is, hence, its hybridity resulting from the collusion between two contradictory narrative positions, each being characterised by facticity and invention. Dervila Cooke (2005) summarises the difference between the definitions of Doubrovsky and Colonna by pointing out that Colonna's version of autofiction is predominated by invention whereas Doubrovsky is more concerned with verifiable facts (p. 80).

With his emphasis on fictionalisation of the self, Colonna expands significantly the scope of autofiction. According to his formulation, the events and characters in autofictional works are disguised projections of the author's own life and personality. Even though the writer has the liberty of employing

---

5   According to Dix (2017), this fact may help explain the prevalence of scientific and structuralist impulse among theoreticians to categorise and classify autofiction despite Doubrovsky's attempts to disrupt Lejeune's alike efforts to classify different forms of autobiographical writing (p. 167).
6   Colonna describes this narrative position as "a fictionalization of oneself" in *L'autofiction, essai sur la fictionalisation de soi"* (1989, as cited in Snauwaert, 2020, p. 3).
7   For Colonna, Marcel Proust's *In Search of Lost Time* (1913/1992) must qualify as autofiction for the reasons that the protagonist shares a nominal identity with the author, and is a largely fictional alter ego of Proust himself (Cooke, 2005, p. 80).

fictionalisation strategies, the protagonist and story events remain still relatable to the real author and his life. However, the calculated inclusion of unreal content in an autobiographical narrative raises the question of difference between autofiction and autobiographical novel. Colonna argues that the fiction of oneself is distinguished from autobiographical novel by the virtue of "its subject matter, its intimate inscription and its discursive strategy" (as cited in Snauwaert, 2020). As distinct from Doubrovsky's formulation, in such a discourse, the content of the story is fictitious, and the author does not pretend to seek the truth. What autofiction in Colonna's version attempts to achieve through the practice of fictionalisation is a distortion of reality, a "free play of imaginative forces" (as cited in Snauwaert, 2020). By disrupting narrative codes, it aims to create an ambiguous setting which gets the reader involved in an intellectual play through ceaseless misleading and the raising of doubt at every possible occasion (Snauwaert, 2020, p. 4). Autofiction, in Colonna's formulation, strives to provoke perplexity in the reader by means of the ambiguity that arises from the clash of opposing narrative strategies. While autofiction announces itself as a novel, it also seems to suggest conforming to an autobiographical pact through the onomastic relationship between the author, narrator and character. This undetermined quality of autofiction propels the reader to vacillate between the opposite poles of narrativity. Autofiction's in-between narrative position, thus, affords mechanisms of hesitation that mystify the boundaries between veracity and invention. By alluding to the referentiality of the author and at once giving a fictional account of his/her real life, autofiction generates confusion, which leads the reader to question the surrounding reality (p. 4).

Colonna calls attention to the affinity between the autofictive and the fantastic by proposing a distinction between "autofiction biographique" and "autofiction fantastique". The former of the two categories conforms to the autobiographical identity which assumes that the author, narrator and protagonist are different facets of the same person, and it narrates events that are strictly real in Doubrovskian sense, although they can be fictionalised as needed. It intends mainly to give as truthful an account as possible, including referential information about the author and his/her life such as dates, facts and places (Fraser, 2015, p. 23). *Autofiction fantastique,* on the other hand, allows the author to invent alternative identities and lives for themselves (Dix, 2018, p. 6). Colonna suggests that such works should not include any indices hinting at a shared identity between author and character (Fraser, 2015, p. 22). Although the writer is positioned at the centre of the text, his/her identity and existence are transfigured into fiction, as the result of which "no one would think to draw a likeness to an image of the author" (as cited in Snauwaert, 2020). Colonna identifies two more subcategories of autofiction which he names as "autofiction spéculaire" and "autofiction intrusive/auctoriale". In the former, the author is not placed at the centre of the text, but can be found in some portion of the narrative. In this version, the character must reflect the personality of the author (Fraser, 2015, p. 23). The last category refers to third person narratives in which the narrator is present on the edge of the narration. Rather than the main character, this form relies on the existence of a narrator that reflects the writer's identity (p. 24). This author/narrator exists as a solitary and disembodied voice along the unfolding of the story.

Colonna's taxonomical attempt by splitting autofiction into four varieties overreaches its boundaries, and results in a literary classification that proves to be comprehensive of a wide range of self-writing forms. While attempting to map out all possible varieties of autofiction, with clear boundaries set around them, Colonna makes it more problematic to pin down the fundamental principles common to all autofictional texts. Furthermore, Colonna's definition of autofiction differs markedly, in certain respects, from the one that Doubrovsky set forth. Whereas the former uses the term to designate texts in which the author invents different versions of the self, the latter views autofiction as a means of arriving at a deeper understanding of the self (Jones, 2010, p. 178). Colonna fictionalises events to imagine alternative identities and experiences, while Doubrovsky uses the same strategy to evade the problems of truth and memory (Fraser, 2015, p. 21). Although Colonna and Doubrovsky seem to foreground different aspects of autofiction and impacts of fictionalisation, Menn (2018) significantly notes that writing about a life retrospectively with fictive techniques, whether for self-imagination or self-conciliation, is driven by a desire for searching for the self through narration. Autofiction allows the author to imagine the self in any chosen way, and thus, to arrive a more profound sense of selfhood and identity (p. 166). Moreover, the incongruities in various attempts at defining autofiction reveal an ontological and epistemological instability surrounding the autobiographical mode of self-presentation. It becomes evident that there is not only one way of narrating the self. Being a strategy of playing with the expression of subjectivity, autofiction accentuates a pluralistic self-conception that assumes there is a multitude of aspects of subjectivity to be told and retold. That way, autofiction eludes conceptions of fixed truth, giving way to instances of multi-faceted self-narration (p. 167). Colonna's conception of autofiction is relevant to this book particularly in the way that it incorporates non-referential elements in an autobiographical narrative, upsetting the readers' narrative expectations, destabilising the idea of an objective and unified reality, and interrogating the assumption of correspondence between reality and its textual reconstruction. In that respect, autofiction blows open the texts that pretend to represent the truth and that aspire to be publicly acknowledged, at times, for hegemonic purposes, as will be discussed in regards to the multi-ethnic experiences of the authors in the case studies.

Differing from the advocates of the definitions above, Gerard Genette (1991/1993) embraces the "fiction" part of the term autofiction. For him, plots of autofictional texts are overtly fictitious despite the onomastic relationship between their authors, narrators and protagonists (Worthington, 2018, p. 10–11). In *Diction & Fiction* (1991/1993), Genette does not mention Doubrovsky, but he proceeds to comment on autofiction and narrative texts where the author shares the same name with the narrator and/or the character. Under the section entitled "Voice", he examines the elements of the relations between author, narrator and character. As Doubrovsky models his conception of autofiction on Lejeune's structural analysis of autobiography, Genette develops his own formulation by expanding on Lejeune's work that propounds a mimetic relationship between the author, narrator and character in first person autobiography. In line with Lejeune's observations, Genette provides various diagrams that illustrate five different possibilities of the relationship between author (A), narrator (N), and character (C). Genette draws on these relational patterns particularly so as to distinguish between factual and fictional narratives. Accepting that there are exceptions, he predicates that when A=N, the narrative is factual; conversely, when A does not equal N, the narrative is fictional (p. 72). Then he notes that nothing, in effect, prevents a narrator who is eponymously identified with the author from narrating a manifestly fictional story, as it is the case in autofiction (p. 74–75). Accordingly, he calls attention to a contradiction in autofictional texts between the fictional quality of the story and the formula A=N → factual narrative (p. 75). He proclaims that this formula does not apply to the situations which he describes as instances of "the functional disassociation between author and narrator" (p. 75). For example, in Borges' story "El Aleph", Borges the author is not "functionally identical" to Borges the narrator and protagonist despite the shared biographical features (p. 75–76). Genette's model of autofiction adopts the formula for autobiography, A=N=C, yet it assumes the disassociation of C into two components, an authentic personal identity and a fictional journey of life, which results in an autofictional subject that is "I" and "not I" at once (p. 76–77). Therefore, he concludes that the equals signs, found in the formula for autobiography, are used metaphorically for autofiction, that is, they do not have precisely the same value (p. 77). Genette sums up his view of the term with the suggestion of an intentional contradictory pact in which the author avows that "I, the author, am going to tell you a story of which I am the hero but never happened to me" (p. 76). Jones (2010) encapsulates the difference between the positions of Doubrovsky and Genette by pointing out that while Doubrovskian autofiction fictionalises the story events in order to uncover the truth about the self, Genette's version fictionalises the self as well (p. 179). On the other hand, Genette makes a distinction between "true autofictions", in which the narrative content is fictional, and "false autofictions" in which the author of autofiction relates "strictly real events" in a novelistic form not to assume responsibility for his articulation of the facts. Therefore, Genette holds Doubrovskian autofiction as being deceptive and unethical (Hughes, 2002, p. 568).

In line with the theorists of autofiction discussed above, Arnaud Schmitt considers autobiography as being characterised by the problems of truth-telling, resulting from the factors such as the subjectivity of the author's experience, the fallibility of memory, and the narrative conventions (Stumm, 2019, p. 451). Accordingly, Schmitt (2010) opposes the theories that confine first person narratives to the realm of referentiality. He asserts that the notion of autobiographical pact itself necessitated for autobiography substantiates the assumption that authors might not be as good as their word (p. 125). That way, he calls attention to the possibility that the author will not adhere to the reality while supposedly giving an autobiographical account of his/her life. Furthermore, in his essay "Making the Case for Self-narration Against Autofiction" (2010), Schmitt accentuates the impossibility of making a clear-cut distinction between the "I-origo" (the real author) and the "I-origones" (the fictional narrator) in today's literary world,[8] which he holds to be the reason for the creation of the concepts of autofiction or autobiographical novels with their paradoxical foundations (p. 124).

As for his stance on the debates surrounding the definition of autofiction, Schmitt (2020) finds Doubrovsky's term intrinsically flawed, if not his formulation. It is because he understands the term *autofiction* as laying stress on the nonreferential part, which he believes accounts for Colonna and Genette's conceptions that incline towards fiction (p. 126). Schmitt (2017) also considers as flawed Gasparini's concept of "simultaneous double reading" which readers need to adopt when dealing with textual hybridity. He argues that it is cognitively not possible to understand a text as being both referential and fictional, "to entertain two contradictory ideas simultaneously", and to ravel in uncertainties (p. 3). He propounds that there is a difference between "experiencing fiction" and "experiencing a factual text"; therefore, readers are rather prone to choose one mode of

---

8   Arnaud Schmitt (2010) forms his argument in contradistinction to Kate Hamburger's strict differentiation between the real author, the "I-origo", and the fictional narrator, the "I-origones" in *The Logic of Literature* (1973) (p. 124).

reading (p. 3-4). Through his concept of contamination, Schmitt contends that when readers perceive a certain degree of fictionality in a referential text, they will decide to read it as a fiction (p. 4). By the same token, Schmitt (2010) opposes the general critical opinion that recognises autofiction as a hybrid genre occupying an indeterminate space between autobiography and novel, on the ground that such a standpoint leads to fruitless discussions on the inextricable question of whether the autofictional subject corresponds to the "je réel" (the real "I") or the "je fictif" (the fictive "I") (Boyle, 2013, p. 287). Schmitt (2010) maintains that rather than attempting to determine whether the author is lying or telling the truth, readers need to ask themselves the question, "Do I get more out of it if I see it as a fiction or as autobiography?" (p. 129). Since he does not deem "autofiction" as a proper term to describe texts not aiming for deliberate fictionalisation of the self and story events, Schmitt suggests the concept of "self-narration" to label the narratives in which the referentiality of the author is preserved, yet a form of poetic licence is allowed (p. 129). Schmitt's term clearly applies to the texts that Doubrovsky sees as autofictional. As in Doubrovskian formulation of autofiction, Schmitt considers narratives of self-narration as referential on account of the absence of a protective distance between the author and the narrator, and as literary because they inescapably have recourse to practises of fictionalisation. For Schmitt, picturing the self is inexorably linked to imagination due to the flawed nature of memory. Like Doubrovsky, he foregrounds the conviction that we forget, misunderstand or partially understand, as a result of which the author of self-narration resorts to imagination in order to overcome limits of empirical experience (p. 129). Finally, in tune with the psychoanalytic focus of Doubrovsky's version of autofiction, Schmitt characterises self-narration with a shift from narration of life to mind (p. 129).

On the other hand, Schmitt (2020) restricts the term "autofiction" to narratives conforming to the definitions of Vincent Colonna and Gerard Genette. He, therefore, considers autofiction as a special form of autobiographical novel in which there is a clear similarity between the author, narrator and main character, onomastic or not, and story events are fictional. According to Schmitt, autofiction is "a hyperbolic version of autobiographical novel" in the sense that it is marked by an overwhelming presence of the author in his/her own fiction. While autobiographical signs are subtle in autobiographical novel, autofiction transforms them into salient signals. Schmitt views this extravagant and playful dimension of autofiction as the principal trait that distinguishes it from autobiographical novel (p. 9). Correspondingly, he perceives the autofictional subject as an avatar for the author who projects himself/herself into a fictional world. He describes an autofictional avatar as the double of an author that is progressively detached from his/her referentiality, and concludes it to be the main raison d'être of autofiction (p. 10). Both Genette and Schmitt attempt to situate autofiction on the fiction/fact axis at a position closer to autobiographical novel whereas Schmitt positions his concept of self-narration somewhere towards the endpoint of classical autobiography.

This book is not concerned with deciding whether the texts in discussion are predominantly factual or fictional. Eluding Schmitt's doubts about the hybrid approach, it is argued that autofiction of multi-ethnic authors largely hinges upon the reader's awareness of two modes of narration, those of autobiography and fiction, present in the text, which are continuously hinted at yet remain indecipherable. While oscillating between the indices of referentiality and fiction, autofiction creates uncertainty in the reader as to whether to categorise the work as autobiography or fiction. Unlike what Schmitt estimates for the texts with hybrid status, readers do not definitively know which enunciations of the author are factual, and which of them are fictional. They simply know that statements belonging to the spheres of both referentiality and fiction coexist within the same text, and that there is no need for identifying them as one or another. The concurrent presence of "je reel" and "je fictif" causes instability in the text, yet neither of them is negated by the other. Although Schmitt's insistence on non-hybrid status of autofiction and his attempt for finding a solution to its generic problem are not relevant to the purposes of this book, his thoughts on the authorial figure provide useful insights into autofiction penned by multi-ethnic authors. Schmitt (2010) argues that it is the authorial persona which is the locus of the instability of autofiction, rather than its indeterminate position between autobiography and fiction. That is because the author is always reimagined by the reader based on pieces of referential information given in an autofictional text, which yields numerous images of the author as readers conjure up individually (Boyle, 2013, p. 287). Despite reading the same information about the author, readers are likely to arrive at different conclusions, creating instability in the genre. In relation to the discussions of multiethnicity in this book, it becomes important that the authorial presence is partly constructed by the reader in contradistinction to representation of a fixed identity. As different from Schmitt's views, however, it is contended that autofiction's constant code-switching between the factual and fictional domains contributes to the instability of genre as well as to the representation of a shifting authorial identity. Autofiction is considered as predicated on the notion of doubt, resulting from both the oscillation between facts and fiction, and the uncertainty surrounding the autofictional persona. It is argued that as multi-ethnic authors of autofiction are not able to fit in rigid racial and ethnic categories, their works are marked by a hesitant literary position and an ambivalent perception of identity that is reconfigured in each new setting.

In "The Limits of Autofiction" (2012), Catherine Cusset points to the fact that autofiction has become a loosely employed concept, and attempts to restrict its use to Doubrovsky's formulation, arguing that only fiction present in autofiction is rooted in language. She conceives autofiction as a project in which real events are narrated, and there is an intention to reach a certain truth (p. 1). Cusset places the notion of truth at the centre of autofictional enterprise; however, she disassociates it from factual accuracy. Like Doubrovsky, Cusset argues for the impossibility of creating a truthful textual representation of reality on the grounds that writing requires a concentration of facts to avoid repetition, and memory fails to provide empirical experiences in their entirety due to its flawed nature (p. 2). Nevertheless, she holds that the writer needs to make a pact with himself/herself "not to lie, not to invent just for the sake of fiction, but to be honest as much as possible, and to go as far as possible in his/her quest for truth" (p. 2). By "truth", Cusset refers to the writer's ability of going deep in an emotion, getting rid of anything that is not related to it, and afterwards, portraying the pure and bare form of this emotion that the reader can adopt. For her, if the author succeeds in going deep enough in the emotion, it becomes universal in the sense that anybody can claim it as their own (p. 2). This is the reason why autofictional works are rarely characterised by chronological timeline. Because emotion is the organising principle of such narratives, Cusset regards autofiction as "a spiralling movement towards the resurrection of a buried fragment of memory" (p. 2). She maintains that these memories are usually centred on painful and traumatic experiences such as death, illness, abandonment, madness and loss, for the reason that the experience of pain is more universally relatable (p. 6).

In like manner, Isabelle Grell (2014) suggests that autofiction has appeared in the wake of various types of crises (Dix, 2017, p. 170). In addition to traumas of war, she identifies the distressing experiences that recur persistently in autofiction as the divided sense of selfhood in postcolonial societies as a consequence of the colonial legacy; the loss of a loved one or friend; and the long-term experience of debilitating disease or sickness (p. 170). She argues that the author of autofiction, as the survivor of a traumatic incident, feels compelled to write the self in the hope that he/she attains a truth revealed through the emotions, and keeps a memory of the experience within himself/herself and the reader (Grell, 2018, p. vii). She also points out the fragmenting effects of these experiences on the subject who loses the integrity of selfhood (p. vii). As a result, the author is not able to capture his/her subjectivity as a whole in the narrative of his/her life. In the same vein, Arnaud Genon (2013) views painful experiences as incentives for the act of narration, and lays an emphasis on the author's conflicting relationship with society. According to Genon, there are four principles characterising autofiction, which are; the experience that provokes the author to write; the attempt to reconcile this experience with the broader narratives of history and society in which the self is located; the experimental use of the speaking "I"; and a tactical reconstruction of the subject (Dix, 2017, p. 171). In other words, Genon associates the practice of autofiction with the feeling of being dislocated within a society that incites the author to attempt to resituate himself/herself as a literary being through narrative. This book will discuss the multi-ethnic experiences of Black British women writers as an incentive to produce autofictional narratives in which they are provided with an opportunity to explore their feelings of divided subjectivity, racial discrimination and social displacement. Autofiction in Doubrovskian sense as a means of arriving at a deeper truth, and autofiction as a hybrid form, as formulated by Gaspirini and Colonna, will provide the theoretical basis for discussions of multiethnicity throughout the book.

As Isabelle Grell (2018) puts it, autofiction is not restricted to French literature, which is evidenced by the existence of books by theorists and authors of autofiction in numerous languages (p. vi). The Norwegian writer Karl Ove Knausgaard's six-volume work, *My Struggle* (published between 2009 and 2011), has been treated by various critics as a seminal exemplar of autofiction outside France. In this regard, Arnaud Schmitt (2016) argues that Knausgaard's book, based on his life, can be read within both referential and fictional frames (p. 555). Although Schmitt considers the term self-narration as the most appropriate label to classify the work, his critical judgements conform with Doubrovsky's formulation of autofiction. Schmitt notes that *My Struggle* is distinguished from an autobiographical novel by the author's overt recounting of real events about real people and his aim of reaching a higher "truth" about himself through the act of writing. On the other hand, it differs from autobiography in that he focuses on narrating a self, rather than a life which is typically found in the latter (p. 555). Schmitt observes that the undisguised self-references illustrate the author's desire to engage with the real as a remedy for his fatigue with fiction (p. 566).[9] Knausgaard (2009/2013) himself declares the purpose of his work to be depicting the reality as it is, stating that he can value only the forms of narratives which contain the voice of one's personality, and which permit the writer to confront

---

9 Knausgaard (2009/2013) expresses his dissatisfaction with fiction in *Book 2* with the words: "So why not write just fiction?... just the thought of a fabricated character in a fabricated plot made me feel nauseous" (p. 490).

with himself/herself (p. 545). Consistent with Doubrovsky's reasons for resorting to the acts of fictionalisation, however, Knausgaard admits that he is not capable of remembering entirely the events he narrates.[10] As a result, the reader gets the sense that Knausgaard as an unreliable narrator invents or omits many significant aspects of what really happened despite giving detailed accounts of the episodes from his life.

According to Schmitt (2016), Knausgaard's confessions of the flawed nature of his memory do not undermine his manifest commitment to reality for the reason that the author regards as trustworthy the fragmentary pieces and traces of past events which seem to be deeply engraved in his mind (p. 566). Knausgaard (2009/2013) expounds the value of his imperfect recollections with the words: "I might not have remembered what people said to me, I might not have remembered what had happened where, however I did remember exactly what it looked like and the atmosphere that surrounded it" (p. 543). No matter how partial and subjective his version of the reality might be, Knausgaard claims it to be a rich mode of retrospection due to the fact that the emotionally intense moments of lived experiences have impacted on his selfhood. As Schmitt (2016) puts it, forgetting or misremembering is an inescapable reality of human memory; therefore, it does not necessarily render a text fiction contrary to the intentions of the author (p. 567). Like Doubrovsky, Knausgaard, in fact, writes in order to remember his life. He relates the act of narration to recalling by pointing out that while writing, a reminder of something often releases something else (Marcus, 2018, p. 119). Even though he has to invent in order to fill the gaps in his recollections of the past events, Knausgaard primarily aims at a realistic rendering of his life. For that reason, he makes use of autobiographical devices such as referentiality and a shared identity between the author, narrator and character. However, some part of Knausgaard's "struggle" is revealed to be about representing accurately his life and subjectivity, which persistently results in failure. The discrepancy rising between the referential world and its textual representation prevents Knausgaard from establishing an autobiographical pact with the reader, and induces him to produce an autofictive text where questions of truth and personal identity ultimately arise (Kunzru, 2014). Knausgaard illustrates that reality is a subjective construct unless one records every moment of the lived

---

10   Knausgaard (2009/2013) confesses the imperfect state of his memory by writing in *Book 1* that "I remembered hardly anything from my childhood. That is, I remembered hardly any of the events in it. But I did remember the rooms where they took place" (p. 189).

experiences, and selfhood is continuously shaped by the memories of the past which are often subject to imagination, and which can be only partly uncovered through processes such as the act of writing.

Published earlier than Karl Ove Knausgaard's *My Struggle* (2009–2011), in *The Book of Laughter and Forgetting* (1979/1981), the Czech author, Milan Kundera, deals with human struggle to either remember or forget the past, by mixing purely fictional narratives with sections of verifiable autobiography in which the author, narrator and character share a nominal identity. Like Doubrovsky and Knausgaard, Kundera expounds on the problematic nature of memory with an emphasis on instances of intentional and unintentional acts of forgetting. Placing the private lives of his fictional characters and his own textual self in the referential social context of the Soviet regime, he illustrates the constructedness of both collective historical accounts and individual life stories. In both cases, the reconstruction of the past becomes subject to manipulation of facts and invention in line with the interests of the teller who deliberately distorts certain aspects of past events. Kundera exemplifies the subjective composition of historical narratives with the insertion of his own real experience of being erased from historical documents due to ideological reasons.[11] He further depicts unintentional processes of forgetting by creating fictional characters who strive to recall past occurrences, yet encounter frequently gaps and chronological confusion. He shows that despite the haziness surrounding memories of the past, traumatic experiences, in particular, linger in mind more vividly than others as a result of the intensity of emotions felt at such moments, which points to the selective quality of human recollection. Kundera reflects the partial and chaotic workings of memory in the book by establishing an associative relationship in the shifts between the fictional and referential fragments of narrative. Kundera's use of some of the significant autofictional strategies in his novel is remarkable chiefly in that he represents the self in relation to politics.

In *Routledge Encyclopaedia of Narrative Theory* (2005), the German comparatist, Frank Zipfel considers autofiction in a poststructuralist context. He describes it as a narrative mode that accentuates the constructed and fictional nature of all autobiographical writing. Autofiction, thus, eradicates the

---

11 Although Kundera was an enthusiastic member of the communist party when he first joined in 1948, he became one of the leading figures of the failed movement the "Prague Spring" of 1968 against the Soviet invasion of Czechoslovakia and totalitarianism, as a result of which he lost his teaching job, his books were banned from publication, and he was stripped of Czechoslovakian citizenship in 1979.

distinction between fact and fiction, and questions the separation of art and life. He significantly notes that autofiction is linked to the dissolution of the concept of a homogeneous personal identity. It is common that writers who are members of social minority groups make use of the paradoxical particularities of autofiction for creative restructuring of minority identities (p. 36–37). In accordance with the contradictions it embodies, in "Autofiktion Zwischen den Grenzen von Faktualität, Fiktionalität und Literarität?" (2009), Zipfel views autofiction as an oscillation between the autobiographical and the novelistic pact, which causes uncertainty in the reader as to how to classify the text while reading it. He concludes that the ambiguous literary situation of autofiction helps the text to gain creatives perspectives, ruling out the possibility of a uniform critical approach (Wagner-Egelhaaf, 2019, p. 3).

In her essay "Does Autofiction Belong to French or Francophone Authors and Readers Only?" (2018), Karen Ferreira-Meyers proffers the most widely accepted understanding of autofiction as the one in which the author blends fiction into his/her life writing, abandoning some of the truth-claims on which autobiography is predicated (p. 31). Ferreira-Meyers maintains that autofiction's embodiment of fiction does not simply result from the assumption of inherent fictionality of all writing. Rather, the author engages in the act of fictionalisation intentionally and strategically, taking liberties with the factual referentiality that is expected to be found in autobiography. Authors of autofiction give themselves a licence to reserve or alter parts of the objective truth in order to represent a subjective self, without feeling constrained by a pact that obligates adhesion to the reality (Ferreira-Meyers, 2015, p. 214). In this regard, she makes a distinction between autobiography and autofiction, pointing out that whereas the former is committed to representing in the most realistic terms a character who really existed, the other is concerned with fictionalising a character who really lived, albeit moving within reality (p. 205). Starting from the facts, the author of autofiction weaves them into imaginative threads so as to interfere with the truth. Hence, Ferreira-Meyers emphasises that there is a difference between the fiction in autofiction and the fiction that is necessarily present in autobiography. It could be argued that autofiction accentuates the unavoidability of fictionalisation in autobiography by exaggerating its presence. Ferreira-Meyers (2018), accordingly, describes autofiction as encouraging the reader primarily "to question the text, its truth and validity", yet more significantly, "the truth and veracity of the self; memory; and the (non)ability to (re)create or invent reality." (p. 40). The fiction that autofiction involves ultimately leads the reader to contemplate on the issues of inaccessibility to the absolute knowledge of the self, status of memory as an imperfect source for recovering the past, and failure of textuality in giving a truthful representation of life. Consistent with her perception of the ends that autofiction serves, Ferreira-Meyers specifies the most prominent characteristics of autofiction as the use of a nominal shared identity between the author, narrator and character; the contradictory and confusing message to the reader who becomes unable to identify fact from fiction; and the manifestation of a fragmented/multiple identity (p. 36). The uncertainties that the author experiences in regard to his/her subjectivity are communicated to the reader in the form of undecidability between fact and fiction, all of which clearly contribute to autofiction's designation as a genre of ambiguity.

In the introductory section to *Handbook of Autobiography/Autofiction* (2019), Martina Wagner-Egelhaaf retraces the changes in autobiography studies, influenced by the development of poststructuralist literary theories from the 1960s onwards, as a result of which critics have read autobiographical works, taking into consideration the deficiencies of memory, narcissistic tendencies of the writer, the interference of imagination, and the narrative structure that necessarily adds a fictional dimension. She points out that the perception of fiction in autobiography has altered with postmodernist approaches since 1980s. While fiction was first regarded as an unavoidable constituent of autobiography, authors later began to play with the fictional element and incorporate it deliberately, which resulted in the emergence of autofiction (p. 2). Accordingly, Wagner-Egelhaaf describes autofiction as a transgressive genre that crosses over the boundaries between autobiography and literature, life and art. Furthermore, she points out that after the era of poststructuralist criticism of essentialism and assumption of linguistically constructed nature of meaning, there is a renewed interest in "real life" motives and effects of literary production (p. 4). She suggests, this does not mean that the thoughts of poststructuralist theorists are to be brushed aside. On the contrary, their critical insights help us attain a better grasp of "experience" and "reality". Therefore, she views signification as not contradicting the reality, but rendering it more comprehensible (p. 4). She advocates for a constructive dialogue between "new realism" and "poststructuralist criticism", in which new understandings of "truthfulness" might be produced. Importantly, Wagner-Egelhaaf relates the reason for the new awareness of the "real" and of people's authentic life experiences to the processes of globalisation in the digital age which threaten to eliminate diversity and heterogeneity (p. 4). Autofiction emerges as a form of narrative that upholds the notion of multiplicity, which lays out the ground for the discussion of multi-ethnic identities in this book.

Autofiction in the Anglophone Context

The discussions over possible definitions of autofiction in France and other countries in the continent have been taken up by Anglophone critics and authors. Thomas C. Spear, in "Autofiction and National Identity" (1998), argues that the form of traditional autobiography, like national identity, is too limited for recapturing the autobiographical truth of an individual. Although his discussions are focused mainly on Francophone authors and their works, his views on autobiography and subjectivity provide useful insights into multi-ethnic experiences of Black British authors. As he opposes to a rigid classification of the frontiers of autobiography, Spear maintains that one's identity cannot be reduced to categories such as "French", "Senegalese", "Asian", "black", "woman", "man", "gay" because the self is constituted by the multiplicity of relations (p. 93). Unlike the unified perception of a subject, as autobiography attempts to represent, he understands the self as being influenced by a wide range of collective forces from nationality, history, religion, language to ethnicity. As such, he contends that the link between individual and community breaks down the hegemonic singularity of the self in autobiography which neglects the plural and composite nature of identity (p. 95). For him, the true autobiography of the individual always contains a composite voice (p. 100).

Spear (1998) points out that writers might sometimes be obliged to express an extratextual reality of the self or nation in a fictionalised form, in such situations as when they do not conform to the norms of a nation, or it is simply dangerous to use the autobiographical first person (p. 91). These works, further, illustrate the limitations of the individualist western form of autobiography, and necessitate a different narrative category which provides a broader space for exploring the multiple layers of the self in its relation to community. In this regard, Spear defines autofiction as a genre in which characters are extra-textually connected to a factual person and/or context in a fictional account. He suggests that autofiction is likely to be adopted by authors who do not dare or care to be bound to a pact of truth/fiction (p. 90). Spear's observations, in Francophone authors' autofictional works, of individual identities that are hybrid and multiple yield significant findings for the purposes of this book. He concludes that collective memory has substantial impacts on the self of multiple heritage. The subjectivity of these authors is shaped by multi-generational histories as much as individual experiences. Their life stories are, accordingly, intertwined with those of family lineages (p. 101). Their biological and cultural hybridity proves to be subversive in that they are ascribed a number of sub-identities by multiple communities, as a result of which their self-characterisation becomes more complicated than the one that would be restricted to a singular representation of the self and nation (p. 104). As will be examined in the following chapters, Black British writers' use of autofictional strategies to explore their multiethnicity and to search for self-definition intersect with collective forces in similar patterns.

In *Encyclopaedia of Life Writing: Autobiographical and Biographical Forms* (2001), Johnnie Gratton identifies the key feature of autofiction as promotion of act-value at the expense of truth-value within the parameters of autobiography (p. 86). Rather than reflecting the past transparently, autofiction renders life writing into a personal performance. In this view, the act of writing gains prominence over a truthful representation of referentiality. Gratton emphasises that the decreasing confidence in truth value and growing investment in act value result in a situation where fiction and autobiography are no longer polarised; on the contrary, they ineluctably become overlapped. As the reality of the real is denied in its textual form, language itself becomes the central event in such autobiographical performances (p. 86). Gratton notes that the conception of autofiction as a performance is based on the post-Freudian view of destabilised subject that demands fresh ways of dealing with subjectivity and referentiality in autobiographical practices, like the one that does not straightforwardly disqualify potentials of fiction. Given that the modern subject's experiences of loss, forgetting and trauma have problematised his/her claims to such memories, Gratton reasons that it would be possible to recover the past events only through the indirectness of fiction (p. 87). In Gratton's explication of the term, the fiction embodied in autofiction functions as a means of exploring the realities that lay beyond the solid referents to which language can correspond.

Like Spear and Gratton, Alex Hughes (1999) calls attention to the limitations of conventional autobiography, and asserts the impossibility of its undertaking to produce a mimetic copy of the referentiality, on the grounds of the unreliable nature of both memory and ego. She considers such a premiss as inciting authors to step outside the frontiers of autobiography, and to problematise the dividing lines between factuality and sincerity in their self-reflexive narratives (p. 3). Hughes (2002), accordingly, defines autofiction as a narrative modality in which the referential is enriched through fictionalisation, resulting in a metaphorical version of the author's life story (p. 567). She perceives such a narrative form as a "monstrous" production in that it loosens the generic boundaries and undermines the pre-established literary classifications. As Doubrovsky accentuates its occupation of diverse places and its openness to other forms, Hughes characterises autofiction as being haunted by what is foreign to it, laying stress on the permeability of autofictional narratives (p. 567).

Referring to Doubrovsky's formulation of autofiction, Elizabeth H. Jones (2007) indicates autofictional works to be often labelled "novel" to signal their partly fictitious contents. She reaffirms the dominant assumption that acknowledging the fallibility of memory and the impossibility of representing a life story truthfully, autofiction does not claim to proffer an entirely sincere revelation of the reality. Authors of autofiction, in fact, create a fictional framework through which they narrate verifiable facts of their lives. In doing so, they blur generic boundaries between autobiography and novel, and blend facts with fiction (p. 96). In "Autofiction: A Brief History of a Neologism" (2010), Jones remarks the potential of autofiction as lying in its venture to bring into conventional autobiography the contemporary critical thoughts of psychoanalysis and constructedness of selfhood. For her, autofiction's treatment of the self as a fractured, incomplete and uncertain entity corresponds to the cultural paradigm of the present era. Hence, she asserts, "Autofiction, as opposed to autobiography, then, is highly attuned with an age in which the subject is no longer accepted to be a unified, simple whole" (p. 177). Recognising the limitations of autobiography that reduces the self and lived experiences to coherent integrities, Jones sees autofiction as a critical approach that deconstructs totalising perceptions of autobiographical narration of selfhood.

Jonathan Sturgeon, in his article "The Death of the Postmodern Novel and the Rise of Autofiction" (2014), notes that there has been a remarkable tendency, in recent years, for publishing autofictions, in which the authors "vigorously reasserted themselves" (n. p.). He professes that the authorial self is no longer positioned in sites of disinformation, entropy, hyperreality or unreality, as it has been in postmodern novel. Literary products of the new current are distinguished as autobiographical, memoiristic and metafictional. Differing from postmodern fiction that often displays a mistrust of metanarratives, Sturgeon identifies autofictional writing as embracing the metanarrative of one's own life, which is made up of the stories the author tells himself/herself and others. Hence, he defines autofiction as pointing to the presumption that the self is composed of fiction. According to Sturgeon, autofiction is not concerned with tensions between the real and the unreal. Rather, it seeks to reposition the relation between the self and fiction. He asserts, "Fiction is no longer seen as false or lies or make-believe" (n. p.). Because it comprises the narratives one tells and the stories one is told, fiction is recognised as an indisputable part of one's life. Turning away from the debates of truth versus reality, Sturgeon propounds, autofiction looks for answers to the questions of how to live and how to create. Ferreira-Meyers (2018) maintains that Sturgeon's standpoint has initiated a new sort of debate on the understanding of autofiction. She observes that while French and other Francophone autofictions are preoccupied with the issues of truth, factuality and fiction, autofictional writing in other world literature puts aside the question of representing life truthfully, and instead inquiries into the ways of living and creating (p. 33).

Juliet Jacques (2016), the writer of *Trans: A Memoir*, acknowledges that she has intended to write her book as an autofiction, in which she narrates her own experiences of transsexuality. Considering autofiction as a transgressive genre, Jacques holds it to be an appropriate form for conveying cross-gender issues. As such, she describes autofiction as a writing that aims to subvert and blur the boundaries of the pre-established literary genres of autobiography and fiction, as transsexuality crosses over the dividing lines between the alleged gender categories. For her, autofiction recounts the referential facts about the author, in the form of a novel. It takes a factual story, and mixes it with invented episodes on account of the assumption that fiction allows a greater deal of truthfulness. As Jacques describes her own work, the resulting text qualifies as a memoir of the author and at once not. Some of the experiences belong to the author, and some of them do not. It becomes the reader's responsibility to decide which parts of the text are factual and which ones are fictional. Jacques responds to the arguments on the death of the novel form, as Sturgeon has brought up, by pointing out that people do not believe in pure fiction anymore as the result of the demystification of the twentieth century that has unmasked the authorial manipulations in those narratives. She sees autofiction as the only place where fiction could recover its status.

With a focus on the American context, Marjorie Worthington develops a definition of autofiction in which she traces the etymological origin of the term to France, yet she maintains the form and content of autofictional works produced in the US as being rooted in metafictional tendencies of American postmodern literature. As American novels from the post-war period employed the trope of a character sharing the same name as the author,[12] Worthington (2018) considers the primary feature of autofiction as the inclusion of the author as a fictionalised character, commonly as the protagonist. In her conception, notwithstanding the onomastic connection between the author and the character, the two are not identical to each other (p. 2). In line with Gerard Genette's formulation, the protagonist of autofiction engages in overtly fictional events (p. 11). For

---

12 Worthington (2018) points to Ronald Suckenick's *Up* (1968) and *Out* (1973), John Barth's *Chimera* (1972), and Kurt Vonnegut's *Breakfast of Champions* (1973) as examples of American metafictional novels and forebears of contemporary autofiction (p. 1).

Worthington, therefore, American autofiction is marked by a blending of the seemingly verifiable biographical facts of the author with the accounts of clearly fictional incidents and experiences (p. 12). As exemplary works of American autofiction, she specifies Mark Leyner's *Et Tu, Babe?* (1992), Philip Roth's *Operation Shylock* (1994), Richard Powers's *Galatea 2.2* (1995), Bret Easton Ellis' *Lunar Park* (2005), Arthur Philips's *The Tragedy of Arthur* (2011), David Foster Wallace's *The Pale King* (2011), and Ron Currie, Jr.'s *Flimsy Little Plastic Miracles* (2013), in all of which eponymous author-characters are positioned in fictional situations. In Worthington's definition of autofiction, such texts are classified as both referential and fictional in that they feature a character who resembles the author in some aspects, but they incorporate intentionally fictionalised story events. Autofictional texts, hence, sustain a tenuous relationship between the author and the character (p. 12). Despite being interconnected entities, the author and the author-character become divergent in the course of narrating fictional events. As such, Worthington (2017) contends that autofiction inhabits a liminal space between fiction and nonfiction, vacillating constantly between biographical facts and pure fiction (p. 472).

Worthington (2017) notes that autofiction is sometimes confused with memoir due to the fact that in both narrative forms, the protagonist shares the same name as the author. Although acknowledging that memoir has experimented, in recent years, with fictionalisation techniques, blurring the boundaries between fact and fiction, Worthington views it as a genre that is predominately referential. Even if it ventures into the realm of non-referentiality, she suggests that memoir never becomes quite fiction in the way autofiction is (p. 472). For her, therefore, the main difference between autofiction and memoir is that the former qualifies essentially as fictional despite its inclusion of biographical facts, the latter remains essentially referential even if it incorporates fictional elements (p. 473). In this regard, Worthington (2018) posits that in the United States, the Doubrovskian kind of autofiction is to be categorised as a memoir for the reason that it purports to present a referential portrayal of the self to the greatest possible extent, rather than crafting a fictionalised version of the authorial persona (p. 10). Worthington expounds on her conception of autofiction by distinguishing it further from autobiographical novels. She points out that an autobiographical novel depicts a character who resembles the author, yet no onomastic connection is established between the two. As a result, biographical information included in autobiographical novels does not cause confusion in readers who read them unambiguously as fictions. On the other hand, autofiction is predicated on ambiguity induced by the presence of a character named after the author and situated in invented story events (p. 4).

Worthington (2017) ascribes the proliferation of autofictional texts to a variety of cultural anxieties, from poststructuralism's rendering all writing into artificial constructs to the author's diminishing power as the arbiter of culture. She argues that notwithstanding the poststructuralist notions of language's fallibility and the unattainability of objective truth, the increasing popularity of memoirs in recent years illustrates that factual stories are still of importance, and "truth" in such narratives is valued by readers (p. 475). Rather than a reaction against the theories that postulate the impossibility of language to communicate the truth, Worthington sees readers' predilection for factuality as an indication of their acceptance of the inaccessibility of objective truth, and therefore, of their longing for personal versions of reality (p. 476). She maintains that because memoir presents the author's individual perspective on a particular episode of life, unlike autobiography claiming to recount the story of an entire life, it provides the kind of truth that readers crave. Such truth transmitted by memoir is not universal or timeless, but highly subjective and transient. For Worthington, readers' interest in the author's specific view of truth results from their awareness that language does not simply mirror the reality, but also constitutes it, giving a new shape to one's perception of it (p. 476). She contends that autofiction complicates this conceptualisation by intentionally joining with and diverging from the facts of the author's real life, with the aim of questioning the idea of an unproblematic equation between the author-character and the extratextual author (p. 476). Depicting a character that is both connected to and separate from the author, autofiction demonstrates the possibilities and limitations of language when representing real-life experiences (Worthington, 2018, p. 6).

Worthington (2018) claims that the emergence of autofictional techniques is closely tied to the declining cultural authority of the conventional author figure, partly with the "death of the author" debates that started in the late 1960s, leading to a reconsideration of the author's hitherto privileged position (p. 6). She maintains that the traditional image of the author as a creatively powerful white male has been further challenged by the inclusion of women and writers of colour in the canon and the democratisation of authorship as a result of new-media technologies. Seeing autofiction as being produced mostly by white male writers in the US, she asserts that these authors convey their authorial anxieties through metafictional insertion of themselves into fictional texts (p. 5). Autofiction's postmodern challenges to conventional conceptions of authority and truth are simultaneously attempts to restore these traditions through recentring the white male author (p. 21). Worthington limits her observations mainly to autofictional works produced by men, and perceives the practice of autofiction as a response to the crisis of masculinity induced by the declining status of today's male authors. Worthington's position has been largely challenged by some of the succeeding theoreticians and practitioners of autofiction.

Hywel Dix (2017) attempts to define autofiction by accentuating the difference between the "I" and "me" of an autobiographical narrative, by which he refers to the subject who narrates and the object who is narrated, respectively. He argues that in autofiction, the "I" as the subject of a text is considerably more active and more questioning when compared to the objectified "me" that is, conversely, more passive and more steadfast. Additionally, the subject of autofiction appears to be constantly in question, which Dix considers as the key feature of the genre (p. 171). As opposed to the object-oriented practice of autobiography, Dix notes one significant purpose of autofiction to be using narrative in order to explore and experiment with the self. Because authors of autofiction engage in reconfiguring ceaselessly the possibilities of first-person narrative, he observes that the "I" of their works eludes lapsing into "me" (p. 171). Autofiction destabilises the conventional subject-object relationship in that the quests of the self result only in an endless deferral of the object. As a result, the subject "I" is dissipated into a number of textual explorations which lead to no final point (p. 172). Dix sees the shifting and unstable subject of autofiction as mirrored stylistically in narrative discontinuities and nonlinearity of time frame. As the subject itself is fractured, autofictional texts are marked by fragmentary aesthetics. According to Dix, the development of the actively questing subject in autofiction ensues partly from the modernist inquiries into the limiting and distorting nature of memory, and partly from critical theories such as psychanalysis that has interrogated the conception of an essential and stable self (p. 172).

Dix (2017) views autofictional writing as a practice in which life, lived experience and work are interpenetrated, that is, the process of writing moves from past experiences of the author and becomes a constituent part of his/her subsequent experiences (p. 173). He significantly notes that autofiction legitimatises the author as the subject of literary practice and critical investigation, notwithstanding the endless deferral of the authorial self, rendering the whole pursuit eventually fruitless (p. 175). For him, they are often traumatic experiences that provoke the author of autofiction to write a fictional self-retrospect. On the grounds that they write and rewrite themselves after trauma, Dix suggests Tim Lott and Julian Barnes as examples of English authors of autofiction (p. 175). Furthermore, he considers A.S. Byatt and Salman Rushdie as autofictive writers, in conformity with Eefje Claasser's observation that the active questing and questioning of the author as subject has always been a prominent feature of works by feminist and postcolonial writers.[13] Dix maintains that these authors have written their own selves in the aftermath of turbulent experiences, resorting markedly to the semi-fictionalisation of the authorial self (p. 175). Unlike Marjorie Worthington who holds the nominal relationship between the author, narrator and character as an indispensable component of autofictional texts, Dix contends that the semi-fictionalisation of the author allows a diverse range of narrative experiments. Situating the fictional avatars of themselves in fictional scenarios, authors explore the themes concerning their own extratextual lives. In this regard, he describes autofiction as exploring "the question of whether the authorial 'I' is singular and inherently stable regardless of context, or whether, when the scenario alters, the attributes of the author alter too" (p. 178). Dix sees autofiction as a practice that interrogates the essentialist perception of selfhood, and that places pressure on the narrative medium to reveal the possibilities which the authorial subject might consist of.

As opposed to Worthington who ascribes the rise of autofiction in the U.S. to the diminishing cultural authority of white male writers and their efforts to reassert partly their authorial power, Dix (2018) enunciates one significant context for the evolvement of autofiction in English as the advancements in women's writing marked by experimental tendencies. He propounds that autofiction provides female authors with an opportunity to engage in a more liberated and liberating experimentation with the expression of selfhood than the established critical schools of thought do. As such, he maintains that many female writers have deliberately turned away from critical approaches such as deconstruction, post-structuralism and even feminism in order to experiment with new parameters, like the ones offered by autofiction, for representing women's subjectivity in the contemporary era (p. 10). By extension, Dix understands the development of autofiction in English as being occasioned by the postcolonial writing that constantly calls for new forms to articulate a wide range of diverse experiences and subjectivities within and across postcolonial cultures (p. 11). This book attempts to extend Dix's observations on the evolvement of autofiction in English to the writings of multiethnicity by Black British authors. It is argued that literary hybridity and ambivalence of autofiction enable these writers to explore and recount their multi-ethnic experiences beyond the conventional narrative

---

13   In *Author Representations in Literary Reading* (2012), Eefje Claasser articulates that "the death of the author and its implications for the author (and reader) have not restrained feminist and post-colonial criticism from focussing their research on the author's identity, gender and ethnicity" (p. 15–16).

forms and strategies. Consistent with Dix's definitions of autofiction, the works of multi-ethnic authors will be examined with respects to the semi-fictionalised authorial "I" that is on quest to explore the plurality of the self, and the interplay between the author's lived experiences and act of writing.

In "How Best to Read Auto-Fiction" (2018), which Tim Parks penned after being criticised for labelling his book *In Extremis* (2017) as a novel despite the obvious similarities to his own life, the writer discusses the idea of having an identity as a perpetual performance. That is, rather than being a singular and stable entity, the self consists of fleeting multiplicity, yet performs only certain aspects of the personality when interacting with other people. In line with Philip Roth's suggestion that a character cannot be identical with the author, but manifests only one possibility of the author's selfhood, Parks asserts that certain kinds of authors, like himself, do not claim to represent the ultimate truth about their subjectivity. On the contrary, they attempt to discover the possibilities of the self that would be unacceptable to perform in real life. For that purpose, these authors reconstruct fictionally the events from their own lives, yet allow their characters to act differently in overtly factual situations, with the hope of gaining a grasp of the concealed possibilities that constitute the reality of their subjectivity. Hence, Parks perceives fictional characters as being connected to the extratextual author but not representing the entire truth of his/her personality. His views of the self as a plural, shifting and performative phenomenon and the act of writing as a means of exploring the unknown aspects of subjectivity are particularly significant for the aims of this book.

As Christian Lorentzen (2018) points out in an article for New York Magazine's "Vulture", the term autofiction has become common in Anglophone literature to describe the novels that are on the lines of the works by certain authors, such as Chris Kraus' *I Love Dick* (1997/2006), Sheila Heti's *How Should a Person Be?* (2010) and *Motherhood* (2018), Rachel Cusk's trilogy *Outline* (2014), *Transit* (2017) and *Kudos* (2018), Ben Lerner's, *10:04* (2014), Jenny Offill's *Dept. of Speculation* (2014), Maggie Nelson's *The Argonauts* (2015), Teju Cole's *Open City* (2011), Tao Lin's *Taipei* (2013) and *Trip* (2018), among others. In all of these novels, the boundaries between memoir and fiction are crossed, and the authors' actual lives and experiences are reflected in those of the protagonists. Lorentzen (2018) emphasises that when reading such books, readers might feel like they are reading a diary in that autofictional texts impart the sense of a somewhat direct inscription of real life onto the page. However, he holds the induced "real life" effect to be a mere illusion. He argues that like fictional novels, works of autofiction have artifice too, but it serves to create the feeling that they lack any artificial craft, which Lorentzen considers as one of the most distinctive features of the genre. Along similar lines, in *Reality Hunger: A Manifesto* (2010), David Shields calls attention to contemporary art's increasing engagement with referentiality and experimentation with the boundaries of genres. For him, such developments point to the formation of a new artistic movement, yet he perceives its composition as being of an "organic" kind. He identifies accordingly the key components of the current as:

> A deliberate unartiness: "raw" material, seemingly unprocessed, unfiltered, uncensored, and unprofessional [...] Randomness, openness to accident and serendipity, spontaneity; artistic risk, emotional urgency and intensity, reader/viewer participation; an overly literal tone, as if a reporter were viewing a strange culture; plasticity of form, pointillism; criticism as autobiography; self-reflexivity, self-ethnography, anthropological autobiography; a blurring (to the point of invisibility) of any distinction between fiction and nonfiction: the lure and blur of the real. (p. 5)

Although Shields does not mention the term "autofiction" anywhere in his book, many of the distinguishing traits included in the list for defining the recent artistic developments are present in autofictional works by Anglophone authors. In regard to the "unartiness", Sheila Heti's *How Should a Person Be?*, for instance, comes with a blurb that describes the book as "complex" and "artfully messy". For the adherents of this "unartful art", a deliberately messy way of writing helps them incorporate more reality in their novels than what artificially created designs can permit. They claim that unartful writing produces texts that are more approximate to real life (Tomson, 2018, n.p.). However, authors of autofiction are paradoxically far from purporting to provide a truthful representation of the reality. As Christ Kraus has remarked on her own book: "Everything that happens in it happened first in life, but that doesn't mean that it's a memoir" (as cited in Hunt, 2017), the narration of real events does not necessarily qualify a text as referential, which autofiction is concerned with demonstrating. Kraus adds that "What makes fiction is not whether it's true or not, [...] but whether it's construed as a work of fiction" (as cited in Hunt, 2017). She emphasises the possibility that referential materials from the author's life can be conveyed in a novelistic form without contradicting itself, which suggests the idea of the artificiality of literary categories as well as the sterility of making a straightforward distinction between fact and fiction.

Authors of autofiction persistently call attention to the referential dimension of their works by writing in the first-person and recounting their own life experiences; however, they also lay emphasis on the divergence between the author-character and the actual author. Sheila Heti (2007) articulates the connection between the author and the protagonist with the words: "as I'm writing, the character or self I'm writing about and my whole self [...] become entwined" (n. p.). She also points to the distance between the two upon completion of writing process, which normally results in the creation of "a different self from the original" (n. p.). Heti's remarks foreground the notion that the self is composed of multiple selves. The textual self-proceeds from the "original" one, yet they correspond to each other only temporarily, which implicates that the self is a constantly evolving entity, constituted by discontinuities, and thus invariably becoming split into multiplicity. As a result, the textual self ends up representing only one of myriad possibilities contained in the actual self. Despite the ineluctable distance between the author and the character, authors of autofiction are mainly concerned with conveying the authenticity of lived experiences. Sheila Heti (2007) states, "Increasingly I'm less interested in writing about fictional people, because it seems so tiresome to make up a fake person and put them through the paces of a fake story" (n. p.). Heti expresses her diminishing interest in creating fictional characters and stories on the grounds that they do not feel realistic adequately. Similarly, Rachel Cusk declares that "I'm not interested in character because I don't think character exists anymore" (as cited in Schwartz, 2018). Like Heti, Cusk emphasises the lack of authenticity in fictional characters. She considers her previous fictional stories as seeming now "fake and embarrassing" (as cited in Kellaway, 2014). That is because, after going through traumatic life events, like her experience of the break-up of a marriage, Cusk finds it impossible to communicate the realities of the self and life through fiction. She remarks, "Once you have suffered sufficiently, the idea of making up John and Jane and having them do things together seems utterly ridiculous" (as cited in Kellaway, 2014). As Chris Power (2018) observes, Cusk's disillusionment with writing fiction recalls Knausgaard's thoughts which she once quoted in a review of volume two of *My Struggle*: "just the thought of fiction, just the thought of a fabricated character in a fabricated plot made me feel nauseous" (n. p.). Consistent with such unfavourable stances against fiction, in the *Outline* trilogy, Cusk writes her life from the point of view of a character named as Faye but who shares a great deal of Cusk's biographical referentiality. By creating a character that is simultaneously both identical to Rachel Cusk and not, and investing this already uncertain textual self with an elusive presence in her first-person narratives, the author demonstrates that fiction is still an indispensable part of the kind of reality she argues for. In a similar vein, Ben Lerner expresses his concern, when he is writing, as exploring "how we live fictions, how fictions have real effects, become facts in that sense, and how our experience of the world changes depending on its arrangement into one narrative or another" (as cited in Lin, 2014). It could be argued that authors of autofiction presuppose the inseparability of facts and fiction. They acknowledge that narration of factual events from a subjective viewpoint renders them inescapably fictive. Although these authors are preoccupied primarily with representing the authenticity of lived experiences, they conceive of the real as partly composed of fictions. In her article for The New York Times, "Our Autofiction Fixation" (2021), Jessica Winter likewise professes that much of writing about the reality results in "pure invention", pointing out that "your subjectivity is all you have. You made it up. It's made of you" (n. p.). Winter calls attention not only to the individual perceptions intervening in representation of the reality, but also to the fictionality inherent in the act of narrating, which she understands as being performed, at times, with "lack of self-knowledge" and "a near total absence of control" over composition of a work. Despite all its nonreferential aspects, however, Winter argues that the practice of autofiction allows authors to see the reality in novel ways, and thus reveals a kind of truth that has not previously been available to the conscious mind. As such, it becomes evident that for authors of autofiction, fact and fiction interpenetrate in many complex ways.

According to Myra Bloom (2019), autofiction's overt play on the line between fact and fiction targets the hierarchal categories associated with masculine high art. As opposed to Marjorie Worthington, who regards autofictional practice as an attempt by white male authors to restore their historically privileged position in the literary field, Bloom relates the development of autofiction to feminist critics' expansion of the study of autobiography to encompass a broader variety of authors and works. She notes that while traditional autobiography was dominated by the Enlightenment conception of subjectivity expressed by white European writers such as Saint Augustine, Jean-Jacques Rousseau and Thomas De Quincey, female practitioners of autobiography have blurred the line between fact and fiction since the late 1980s (p. 2). In this regard, Bloom argues the majority of writers of autofiction to be women, who have adopted autofictional strategies in order to denounce the constraints imposed on them by the patriarchal society. Accordingly, she views experiential tendencies of autofiction as an indication of female authors' need for distinct forms of self-expression (p. 7). Bloom maintains that the stylistic template for traditional autobiography, characterised by a linear narration of the retrospect of a well-known individual, does not apply to many "ex-centric writers" because they are either unable to or choose not to compose coherent and teleological narratives (p. 11). Instead, they seek to subvert the precepts of autobiography for political ends. Through autofictional strategies such as self-fictionalisation, they interrogate the communities in which they are embedded, and imagine new ones structured with more equitable relations that recognise the values of marginalised individuals. Autofiction, thus, allows writers to create spaces for "women, racialized, and queer subjects" (p. 13). In the same vein, the coloured author Tope Folarin (2020) expresses his criticism of the thoughts that attribute autofiction solely to narrative practices by white men. Having written his own autofictional novel, *A Particular Kind of Black* (2019), Folarin asserts that the publishing industry has largely failed to recognise the extent to which autofiction is penned by authors of colour. Although his works and the ones written by other coloured writers are formalistically identical to autofiction, they are categorised as autobiographical fiction. Because autofiction is perceived to be a literary innovation, it is associated with the efforts and creativity of white authors, while coloured writers are left out of the circle, being confined into conventional forms. Starting from the view that women and coloured authors' autofiction is often neglected, this book is focused particularly on autofictional practises by Black British women writers who are liable to double marginalisation.

It is concluded that autofiction by both French and Anglophone authors is primarily concerned with the issues of memory, subjectivity and representation. On the other hand, Dix (2018) observes that French writers are dedicated to searching for an impossible truth in their works whereas Anglophone writers are preoccupied with the construction of the self in writing (p. 20). All the same, autofiction illustrates that the boundaries around autobiography as well as identity are too rigid to capture fully the "truth" and the self. Autofiction, as considered in this book, assumes that the distinction between fact and fiction is inessential; fiction is a part of one's life; the real is composed of fictions; fiction enriches the representation of the referentiality; and established categories can be interrogated and subverted, opening up new spaces for marginalised individuals to exist.

Chapter 2 Theoretical Contexts

Autofiction within Literary Theory

Contemporary theoretical developments such as psychoanalysis, structuralism, deconstruction, poststructuralism, and postmodernism have substantially contributed to the development of theories and practice of autofiction. Critics concur that autofiction has a dialectical relationship with these twentieth century critical theories, which have both laid the foundation for and come in conflict with autofictional mode of writing. In the preceding humanistic approach to literary criticism, the individual was held to be a unified, knowing, and autonomous entity. Authors were accordingly considered as being capable of articulating unproblematically truths about human nature or about the world in general. They were the unique source and origin of texts which conveyed their particular perceptions and individual insights (Belsey, 2002, p. 2). However, the authorial authority which traditional criticism upheld has been put into question by the subsequent theorical advancements. As a result, the omniscience and self-confidence of autobiographical subject have progressively given way to the self-doubt and uncertainty of autofictional persona.

Grounded on the presumption of the post-Freudian subject as unstable, fragmented and shattered, modernist approach to literature has rejected conventional truths and figures of authority, and endorsed detachment of the author's personality from the text, undermining the authority of the autobiographical subject. Structuralist theory, problematising the traditional notion of intrinsic one-to-one correspondence between objects and referents, has maintained language not to reflect a pre-existent or external reality of objects. In this respect, neither objects nor referents possess essential meanings. Rather, meaning is generated symbolically through the signifying practices of language structured as a system of signs. Identically, for the poststructuralist theorists, language is not a transparent medium that can represent the world truthfully. Language is, in effect, utterly problematic. Contrary to the structuralist assumption, however, meaning does not reside in linguistic signs because relations between objects and referents are unstable, changing in every new context. Furthermore, language is capable of blending unintentional meanings and subconscious references into statements. This realisation of the fallibility of language has given rise to the conviction of imperfect nature of authorial power. If the language does not allow the author to communicate his/her intentions, then the author cannot be considered as having a hold on his/her enunciations (Jones, 2007, p. 61). Many critics agree that by simultaneously bringing the authorial presence back to texts but fictionalising it to some extent, and committing to narrate the truth but creating ambivalence around the concept of truth itself, authors of autofiction both affirm and question the poststructuralist dismantling of the traditional perspectives on the concepts of authority, authenticity and truth. They view autofiction as exploring the extent to which language can represent the reality and the extent to which the process is distorted by impingement of such forces as memory, thought, feeling and mood. With the aim of contextualising autofiction within literary theory, the book will attempt to establish the ways in which contemporary critical thoughts have been influential on the development of autofiction.

Before the flourishment of structuralism in the 1960s, traditional criticism assumed that through writing, it would be possible to achieve self-discovery, self-knowledge and self-creation, which would reveal truths about "a universal self". Language was believed to be mimetic in the sense that it mimicked the outside world, giving a direct representation of reality. Ferdinand de Saussure (1916/1959) rejected the mimetic theory of language and drew attention to the composition of language as a system. He asserted that language is determined by its own internally structured rules. For that reason, language does not and cannot imitate reality, or designate objects or ideas through words. Words are not symbols that equal to things. They are simply signs constituted by two parts: the signifier (a written or spoken mark) and the signified (a concept in our minds). Meaning is produced by the relationship between the signifier and the signified, which is arbitrary and a matter of convention. For Saussure, meaning is made possible by differences among signs within a linguistic system. We can know what a sign means only because it differs from other signs, that is, words obtain their meanings through relations among one another within a particular system. Saussure's assumptions that language as a system operates outside an individual and it is the individual who is "spoken by" language have had profound impacts on the following critical systems of thought and on the development of autofictional subject who is presented as being constantly redefined by language.

In line with the structuralist stance, Jacque Derrida and other poststructuralists maintain that there is nothing outside of the text because for humans everything is mediated by language. However, poststructuralism breaks with structuralism at a crucial point. Derrida significantly posits that there is not an innate relationship between the signifier and the signified, and therefore, language is not so stable as structuralists believed. As Saussure suggested, a signifier differs from other signifiers, but it also defers the meaning it produces because every signifier takes place of the signified in a different context. In Saussure's concept of sign, the signifier is tied inseparably to a single meaning, yet Derrida destabilises this relationship with the postulation that signifiers constantly transform into signifieds. For him, sign and meaning are never identical. A sign can appear in many contexts with different meanings. As a result, meaning is continually relegated by the signifier, leading to what he calls "différance".[14] That is to say, meaning is both generated by differences among signifiers, and it is deferred in an endless play of signification. The free play of meanings, in which a signifier leads to a signified that becomes a signifier for another signified, undermines the unity and coherence of a text. Given that words carry multiple meanings and traces from related words in other contexts, language cannot be a transparent medium of representation. Language produces meanings that are always elusive and transitory. Being inherently unstable, meanings constantly slide away. Because nothing escapes from language, authenticity and truth become impossible. In this regard, the truth claims of the author of classical autobiography inevitably precipitate the birth of the autofictional "I" that admits offering a kind of truth which is different from its conventional definition. Rather than aiming for an indisputable and universal truth, autofiction acknowledges providing a highly subjective version of truth that can be barely conveyed as the author intends due to polyvalent nature of language.

For Derrida, logocentrism of Western philosophical tradition longs for a transcendental signifier that corresponds to a stable transcendental signified. He notes that Western thought systems are founded on a ground or a first principle which is accepted as the essence, or truth. Poststructuralist view of impossibility of truth yet collides with this desire for a centre. Derrida (1970/2002) defines a centre as a principle that organises a structure and permits a limited play of signification because centre creates boundaries. Centres of meaning temporarily stop the infinite flow of signification. Derrida further points out that first principles are often marked by what they exclude. When there is a centre, there is also something which does not belong to it. Setting up centres, thus, generate hierarchized oppositions in which one concept is privileged over the other. There are plenteous sets of oppositional terms in Western culture, such as good/evil, nature/culture, thought/feeling, pure/impure, same/other, masculine/feminine, and the notorious white/black. One concern raised by oppositional terms

---

14 The French word "différence" homonymously means either difference or deferral. Derrida (1972/1989) has invented the term *différance*, spelt with "a" instead of "e", to signify both difference and deferral simultaneously. He uses the term to refer to his presumption that meaning in a language is produced by a word's difference from other words, and at the same time, it is inevitably postponed through an unending chain of signifiers.

is that they are intimately linked to negative stereotyping, repression, discrimination, social injustice and other undesirable practices (Bertens, 2014, p. 113). Deconstruction intends to dismantle these binary oppositions in order to lay bare that they are not naturally given, or guaranteed by any existing authority. All language systems are fundamentally unreliable cultural constructs; therefore, hierarchies they create can be challenged and changed. By subverting conceptual opposites, deconstruction democratises language and moves meaning towards undecidability. The Western tendency to create binaries and boundaries is clearly seen in literary categorisation too. Autobiography and novel are strictly set apart from one another, which immediately creates the binary opposition of fact and fiction. Autofiction serves to demonstrate the constructed nature of literary categories by blurring the dividing lines, which renders it as a subversive genre that deconstructs pre-existing conceptions with creation of ambivalence around them.

Deconstruction, rather than setting new centres in the process of subversion, unveils a strange complicity in which oppositional terms become engaged. The existence of a concept is revealed to depend on the existence of another concept. For example, it is argued that without darkness, it would not be possible to recognise the light. Hence, deconstruction assumes that presence of a term is always tainted by an opposite one. The idea of purity of a concept or transcendental meaning is nothing but a fiction. The two terms in any set of opposites are defined by each other, which points to the structuralist and poststructuralist presumption that meaning depends on difference. In like manner, autofiction aims to illustrate the inseparable links that bind fact and fiction together. In autofiction, the imaginary appears at times as more real than the factual, and the referential is always constituted by some elements of fiction. It contests the "purity" of literary genres with a focus on possibilities that lay outside conventional thought.

Derrida contends further that any linguistic system is subject to *différance* because of countless connotations words have. Deconstruction draws attention to the ambivalence around words and discrepancies between meanings and intended messages as the result of the differences at play within a language. It argues that multiplicity of meanings contained in words lead to a proliferation of interpretations, and none of which can be ever considered as more valid than the others. In this regard, deconstruction disarticulates traditional understandings about the author and the work. The work now becomes the text, the conventional notions of stable meaning and truth are replaced by the unending play of infinite meanings that exceed the author's intentions and control. In this respect, the author of autofiction relies on multiplicity of meanings created by language, not to inscribe a foreknown objective veracity as in traditional autobiography, but to engage with the processes of both discovering and constituting a kind of truth that is neither preconceived nor absolute.

In accordance with Derrida's assertation of the split between the signifier and the signified and free play of meanings within a linguistic system, Paul de Man (1973) points out the unreliability of language as a medium for communicating truths because of its rhetorical and figural dimensions. Figures of speech enable the author to achieve meanings that are different from the literal statement; therefore, they problematise the relationship between words and their referents. For de Man, all texts have both grammatical and rhetorical structures with separate meanings. Reading a text grammatically produces one meaning, and reading it rhetorically gives another. Every text has at least two possible meanings. Along these lines, autofiction never purports to convey one singular truth. It acknowledges that the moment when embodied experiences are translated into language, alternative "realities" are brought into being as a result of creative potentials of language. Therefore, autofiction is distinguished markedly from autobiography by its capacity to hold a variety of meanings of "facts". Concordantly, Roland Barthes (1970/1974) defines the ideal text as containing instability, plurality and dispersion of meanings, that has "a galaxy of signifiers, not a structure of signifieds" (p. 5). It is the kind of text which embodies blanks and fragments, permitting "both overlapping and loss of messages" (p. 20). It engages readers and critics to produce infinite number of meanings. In this respect, Barthes (1971/1977) makes a distinction between the work and the text. Unlike the former that intends to communicate a pre-determined meaning, the text does not close on a signified. On the contrary, it offers an endless deferment of meanings with disconnections and variations between the signifier and the signified. Barthes' delineation of the dissimilarity between the two types of writing can be applied to traditional autobiography and autofiction. While autobiography aims to convey a certain singular truth, autofiction permits language to produce unceasingly different versions and possibilities of the factual.

As Barthes (1966/1977) stated earlier, the function of narrative is not to represent, to show or to imitate an external reality. What the text concerns itself with is "language alone, the adventure of language" (p. 124). In his definition of autofiction, Doubrovsky directly refers to Barthes's description of the text. Rather than representing life events, autofictional works as "texts" engage with creative possibilities of language to discover their meanings. According to Barthes (1973/1975), the text transcends all types of boundaries, such as the ones present among social relations (i.e., author, reader and critic) and linguistic relations (i.e., multivalence of signs). *Texte scriptable* explodes literary codes and destabilises the reader's expectations, inviting them to participate actively in the construction of meaning. The writerly text, thus, blurs the distinction between the reader and the author. Besides, the writerly text deviates from the status quo in style and content. It seeks forms of representation that obscure the divisions between the real and the artificial. For Barthes (1971/1977), because traditional literary categories set bounds to the flow of language, the writerly text poses problems of classification. In this regard, autofiction's significant emphasis on figures of speech, unusual writing styles and mixing of genres provide the author with the liberty to experiment with language and to explore the "reality" outside conventional ways of thinking. It challenges all boundaries in order to make space for emergence of alternative interpretations of embodied experiences, which can provide insightful perspectives to the authors themselves.

As opposed to the humanistic approach that situates the origin and true meaning of works in the author, poststructuralism posits that the text can be read without the knowledge about the author, who is no longer the origin and owner of his/her work. In his well-known essay "The Death of the Author" (1967/1977), Roland Barthes reduces the authorial position to that of a scriptor. The modern author does not express anything but brings together threads from existing writings, weaving them into a new text. The scriptor, therefore, exists only to produce the work, and not to explicate its intended meanings. For Barthes, the traditional concept of author imposes a limit on the text, ascribing to it a final meaning. By contrast, the scriptor comes into existence with the text and disappears upon completion. The origin of the meaning resides only in language and its influences on the reader. The text does not have a single message that requires to be deciphered. It can be explained only in relation to other texts and subjective responses of readers, that is, the meanings of the text perpetually proliferate rather than being reduced to certain signifieds. Being stripped of the authority over the writing, the author can exist in his/her own text only as a textual element (Barthes, 1971/1977, p. 161). In "What is an Author?" (1969/1984), Michel Foucault identically targets at the humanist notion of the author which he believes to be an outcome of the "privileged moment of *individualization* in the history of ideas" (p. 101). Like Barthes, he views today's writing as being freed from the restrictions imposed by the authorial authority and textual closure. The text is now conceived as referring to itself without being confined to its interiority, that is, it becomes identified with "its own unfolded exteriority" (p. 102). In other words, the text is seen as an interplay of signs arranged according to the free-floating nature of signifiers rather than its signified content. As a result, the text invariably exceeds its rules and transgresses its limits.

As Barthes declared the death of author, Foucault (1969/1984) asserts that the work holds "the right to kill, to be its author's murderer" (p. 102). Like Barthes, he stresses that the author is no longer the centre of the text but only a part of the narrative structure. The author has to be cancelled out because his/her individuality is as much problematic as the conventional ideas of unity of language and text. For Foucault, a proper name, a signifier that indicates a specific historical figure, does not have a single signification. It oscillates between the two poles of designation and description. While the former refers to the person, the latter refers to the ideas and the work associated with the name. As a signifier, then, the proper name can take on either the signified of the actual person or the signified of the ideas/work. Through what he calls "author-function", one can limit, choose and exclude interpretations. It is a certain functional principle by which the free circulation of meanings is impeded. In this respect, the author can be considered as an ideological figure that marks the anxiety of proliferation of meaning. Both Barthes and Foucault reduce the author to mere textuality by challenging his/her traditionally privileged position as unique source of meaning. Fictionalising the author partly, autofiction attempts to remove limitations on proliferation of meanings in alignment with the poststructuralist views; however, its preservation of certain factual aspects of the author can be considered as a divergence from the idea of pure textuality. In this regard, many critics conceive the presence of the referential author in autofictional works as an effort to restore the authorial authority. Even if authors are not the unique sources of meaning, autofiction emphasises the value of their perspectives and the way they do and could experience the world.

As poststructuralism deconstructs the traditional views of language, work and author, it problematises the concept of truth that has been thought to be accessible through the words of the writer. Because language is now considered as unstable and multivalent, and the author is a mere construct, poststructuralist critics posit that there is not any form of truth that is reliable. Derrida has interrogated the relationship between language and truth based on the instability and multivalence inherent in language. He maintains that language is not capable of giving us access to truth as logocentrism of the Western philosophy has held. What language can provide is nothing more than signs that are culturally constructed (Derrida, 1967/1976, p. 50). Derrida accordingly argues that the binary oppositions generated by logocentrism are always defined by power relations. Identically, based on Ferdinand de Saussure's system of signs in which the relationship between the signifier and the signified is arbitrarily established, Barthes (1957/1972) proposes that signs are elevated to the level of myths when they are used as signifiers attached to new signifieds. For him, this secondary level of meanings or connotations added to signs are less arbitrary because they are meant to serve the ideologies of those in power. Far from reflecting reality,

Barthes views language as creating myths that help to naturalize particular worldviews. Like Derrida and Barthes, Michel Foucault maintains that there is not any truth outside power. In *Discipline and Punish* (1975/2012) and *The History of Sexuality* (1976–2018/1978–2021), he influentially argues that power, knowledge and the subject are interconnected. Through language, power designates what is acceptable and what is not, and through disciplinary institutions, makes sure that individuals become "subject" to its truths. In fictionalisation of certain parts of the referential, autofiction casts doubt on the concept of truth in line with the poststructuralist claims of the constructedness of any knowledge. On the other hand, the fact that Doubrovsky employs autofictional writing to grasp "deeper realities" suggests that a certain type of truth is still possible. Although autofiction acknowledges that language constructs the reality, it can carry meanings of great significance for the writer.

According to Marjorie Worthington (2018), autofiction has developed partially from and as a reaction against the modernist ideas of impersonality and universality and the poststructuralist "death of the author" debates. For her, autofiction's continual references to the extratextual person of the author mark an attempt to reassert authorial authority while simultaneously acknowledging the limits of that authority (p. 21). In accordance with Derrida's contention that meaning is always drawn from outside, from context, autofiction rejects the idea of the text as containing meaning within itself and resuscitates the figure of author. By accentuating the paratext for meaning, autofiction proposes that the link between the author-character and the actual author is undeniable; however, by problematising the representation of the author-character, autofiction recognises that there is always a distinction between the two, resulting from the poststructuralist assumption that the author is not fully in control of language (p. 3). As a consequence, autofiction both reaffirms the authority of the author, and at once, repudiates it.

Furthermore, because it claims to be a novel and yet maintains a certain connection to the extratextual world, autofiction demonstrates both the possibilities and limits of language as a means to represent real-life experiences accurately (Worthington, 2018, p. 6). The poststructuralist narrative theory holds that to narrativize is inherently to fictionalise. All writing is by its nature merely a representation of reality, not the reality itself. Rendering factual events into a verbal format and a narrative structure necessarily requires the reconstruction, and therefore, fictionalisation of those events. Language and narrative are not transparent modes of representation. Language does not communicate any preexisting meaning; on the contrary, it produces meaning. Although autofiction recognises the creative capacity of language, it departs from the poststructuralist view of inherent fictionality of all writing. In order to disrupt this position, authors of autofiction intentionally incorporate biographical facts in their narratives, and yet they simultaneously problematise the representation of their referentiality. These authors accept that language falls short in portraying the reality truthfully; however, at the same time, they maintain that what language creates is still connected to the reality of the author's person and his/her life. In this regard, Doubrovsky describes autofiction as a narrative that arranges facts in a certain order, and in the process, strays inevitably from historical accuracy, for putting an event into words brings along the questions of which details to depict and how to depict them. Doubrovsky stresses that autofiction, nevertheless, adhere to narration of strictly real events, rather than fabricating them, and embraces the creative possibilities inherent in the act of writing (p. 6). For Doubrovsky, hence, autofiction refers to a verifiably referential text that engages in alterations and inventions as necessitated by the practice of transcribing factual events into textuality (p. 7). Even though narrativization inescapably fictionalises all writing, autofiction does not deem it as cancelling out completely representation of reality.

Moreover, by constantly crossing over the borders between fiction and nonfiction, autofiction calls into question the constructed nature of literary categories, but it also accentuates that there is a dividing line between these two modes of narration (Worthington, 2018, p. 21). Requiring readers to shift constantly their reading strategies, autofiction demonstrates that there are decidedly different readerly expectations for fiction and nonfiction (p. 14). As such, contrary to the poststructuralist assertion of fictionality of all writing, autofiction maintains a distinction between a factual story and a fictional story while simultaneously showing that any demarcation between fact and fiction is a construct that can be easily breached. Autofiction's distrust of conventional literary classifications is evinced in its interrogation of the validity of the autobiographical pact too. By presenting an author-character who shares biographical elements with the real author yet diverges remarkably from the latter, autofiction demonstrates that there is a difference between a textual character and a real person, and autobiography relies upon a narrativization process that is not transparently referential (p. 16). Autofiction, thus, raises significant questions about the nature of authorship and of reality in narrative that are both in agreement and contradistinction to the poststructuralist theories. It proposes that even though the fallibility of language renders impossible representation of objective truth, not all writing is deprived of authenticity. Autofiction conveys a kind of truth that is highly personal and specific to the author's view of events, for that very reason, truth in autofiction could be argued to be, to some degree, real. As Doubrovsky puts it, fiction can portray a richer version of the reality, or in Tim O'Brien's words (1990/2009), "story-truth is truer sometimes than happening truth" (p. 171).

In the same vein, Hywel Dix (2018) argues that as opposed to Lejeune's autobiographical pact, foregrounding the mediated nature of the content of any narrative in accordance with the poststructuralist position, autofiction concerns itself with the intersection of truth and imagination. In doing so, however, autofiction does not reject the existence of truth entirely. Instead, autofiction claims to convey a kind of truth that exists in order of symbolic meaning, that is subjectively constructed by virtue of being expressed in the form of narrative (p. 13). In addition, Dix (2017) emphasises that autofiction disavows the notion of absolute truth on the grounds that flawed nature of human memory and influences of emotions prevent textual reconstruction of any actual event (p. 79). In his autofictional works, Doubrovsky accordingly commits himself to narrating the truth while also he thematises the dubious nature of truth itself (p. 70). Problematising thus representation of referentiality, autofiction upholds the poststructuralist view that language and narrative cannot reflect truthfully reality of the external world. As distinct from poststructuralist approach, autofiction embraces meanings of subjectively constructed perceptions of reality. The act of writing in autofiction functions as a means of constructing and exploring what events mean for individuals, rather than reporting what really happened. Unlike poststructuralist negation of truth claims, autofiction recognises importance and relevance of individual accounts of the truth. As the French writer Christiane Chaulet-Achour conceives, the representation of tensions between truth and imagination is the aesthetic aim of autofiction (Jensen, 2018, p. 71). Rather than creating difficulties, these pressures provide authors of autofiction with opportunities to interrogate the reality and voice their own versions of the truth shaped by lived experiences. For this purpose, as Meg Jensen (2018) points out, autofiction simultaneously highlights and obscures veracity. It presents a narrator that is and is not the author, events that are and are not representative of real life, and voices that are both human and textual. The resulting ambiguity between factuality and fictionality constitutes the essence of autofiction (p. 74).

As autofiction opposes to any form of writing, like autobiography, that claims a truthful portrayal of external reality, it rejects humanistic representation of the self as a coherent, unified and stable being or consciousness. Recognising the self instead as a shifting, fragmented and unstable entity, autofiction in Doubrovskian sense commits to a sincere exploration and revelation of the psychic truth of subjectivity, drawing largely on psychoanalytic theories as formulated by Sigmund Freud and Jacques Lacan. Freud's conception of the self is radically at odds with the humanistic view of the subject as autonomous, ruled by reason and morality. For Freud (1899/1999), human mind is far from being a unified whole, divided between the conscious and the unconscious parts. The latter stores many painful memories of the past, particularly of childhood, repressed desires and wishes which continually influence the way one acts, thinks and feels. The contents of the unconscious are revealed in different forms, such as dreams and art, when the censorship of the conscious is relaxed, and always through symbols instead of direct expressions. Freud therefore makes a distinction between the latent content and the manifest content of dreams where the unconscious thoughts are translated into dream images. Through psychoanalytic techniques including dream analysis and talking cure, Freudian psychoanalysis attempts to identify unresolved conflicts hidden in the unconscious mind. Comparing to the dream-work, Freud regards a work of literature as the external expression of the author's unconscious mind, and suggests that psychoanalytic techniques can be applied to the text to unveil the author's repressed thoughts and feelings. Accordingly, autofiction in Doubrovskian sense relaxes the constrains imposed by conventional ways of narration, creating a dream-like state for the unconscious thoughts to come up to the surface on the page. That way, autofictional writing practice allows the author to examine psychoanalytically his/her past experiences, particularly childhood memories, which leads Doubrovsky to define autofiction as functioning like a writing cure.

Like Freud, Jacque Lacan (1973/1998) views the subject as decentred and fragmented. Based on Freud's Oedipal model of psychosexual development, Lacan proposes a developmental scheme for human beings, by which he explains how individuals come to perceive themselves as unified wholes despite being, in effect, defined by a "lack".[15] According to his model of maturation, at the *imaginary* stage, the pre-Oedipal infant cannot yet speak, it is subject to impressions and fantasies, urged by drives and desires, and does not have any sense of boundaries and limitations. It has an organic continuity with the mother and the world with no sense of distinction. At the *mirror* stage, children think they see themselves as an entire being, an individuated person, disconnected from the oceanic unity of the maternal body. For Lacan, such recognition of wholeness is a "misrecognition". The mirror stage is thus marked by a discord between the integrated image in the mirror and the reality of the child's

---

15 Specifically, the lack is an outcome of the child's separation from the mother. More generally, human subjects experience the lack upon entering necessarily in the pre-existing symbolic order that they cannot control (Barker & Jane, 2016, p. 111).

uncoordinated body image. Ultimately, the child ascends to the *symbolic* order where he acquires the language and discourse of the Other.[16] This big Other exists outside us and does not belong to us. It provides subject positions from which one may speak, but it does not allow to express definitively one's desires and wishes as they do not quite fit the signifiers of language. As a result, a gap opens between human as an organism and the signifying subject. In submitting to language and accepting "reality", we lose the original feeling of wholeness. We live ever after with a lack. Lacan argues that what is lost here is *the real* which is different from reality. Reality is constituted by language and culture while the real is the domain outside signification which we do not have an access to because it does not have any signifiers in the world of names we inhabit. For Lacan, the unconscious comes into being as the result of the imposition of the symbolic order on the real of the subject. Rather than representing the "reality", Doubrovsky aims in autofiction to engage with the "real", unconscious contents of mind. Transgressing man-constructed boundaries and limitations, he attempts to go back to the real in the imaginary stage. During the process of narration, however, he acknowledges that the language of the Other falls short in expressing fully what is repressed by the symbolic order.

Upon entering in the domain of language, like Saussure, Lacan views human beings as being caught in a system of signs, in a symbolic world. Meaning and subjectivity are generated relationally along a network of differences. However, he disagrees that language is stable, that is, there is one-to-one correspondence between words and objects. For Lacan, language is chiefly figurative, and always fails to express one's desires in that the signifier and signified are never united. There remains a perpetual gap between utterance and its enunciation. Because meaning is always displaced, truth is rendered impossible to utter. The signifying chain can mean something different from what is intended. Lacan's poststructuralist revision of Freud in the light of Saussure's structural linguistics proposes that the unconscious functions like a language (Lacan, 1957/2006). Analogous to language, the unconscious is a site of signification, defined by the mechanisms of condensation and displacement that correspond to the linguistic functions of metaphor and metonymy.[17] Dream images can be taken as signifiers that are

---

16   Lacan uses a capital O to make a distinction between the Otherness of language and culture and the otherness of other people (Belsey, 2002, p. 58).
17   Lacan draws on Roman Jacobson's analysis of the two poles of languages; metaphor and metonymy in his essay "The Metaphoric and Metonymic Poles" (1956/2002). In metaphor, a signifier substitutes for another signifier in an attempt to articulate what cannot be expressed, the signified while in metonymy, a signifier is replaced

always elusive because of the perpetual barrier between the signifier and signified. Both language and the unconscious are characterised by constant deferral of meaning. Lacan (1956/2006) accordingly draws attention to the rhetorical nature of the "talking cure" in psychoanalysis, that is distinguished by tropes and figures of speech, which illustrates the close affinity between the structures of the unconscious and language. In this respect, Doubrovsky reasons figurative capacity of language to mirror the unconscious part of mind in that both are patterned in the same way. However, for him, the act of narration and unconscious thoughts are identically elusive, unable to reveal a whole picture of the self and life.

In line with psychoanalytic and poststructuralist theories, Doubrovsky recognises the human subject as being "broken into pieces", and that the self is largely inaccessible because of the veiled unconscious part of human psyche and nonrepresentational nature of language (Célestin, 1997). Being informed and inspired by the works of Freud and Lacan, Doubrovsky approaches the subject as a fissured and occult entity that is debarred from the knowledge of repressed thoughts and feelings constituting part of the truth about one's being. Autofiction emerges from this impossibility of grasping the self in complete transparency. Autofiction hence undermines the foundations of autobiography by putting in question the idea of theological and coherent development of the subject's identity and unproblematic transcription of external or psychic reality into words. Although the Freudian position assumes that psychoanalytic techniques such as talking cure and dream analysis may help to uncover the hidden contents of the unconscious, and provide illuminating insights into the nature of one's subjectivity, Lacan's poststructuralist reinterpretation complicates the notion of truth about the self by laying emphasis on the function of language as not representing subjectivity but constituting it. Autofiction in Doubrovskian sense accordingly proposes that writing can function as a writing cure, allowing one to explore, to some extent, the contents of the unconscious. At the same time, it acknowledges that because the real needs to be transformed into the symbolic, the meaning language provides always remains a prophecy (Gronemann, 2019, p. 1985).

Despite failing to represent authentically, language exists as the only medium for inquiring into the unconscious. Through writing, the author of autofiction discovers something that is connected to his/her personality and life, and also constitutes constantly his/her subjectivity, which permits exploration of the

---

by another that is closely associated with it. Both function by signifying something other than they claim.

possibilities of him/herself. For the authors of autofiction, the only "truthful" way of representing the self is a fragmentary writing which imitates the structure of the unconscious. As Doubrovsky talks about narrating the truth of his subjectivity, he adopts the Freudian notion of allowing the unconscious to emerge from the gaps that open when the control of the conscious mind is temporarily suspended. Foregrounding figurative aspects of language, he employs a spontaneous and associative style of writing regardless of syntax, punctuation and structural coherence. By that means, he seeks to "give initiative to words", that is, he steps back from the authorial control over language to allow it to reveal something new about himself (Hunt, 2018, p. 184). Fictionality of his writing, on the other hand, rises from the symbolic function of language in the process of translating lived experiences into a text. The author is aware that he/she cannot portray truthfully a life in narrative, but can endlessly produce subjectivity through language. As a result, writing becomes a part of the author's existence which language operates not to reflect but to create.

Like poststructuralist and psychoanalytic theories, postmodernist thoughts have contributed significantly to the development of autofiction. Jean-François Lyotard, in *The Postmodern Condition* (1979/1984), attempts to define postmodernism by calling attention to a change in the status of knowledge in the postmodern era. In modern times, he notes that a number of "grands récits" (grand narratives) provided Western societies with clear meaning systems that helped to establish norms and beliefs and to organise societal activities. Since the 1950s, however, the predominance of these totalising, closed systems of reasoning have diminished as they have been exposed as fictions. As a result, the postmodern world has become dominated by "an incredulity towards meta-narratives" (p. xxiv). Scepticism has replaced idealistic notions such as scientific advancement, technological development, human progress and universal truths. In place of grand narratives, multitudes of equally weighted "local" narratives have emerged, which have often conflicted with each other, leading to incommensurability and undecidability.

Lyotard's proposition of the collapse of grand narratives that give stable meanings to society is considered as a fundamental principle of postmodern theory, from which many of the other characteristics of the postmodern ensue (Jones, 2007, p. 36–7). Because postmodern societies are no longer held together by collective designs and coherent doctrines, they are increasingly prevailed by heterogeneity and diversity. "Fragmentation", "plurality", "difference" and "change" invariably characterise all aspects of the postmodern world that is decentred and structured with complex networks of relations rather than conventional hierarchies. In line with the negation of singular and universal truths, postmodernism undermines the humanist view of individual identity as unified, stable and coherent. Subjectivity is understood as shifting, fragmentary and "in-process", that is, the self is never a singular, fixed and finished phenomenon. While identity was traditionally held to be constituted by an irreducible essence, postmodern perception foregrounds the influences of social and historical circumstances on formation of individuality, and opens up the possibility for a fluid understanding of identity. As such, postmodernism recognises individual to be complex, plural and unstable rather than being grounded in an unchanging essence (p. 38).

At both individual and social levels, the breakdown of unifying metanarratives and their replacement by fragmentation and plurality bring along feelings of disorientation and confusion, which are emblematic of the postmodern world (Jones, 2007, p. 38). Space in postmodernism is accordingly characterised by loss of a unified plan, discontinuity and constant border crossings. The blurring of spatial boundaries undermines the conventional view of nations as being clearly demarcated and containing distinct peoples with "pure" cultures (p. 47). Accentuating the porosity of boundaries, postmodernism embraces cultural mixing, heterogeneity and multiplicity of histories and cultures.

In *Simulacra and Simulation* (1981/1994), Jean Baudrillard influentially associates postmodernity with a crisis in how we represent and understand the world. For Baudrillard, the conflicts and dilemmas created by the postmodern condition are both real and "hyperreal".[18] They are real to the individuals who have been involved, and yet, at the same time, unreal because in the postmodern age, there no longer exists a distinction between reality and its representation. It is often the latter that precedes and determines the real. Therefore, Baudrillard stresses that reality at some point becomes unreal, a simulation. The real and fiction are blended together, rendering it impossible to distinguish where one ends and the other begins. The boundaries between facts/history and fiction are problematised. Correspondingly, Linda Hutcheon (2006) identifies the postmodern art as being characterised by the blurring of the boundaries between established genres, popular and high art, mass and elite cultures. She emphasises that this mixing of elements from distinct categories of culture creates a state of "in-betweenness". The ensuing formal and thematic hybridity challenges notions of homogeneity and uniformity in art and theory (p. 123).

---

18 Jean Baudrillard (1981/1994) defines "hyperreal" as "the generation by models of a real without origin or reality" (p. 1). It is a representation or a sign without an original referent.

As Elizabeth H. Jones discusses in *Spaces of Belonging* (2009), there are a number of affinities between autofiction and postmodernism. The breakdown of grand narratives and overarching belief systems, as Lyotard suggested, has led to the questioning of traditionally stable elements of life writing, such as history, truth and subjectivity (p. 94). Autofiction destabilises such conceptions by creating uncertainty around them, mixing the referential with the fictional. In line with postmodernism's defiance of dominant systems of thought, autofiction problematises Lejeune's totalising formulation of autobiography through transgressive tendencies, playful crossings of the boundaries between fact and fiction, between autobiography and novel, and emphasis on gaps and inconsistencies in autobiographical writing. Moreover, autofiction challenges the traditional assumption that referential writing necessarily excludes aesthetic beauty and literary merit, through stylistic experimentation, which is a typical feature of postmodernism (p. 91). Besides, Jones notes that postmodernism has contributed to the denaturalisation of the white, heterosexual male "ideal" subject of autobiography, which is reflected in autofiction's openness to the stories of people previously excluded from classical autobiographical writing (p. 94).

Postmodernism challenges the modernist assumption that art and life are separate realms. In that regard, autofiction provides a literary arena where some of the crucial questions from life such as "identity" and "belonging" are discussed (Jones, 2009, p. 259). Rather than giving an account of a pre-existing objective truth, autofictional mode of writing concerns itself with exploring not only the external reality but also the aspects of life that remain outside the conscious part of mind. Furthermore, just as postmodernism foregrounds multiplication of meaning, autofiction is preoccupied with fragmentation and plurality. Grasping the subject in fragments and employing a complex style of writing with discontinuities and digressions, autofiction typically conveys a fissured and partial picture of a life story rather than totalising and explaining it fully (p. 260). As postmodernism refuses the notion of singular and coherent selfhood, autofiction challenges the stability of the narrator's identity, evincing adherence to the postmodern view of plural and shifting subjectivity. Autofiction accordingly presents the author-character as negotiating boundaries between past and present selves, past and present lived experiences (p. 269).

Finally, postmodernism is characterised by the disavowal of the concepts of unity and homogeneity, which autofiction identically challenges through hybridity of the referential and fictional modes of narration. Although autofiction employs amply postmodernist techniques, according to Myra Bloom (2019), as distinct from postmodernism that aims to destabilise the subject and the mimetic abilities of narrative, autofiction uses these techniques in order to capture better the complexity of the subject's psychic and physical worlds. In contrast to the postmodernist focus on irony, autofiction emphasises sincerity of the author and a renewed faith in the possibilities of personhood (p. 8). Similarly, Ferreira-Meyers (2018) remarks that autofiction blurs the boundaries between fact and fiction not for the sake of invention but in an attempt to reflect the world with justice, which is to say that autofiction aims to communicate a certain kind of truth (p. 28). In respect to the purposes of this project, it could be argued that autofictional strategy of crossing over the boundaries between fact and fiction highlights the fragmented nature of memory, inability to belong and identity crisis. Therefore, "memory", "belonging" and "subjectivity" will be employed as the organising conceptions of the book.

Conceptual Framework

Memory

As opposed to the conventional idea of memory as a storage place, the modern perception recognises memory to be flawed, discontinuous and unreliable, which autofiction embraces as a reaction to truth claims of classical autobiography. As early as the eighteenth century, Jean-Jacques Rousseau (1782–1789/1953) treats memory as an act of imagination. He assumes that the process of recollection involves necessarily invention to fill the gaps in remembered fragments of the past as well as unintended fiction caused by the chaotic nature of mind where original memories are blended with one another and distorted by factors such as subjective perceptions and feelings. Rousseau lays particular emphasis on the role of emotions in retrieval of memories. For him, the past instances without emotional significance are more likely to be erased from memory than the moments at which the heart is touched. As such, he understands memory as recalling a succession of feelings rather than accurate dates or facts. Rousseau and other Romantics like William Wordsworth maintain that recollection of the past can occur voluntarily through the restoration of emotion in states of tranquillity. They find particularly memories of childhood as resurging vividly, which is elaborated by Sigmund Freud's theories at the turn of the twentieth century. In "Screen Memories" (1899/1953), Freud describes our childhood memories as mere screens that hide repressed and emotionally significant events. "Screen memories", as Freud terms them, are therefore displaced versions of essential occurrences. Memories of these events, as we remember them, carry deeper, underlying meanings which we are not aware of. Later in "A note upon the 'mystic writing pad'" (1925/1953), Freud suggests a distinction between the unconscious long-term memories and the conscious short-term memories, the former of which are repressed and prevented from reaching the consciousness, yet can be unveiled partially through psychoanalytic techniques such as talking cure and free association. In line with Freud's assumptions, autofiction in Doubrovskian sense seeks to present a more authentic account of the "truth" of the self than classical autobiography, treating life writing as a platform to explore the unconscious contents of mind. Doubrovskian autofiction is further influenced by Marcel Proust's engagement with spontaneous, involuntary memory. Drawing on the philosopher Henri Bergson's distinction between "pure memory" and "habitual memory" (1896), which are connected respectively to involuntary and voluntary memory, Proust (1971) distinguishes between two forms of self; "le moi profound" and an everyday self-manifested in daily habits. As put in Bergson's terminology, Proust gives priority to pure memory, the deep knowledge of the self rather than the memory of the habit. He attempts to recover the former, allowing sensory triggers involuntarily to evoke memory events which he calls reminiscences (Nalbantian, 2003, p. 63). For Proust, voluntary memory cannot revive the past authentically because it cannot evade colouring the past events with the present, and thus, tainting the real past (p. 67). Accordingly, he conceives the past as being hidden beyond the reach of the intellect, and depending on chance for its revelation (p. 68). Similarly, autofiction understands memory not as transparent or sequential but fragmented and fleeting. Moreover, autofiction assumes memory to contain profound realities about the self that are uncovered at times through involuntary processes.

When probing the unconscious contents of memory, authors of autofiction employ extensively the surrealist writer André Breton's method of automatic writing (1933), which operates to suppress the conscious control over writing process and to allow a free uninhibited transcription of thoughts from the unconscious without the presence of any exterior trigger. By this means, psychic automatism corresponding to a dream state opens up to the real through the emergence of unconscious memories, which attests to the intricate links between reality and dreams as authors of autofiction often cannot distinguish decidedly between the two. Furthermore, as psychoanalysis proceeded from Freudian signified to Lacanian signifier, with some modernist writers, there has occurred a shift from the perception of memory as lived and hidden experience of the signified to the notion of memory as a play of linguistic signifiers (Nalbantian, 2003, p. 117). In the latter understanding of memory, craft of writing functions as a catalyst for the retrieval of the fragments of the past. Through the intermediary of language, memory traces are pursued and excavated. Words probe into the past and reproduce it for the writer. However, memories are retrieved not as pictures of the past but as verbal signifiers, which is to say that memory becomes an invention of writing, an act of creation, where language exists as the only reality. Despite regarding autofictional mode of writing as a practice of remembering the lived past and exploring the self, Doubrovsky asserts memory to be essentially fictious in that language on its "adventure" reinvents meanings of life that escape the author, and narrativization of memories renders them inescapably fictions that are based on the author's authentic experiences as well as fantasies. Along similar lines, American psychologist Daniel Schacter (1995) points out that personal memory is naturally and commonly vulnerable to distortions. He maintains that original memories can be easily impaired, leading to "confabulation" or false recollection of events that did not in fact happen. Besides, subjective element of experience may intervene in the process of recollection, introducing a further distortion. Schacter emphasises the possibility that the same event can be experienced and remembered differently by different people due to elements of personality. In tune with these assumptions, authors of autofiction explicitly disclaim articulation of absolute veracity of their lives, and often call attention to failures of memory and fictional aspects of their writing.

Conforming to modern understandings of memory, autofiction foregrounds the idea of blurred boundaries between memory and imagination. It draws on the fictional primarily to compensate for the shortcomings of memory. Fictionalising deliberately certain aspects of a life story, autofiction avoids creating an illusory image of unflawed and coherent memory. Accordingly, autofiction often presents discontinuous series of moments altering between the past and present, mixed with the fictional, in contradistinction to chronological and supposedly accurate recounting of the past in autobiography (Jones, 2009, p. 96). In order to portray memory "truthfully", autofiction engages with the unconscious part of mind, exploring and incorporating psychoanalytic experiences of the author. Imitating the way spontaneous, unconscious memory functions, autofiction accentuates the process of writing freely as remembering the discontinuous moments of the past, in which there exists no clear distinction between reality and dreams. Moreover, as Arnaud Schmitt (2010) puts it, the author of Doubrovskian autofiction is allowed "flights of imagination […] because this is what the real self is about" (p. 126). That is to say, the autofictional author has the liberty to alter and manipulate the veracity of his or her life for the purpose of carrying out an internal quest for identity that comprises fantasies and possibilities of the self. Therefore, as autofiction calls readers to question the authenticity of memory, it also emphasises the significance of telling one's history on the development of the self and identity. Autofiction suggests that both memories and stories carry meanings relevant to subjectivity despite their constructed nature (Vinson, 2018, p. 153). Thus, rather than offering unproblematic access to the past, memory is recognised as a source of new realities about the self and as a mode of creation in that remembering always involves reinterpretation of the past events. The rememberer reworks and orders them in a highly selective and subjective manner, which always includes reconfigurations by imagination (Cooke, 2005, p. 72). In this regard, recollection resembles a process of narrative construction in which half-remembered fragments of the past are constantly reorganised into stories with different sequences, which denotes the fictional quality of memory (Menn, 2018, p. 173). Writing past events into narratives problematises further the authenticity of memories. Representations or narrativizations of memories inescapably turn them into things other than the originals (Saunders, 2008, p. 323). Memories are accompanied by invention whenever they are put into writing. Therefore, it could be argued that both remembering and writing are identically creative processes.

Although autofictional practice fundamentally rests on memory, its reliability is constantly questioned and critiqued. As Dix (2017) points out, autofiction emphasises memory to be inherently unreliable at both an individual and a collective level. Accordingly, autofictional narratives commit to explore the barriers preventing representation of authentic truth of a past event rather than offering an objective account of it (p. 80). On the individual level, autofiction foregrounds the dual identity of autofictional subject, split between the remembering "I" and remembered "I", caused by flawed nature of memory. On the collective level, autofiction asserts that the ways in which the past is memorialised are culturally and selectively constructed (p. 79). As Hayden White (1985) argued that writing of any historical narrative selects what is to be remembered collectively, and Benedict Anderson (1983) set forth that historical narratives serve the purpose of nation building, constructing a common history, autofiction disavows collective memories as absolute truths. Rather than establishing what really happened in the past, autofiction utilises the act of writing to construct and explore the meanings of events and experiences for individuals (p. 79). By doing that, autofiction moves the parameters of representation away from questions of truth and accuracy towards questions of significance and value (p. 80). Autofictional narratives make use of creative possibilities inherent in fiction to ascribe individual meanings to social events. In this regard, autofiction conceives the self as a kind of archive that generates testimonies with the potential to challenge collectively accepted historical narratives while stressing the inevitability of distortions and digressions in acts of remembering and narrating (p. 83). The autofictional author's claims of sincerity are attended with an acknowledgement of fictionalisation occasioned by the unconscious, the deficiencies of memory, and the narrativization of events. Autofiction is thus characterised by ambiguity between memory and imagination, and tendency to highlight the gaps between memory and life, and between text and experience. Being neither entirely factual nor fictional, autofiction as an in-between genre represents, in one respect, the author-character's status as "in-between".

Belonging

The contemporary approaches to space reject the conventional perception of it as a neutral and passive ground where events simply occur. Instead, they recognise space as playing an active and crucial role in the formation of individuals and societies. As the contact between spaces, and therefore between cultures, increasingly grows thanks to developments such as modern transport and telecommunication technologies, spaces are held to be pervaded by ideological considerations and power relations structuring the entire world. In this regard, the state of expanding interrelations between spaces produces significant implications for national and cultural identities which are constructed in compliance with political purposes, and therefore, can always be challenged. As such, the sense of belonging that these identities provide is understood to be illusionary. Furthermore, given the fact that spaces are subject to global forces, they become imbued with multiplicity of meanings and complexity of transnational networks, which disorients individuals, contributing to the loss of a sense of belonging. As an "in-between genre" that cannot fully belong to any of traditional literary classifications, autofiction can be argued both to reflect the unbelonging of individuals inhabiting multi-layered and multi-coded contemporary spaces, and to provide an arena for authors to negotiate their positions in the world, which may open up new possibilities for wayfinding that replace traditional maps.

One significant outcome of the poststructuralist and postmodernist reasoning in regard to the notion of space is the dissolution of the prevalent myth that the world is divided into spaces with definite borders, each holding a pure and authentic culture. In *Imagined Communities* (1983), Benedict Anderson rejects the idea of the nation as a natural and inevitable social composition. Conversely, he asserts the nation to be a cultural construct ensuing from the fall of monarchies and empires, as well as technological and economic advancements in the eighteenth century. He describes nationalism as "the pathology of modern developmental history" because the modern world necessitates everyone to belong to a nationality (p. 5). According to Anderson, nations are simply "imagined political communities" in that most of their members will never meet one another in person, and yet imagine themselves as being part of a communion with shared origins and mutual interests (p. 6). He points out that nations are always imagined as limited, for they do not claim to encompass everyone in the world. They consider certain individuals as fellow members, to the exclusion of others (p. 7). On the other hand, Anderson significantly argues the nation to be simultaneously open and closed, based on the possibility that new people can join the nation, for example, by learning the language and naturalising (p. 146). Making clear the distinction between nationalism and racism, Anderson maintains that the latter emerges when the idea of "contamination" to the purity of the nation is advanced and used as a tool of oppression against people with other racial or ethnic heritage (p. 149). Against the claims for naturalness and pureness of nations, Anderson stresses the role of language in creation of the deep ties that bound people together within nations, through inscription of national myths and narratives of national identity (p. 205).

In line with Anderson's arguments, Homi K. Bhaba (1990) contends the notion of a nation to be a product of "double narrative", which he terms as the pedagogical and the performative. According to his preposition, the people in a nation are both constructed by the nationalist discourses and actively participate in the construction. Not only are they the historical objects of a pedagogy, describing the nation which they belong to, but also the subjects of a signification process in which they reproduce the nation through their actions. The pedagogical narrative aims to constitute the nation as a permanent entity that uninterruptedly progresses through time and space, and therefore, considers its members as composing a collective community of a homogenous nature. The performative, on the other hand, contests the perception of the people as static historical events by accentuating the diversity of interests and identities among the people of a nation, which disrupts essentialist considerations of nationhood. Questioning the idea of the people as a permanent conception, the performative problematises the pedagogical narrative of the fixity of the nation (p. 297). As Bhaba puts it, "The performative introduces a temporality of "in-between" through the "gap" or "emptiness" of the signifier that punctuates linguistic difference" (p. 299). As opposed to the pedagogical assumption of the permanence of the national sign, the performative stresses its shifting nature, articulating the inconstancy and heterogeneity of the population within a nation. For Bhaba, thus, there is an inherent split, an ambivalence in the production of the nation. The tension between the pedagogical and the performative in narrative is fundamental to forming any knowledge of the nation. Bhaba's presumption that the double writing of a nation, or *disseminNation*, involves an incessant play between boundaries and disruptions renders it a liminal space where contending histories and narratives of difference run counter to totalising powers of the national authority. As such, Bhabha employs the barred Nation *It/Self* to signify a national space that is marked by cultural diversity of its peoples, and to suggest a liminal form of social representation (p. 299). In this regard, Bhabha argues the modern space to be "plural", a heterogeneous site of cultural differences encompassing the histories of minorities, the marginal and the emergent, in contradistinction to the political imagination of the oneness of people (p. 300). Refusing the possibility of any coherent totality of the nation, Bhabha recognises the anonymity of the modern community and its temporality. This new space, where normative descriptions of the nation collapse, engenders the in-betweenness of cultural identities. In *Location of Culture* (1994), Bhaba expounds that all cultural statements and systems are constructed in the "Third Space of enunciation" (p. 37). He describes it as an in-between space where cultural identity emerges from hybridity of multiple interacting cultures, which negates the ideas of "pure" national identities and belonging to fixed categories of identification.

Fredric Jameson (1984) asserts that the contemporary thinking of space, defined by the undermining of national boundaries and separation of distinct cultures, is linked to the emergence of the postmodern era. As such, he describes postmodern spaces as being characterised by depthlessness, flatness and fragmentation, where people are deprived of spatial coordination and no longer able to map their positions in the world (p. 89). In a similar vein, James Clifford (1997) associates postmodernity with "the new world order of mobility, of rootless histories" (p. 1). He observes the increasing cultural contact and the state of inhibiting multiple spaces to be emblematic of the postmodern mode of existence. He significantly argues that identities of individuals are formed not only by "roots" but also "routes", which complicates their belonging to "original" spaces. As Elizabeth H. Jones (2007) notes, postmodern spaces are marked by the blurring of categories and the porosity of boundaries (p. 47). The growing conditions of mobility and displacement across geographical places inevitably bring along mixing of cultures, heterogeneity of populations, and erosion of the conventional ideas of nation and nationhood. The disorienting reality of the postmodern world where coherent systems of meanings are replaced by plurality and difference, gives rise to quests for identity (p. 51). Because postmodernity undermines the conventional ways in which identities are understood, the contemporary world is pervaded by a feeling of unbelonging. As people increasingly occupy in-between spaces, they long for a place of belonging, along with the acknowledgement that no place can ever be considered as uncontaminated location of sameness.

Doubrovsky's autofictional works illustrate the contemporary experience of national and cultural unbelonging, and the consequent urge for finding a "home" space. As an author whose life was intersected by multiplicity of geographical locations, ethnicities, languages and cultures, Doubrovsky's autofictionally rendered self epitomises the prevalent state of uprootedness and dispossession, coupled with a strong desire to belong. Accordingly, Doubrovsky's textual avatar is presented as being perpetually on a quest for "a place", both literally and figuratively (Jones, 2007, p. 182). Autofiction in the Doubrovskian sense, therefore, provides an arena for the author to explore the complexities of his/ her selfhood interwoven with the multi-layered significances of postmodern space. In a sense, autofictional mode of writing serves as a medium for orienting the self and forging a sense of belonging in opposition to the confusion of the postmodern world (p. 255). The author of autofiction engages in a search for identity in the form of a quest for spaces of belonging. For this purpose, the author-character is frequently depicted as making trips to places that are imbued with personal memories and associations. Revisiting these sites through the journeys of the author-character, the author attempts to negotiate the boundaries between his/her past and present selves and lived experiences, as well as to secure a stable place in a fluctuating world despite the weight of multi- national, ethnic or cultural heritage (p. 269). According to Jones (2007), the topic of a quest for spaces of belonging is crucial to autofictional writing for the reason that it allows the author to reinsert himself/herself in the sites from which he/she is excluded by ideological forces (p. 291). Hence, it could be argued that autofiction is a useful genre particularly for the authors with multi-ethnic identities to explore the multiplicities that constitute their subjectivity, to come to the terms with their ethnic and cultural differences, and to challenge the discourses that ideologically confine them to particular identities, or exclude them from certain positions.

Plurality of the Self

The contemporary approaches to the self challenge Enlightenment and humanist ideas of subjectivity which conceived of the individual as a rational and unified consciousness, in control of language and meaning. In contrast to humanism, the recent political, philosophical and cultural movements assume the modern subject to be fragmented, elusive and decentred by various social structures and discourses. The Marxist tradition, which developed from the 1840s onwards, assumes subjectivity to be produced and governed by ideology. According to the classical Marxism, economic relations shape not only the society but also the individuals within it. In modern capitalist societies, the relations between capital and labour appear in the form of contracts between workers and employers. These relations established on an economic basis are maintained by ideology that is embedded in social and cultural practices. Although individuals may feel like they are free to decide on their own lives, ideology directs all their thoughts and actions, creating "false consciousness".[19] Marxism, therefore, understands class position to be a crucial determinant in the formation of subjectivity. Psychoanalytic theories, as Sigmund Freud formulated towards the end of the nineteenth century, undermine further the humanist notion of the sovereign rational subject. According to Freud (1899/1999), the subject is inherently split between the rational and the irrational aspects of mind. That is, he/she leads a life that is torn between socially and culturally integrated processes of the conscious and threatening or unspeakable impulses of the unconscious. In this regard, Freud points to the doubleness of the self constituted by the tension between learned societal norms and inborn instincts.

Louis Althusser's theory of subjectivity (1970/1971) suggests that individuals are reproduced as subjects within ideology and language. In his theorisation, what Althusser calls ideological state apparatuses, such as religion, education, the family, the law, politics, culture and the media, generate the ideologies within which individuals are assigned identities. Through the mechanism of interpellation, ideology makes individuals identify with the identities it determines. In other words, ideology transforms individuals into subjects who are impelled to internalise these identities. Drawing on the Lacanian psychoanalytic theory of the subject, Althusser asserts that "ideology represents the imaginary relationship of individuals to their real conditions of existence" (p. 162). In Lacanian terms, ideology results in imaginary misrecognition of the ego. Individuals see themselves as ideology represents them. Moreover, because they disguise the real nature of social relations, ideological formations produce a double distortion of reality. Althusser emphasises that when the individual is interpellated as a subject within an ideology, the "I" speaks and acts in compliance with that ideology. As a result, the subject becomes split between the "I" who speaks and the "I" who is spoken. The subject who says "I think" is not the same as the one whose existence is assumed in the act of thinking. Therefore, the subject cannot be considered as unified and the source of truth. For Lacan, the split between the ego and the speaking "I" points to the subject's inability to control language in the symbolic order (Weedon, 2004, p. 12).

Reinterpreting Freud's theories of sexual development, Lacan (1973/1998) argues subjectivity to be produced through identifications based on a structure

---

19 Friedrich Engels (1893/1949) uses the term "false consciousness" to describe the situation in which a subordinate class willingly adopts the ideology of the ruling class, unaware of being exploited (p. 451).

of misrecognition. In his theorisation, the infant in the pre-Oedipal stage is governed by a fragmented sense of body until it identifies with a mirror image, misrecognising itself as whole and unified. The process of misrecognition continues to underline further identifications in the symbolic order of language. Despite seeming autonomous and unified, Lacan contends the subject to be divided for the reason that he/she is obliged to speak the language of the Other. Accordingly, he concludes that assuming subjectivity within language provides only an illusionary sense of sovereignty. Derrida (1976) uses the term "metaphysics of presence" to describe the situation in which the speaking subject appears to be in control of language and the source of fixed meanings (p. 49). The poststructuralist theories, like the ones developed by Lacan, Derrida and Foucault, maintain that the speaker is not the master of language. On the contrary, language pre-exists and allows him/her to take up a subject position within itself. Thus, it is the language that produces subjectivity, identity and meaning. Language in the form of competing discourses presents different regimes of meaning and forms of identity. When a particular discourse is recognised as true and held over others, the individual becomes a subject who internalises the meanings and adopts the identities it offers. In poststructuralist approach to selfhood, therefore, rather than reflecting or expressing, language plays an active role in constituting subjectivities and identities. As Foucault (1980/1984) argues, discourses creating subject positions are always structured through power relations of inclusion and exclusion. Some discourses have greater power than others, and they define norms in relation to those who are "different". Hegemonic discourses of race and gender within Western societies, for example, assert the supremacy of white men in opposition to coloured individuals and women. For Foucault, however, all discourses involve the potential of resistance since discursive fields produce meanings and subjectivities which are not homogenous. They include discourses that may conflict with one another, which creates space for new forms of knowledge. As Chris Weedon (2004) articulates, power relationships structuring discourses limit the possibilities of subjectivity, providing individuals with a singular meaning of who they are and where they belong. On the other hand, identity must be considered as plural by the virtue that it is fractured and constantly reconfigured by gender, ethnicity and class relations (p. 19-20).

In line with the pluralistic perception of the self, autofiction accentuates the subject to be multiple and divided through creation of distance between the narrated "I" and the narrating "I". Autofictional strategy of fictionalising certain aspects of the author's life story and personality points to the discrepancy between the real author and the author-character despite the undeniable connections between the two. By this means, the latter is suggested to be one possible manifestation of the author's multiple selves. Autofiction assumes that the blurring of the distinctions between the referential and the fictional helps to illuminate the split nature of the ego, allowing the author to imagine possible versions of the self. Thus, autofiction's inherent duality provides the author with a space to exist as a multifaceted subject. The ambiguity of the authorial position, created by constant vacillation between fact and fiction, destabilises the idea of a unified and coherent self, and suggests subjectivity to be an elusive and composite entity. In this regard, Doubrovsky enunciates the individual to be a broken subject. For him, the only realistic way of representing the self is rendered through a fragmentary form of narration where chronological sequence and literary categorisation are disrupted, picturing the subject in fragments (Célestin, 1997, p. 400). As such, autofiction gives an account of the authorial self in its plurality, searching actively for identity. In accordance with the poststructuralist assumption that language produces subjectivity, autofictional writing allows words to constitute the self, creating a new awareness about the author's being. As the author tells stories about him/herself, the narrated self is constantly recreated. Loosening the boundaries between the factual and the fictional, autofictional mode of narration eludes fixed truth conceptions and singular meaning of subjectivity, which gives way to revelation of multiple facets of the self. In autofiction, therefore, the self is refused to be a single story. On the contrary, the self is viewed as a plural and shifting phenomenon that is ceaselessly searched, explored and constituted.

Autoethnography and Postcolonial Theory

Foregrounding the contemporary assumptions of the plurality of the self and the constructed nature of any knowledge, autofiction has led to a new direction termed as autoethnography. Deborah Reed-Danahay (1997) describes the subsequent development as a form of self-narrative which locates the self in a social context (p. 9). That is, autobiographer recounts the story of his or her life with respect to the social circumstances in which it has been lived. Stressing the multiple and shifting nature of selfhood that is constantly reshaped by locations, autoethnography breaks down the distinction between autobiography and ethnography. As a result, coherence of the self in the former and objective observer position in the latter are put into question. The dual nature of autoethnography hence interrogates the binary of self/society as well as the boundary between the objective and the subjective. Danahay indicates the genre to be raising a number of questions. First, it lays emphasis on the postmodern/postcolonial conception of the self and society in which an individual is ascribed multiple identities (p. 2). Second, by blurring the dividing line between the personal and the collective, autoethnography contests the claims for authenticity of representation (p. 3). Lastly, it calls attention to the cultural displacement relating to issues of sociocultural change, globalisation and transculturation. In line with the postmodern condition of the world, Danahay articulates an autoethnographer not to be completely "at home", and that the present era, marked by fragmentation and plurality, requires new ways of writing about the self and the social (p. 4).

In the same vein, Julia Watson (2001) notes that autoethnography understands identity as being formed in social spaces which are "contact zones" of diverse cultures. Autoethnography, therefore, problematises the conventional perception of community as coherent and unified, through a narrator with multiple identities that are culturally constructed and often conflicting with one another (p. 83–4). Accordingly, Lisa Shepperd (2018) uses the term autoethnography to refer to the type of autofictional texts which explore the manifold connections between places and people. She remarks that because both are characterised by plurality, instability and contradictions, autoethnography is concerned with portraying the tensions, rather than harmony, between individuals and societies to which they belong. As autofiction creates ambiguity around the concept of "truth" by constantly crossing the borders between the factual and the fictional, autoethnography draws on autofictional uncertainty to suggest an ambivalent understanding of identity and community. They are assumed to take new forms, depending on the perspectives from which the individual and the society are seen (p. 88). Being never pure or singular concepts, cultural hybridity of people and communities emerges as a recurrent subject in autofictional and autoethnographic texts. In this regard, Mary Louise Pratt (1992; 1994) places autoethnography in the postcolonial context, as a mode of resistance to dominant discourses of the coloniser. Disrupting the Western forms of autobiography and ethnography with their accompanying regimes of truth and identity, autoethnographic writing asserts alternative forms of meaning and of representing the colonised (Reed-Danahay, 1997, p. 7).

Western historicism has homogenised colonial subjects in an attempt to preserve the "difference" between colonisers and the colonised, grounded on the notions of racial and cultural "purity". On the other hand, postcolonial critics argue colonialism to have instead provided the impetus for numerous crossovers that result in mixing or juxtaposition of elements from dominating and subordinated communities. Through the term "double consciousness", W. E. B. Du Bois (1903/2007), for example, points to the situation in which self-perception of colonised people becomes divided in that they begin to view themselves from the perspectives of two distinct cultures. They are impelled to develop a sense of self-image based not only on value judgements of their own ethnic heritage, but also on perceptions and treatment of the coloniser. As the coloniser's culture is imposed on the colonised, oppressed subjects learn and internalise Western prejudices and stereotypes against themselves, which inevitably shapes their selfhood and life experiences. The fact that the colonised are ascribed different identities by different communities makes it difficult to maintain a unified sense of self. The double consciousness of the colonised encompasses a perpetual state of "two-ness"; "two souls, two thoughts, two unreconciled strivings, two warring ideals in one dark body" (p. 8). Within the context of race relations in the United States, Du Bois calls attention to African Americans' struggles to reconcile their African heritage with American cultivation, and their desires to preserve the selves provided by both when trying to attain a better self-consciousness. Likewise, Franz Fanon (1952) points out that the system of colonialism forces the colonised subjects to assimilate the culture of the colonial power, considering native culture to be inferior and conflicting with the Western civilisation. As such, black people are caught between "two frames of reference" within which they have to place themselves; the frame of the African ancestors whose customs and habits have been wiped out, and the frame of the white community which denies to see the colonised as equal human beings (p. 83). Although colonised individuals are made to disown their native culture and to identify with that of the coloniser, they are constantly reminded that the black are not, and can never be truly *white* because of their skin colour. By stereotyping them, white men homogenise black subjects regardless of their personal qualities, and define the way they are seen in a white-dominated world. Straddling the white world, which traps them within stereotypes and the African ancestors, with whose past they cannot identify, black colonial individuals are pushed into an impossible bind where they are unable to achieve a unified identity. Their subjectivity remains ambivalent, neither white nor wholly black (p. 106). On the other hand, Fanon emphasises that the wholeness of the self cannot be recovered by appealing to essences because not all black individuals experience the world in the same way. In Fanon's words, "Negro experience is not a whole, for there is not merely one Negro, there are Negroes." (p. 104). Refusing the fixed categories of identity created by the white, Fanon recognises the influences of both Western and African cultures on his formation. He celebrates "the zebra striping of my mind" (p. 45). Thus, Fanon suggests a model of hybrid identity where different ethnicities are juxtaposed in the colonial subject's selfhood. One can be both black and white without having internal conflicts.

Adapting from Michel Foucault the argument that discourse as the medium of power constructs the objects of its knowledge, Edward Said (1978) contends that cultural-geographical concepts such as the "Black" and the "Orient" are not facts of nature. Rather, they are discursive constructions that create a particular kind of "reality" serving the interests of political power. In regard to the West's perception of the East, Said postulates a set of Western discourses to have invented the Orient with the aim of legitimising Western imperial power. These Orientalist discourses produce knowledge about the East which is consistently put at the service of the colonial administration to control and to manipulate the colonised. Stressing thus the intimate relationship between knowledge and power, Said argues that Orientalism sustains the West's hegemony over the East by constituting the latter discursively as the West's inferior "Other" while at the same time affirming the West as a superior civilisation. Orientalist discourse differentiates and essentialises the identities of the East and West through a system of representations which produce stereotypes along with the feeling of a rigid distinction between the coloniser and the colonised. East and West form a binary opposition in which both parts define each other. The West's stereotyping the Orient as sensual, irrational, primitive, passive, and undisciplined not only homogenies the colonial subjects, but also allows to construct the image of the West as rational, enlightened, active, and disciplined. In Said's contention, entities such as races, nations, and ethnicities are produced ideologically by language, signs, and discourse; therefore, they cannot be considered as all-encompassing objective truths. In contrast, they must be understood as mere representations. He challenges further the Western categorisation of individuals and spaces into distinct and uniform divisions by asserting any form of culture to be quintessentially hybrid. Said (1994) maintains that the contemporary globalised world is marked by overlapping territories and intertwined histories that concern the coloniser and the colonised alike. Like Du Bois and Fanon, opposing to the West's essentialist understanding of identity, Said (1999) proclaims experiencing himself "as cluster of flowing currents" (p. 295). Rather than assuming a singular identity, he acknowledges the influences of multiple cultures on his subjectivity.

Homi Bhabha (1994) propounds the shifting and hybrid nature of the self by pointing to the coloniser's insecurities about his own "supposedly stable" identity. Bhabha argues that colonialism with its consequent displacements and uncertainties affected not only the colonised but also the coloniser. Colonial relations are therefore determined by complex patterns of psychic processes which contradict the presumptions of fixed and unified identities of the coloniser and the colonised, and that they are absolutely separate from and invariably in conflict with each other. Drawing on Lacan's views of identity formation, Bhabha maintains that the coloniser's identity is constructed partly through interaction with the colonised. The fact that Western colonisers develop a sense of selfhood in opposition to the colonised subjects demonstrates identity to be a product of relations and to have no origin. Because the coloniser's identity is partly dependent on the Other, Western subjectivity can be argued to be inherently ambivalent. In this regard, the coloniser's stereotyping of the colonised serves to confirm the former's identity. As acts of stereotyping are repeated over and over again, the stereotyper is understood not to be certain about the truthfulness of the stereotype as well as his own identity, which is revealed by contradictory meanings of stereotypes. For example, within Western perception, the colonised subject can be simultaneously both savage and yet innocent as a child, both uncivilised and yet obedient. For Bhabha, such contradictory psychic responses to the colonised Other fracture and destabilise the coloniser's identity. Furthermore, they demonstrate that the coloniser's discourse is less stable than he thinks, as his language is subject to *différance*. Bhabha contends that cultural encounters cannot escape interaction, which results in fusion of cultural forms. Therefore, neither the colonial nor the colonised cultures and languages can be considered as pure and distinct from one other. He uses the term *hybridity* to propose the idea that all cultures are mixed and impure. Intervening in the exercise of authority, hybridity indicates the impossibility of an inert and solid identity, and represents the unpredictability of its evolvement (p. 114). Hybridity as an in-between position, points to the intersection of two cultures that are of equal weight and power, which allows suppressed histories to enter upon the dominant discourse.

Postcolonial theories have significant impacts on the development of alternative forms of life writing inasmuch as they put the Western norms of truth, identity and experience into question. Accentuating the sterility of the claims for objectivity of knowledge and purity of cultures, they encourage interrogation and transgression of discursively established borders, and embrace the possibilities of contiguity or mixing of distinct cultural elements. Moreover, postcolonial perspective of cultural heterogeneity disrupts stereotypical representations of subjectivities, enabling new forms of being to emerge in which the self is recognised as plural and shifting. Identically, the transgressive tendencies and hybridity of autofiction/ autoethnography problematise conventional literary forms, dominant discourses and unifying categories of the West. They allow authors to relate their personal history to the collective history of the ethnic communities to which they belong, and to inquire creatively into "objective" accounts from their own perspectives and experiences which are often excluded from Western historical narratives. In addition, autofictional/autoethnographic writing enables writers to explore and experiment with new concepts of subjectivity that are hybrid, transcultural, diasporic, and nomadic. They are liberated to express impacts of various cultures on their selfhood and meanings of having multiple cultural identities, as postcolonial theorists have articulated. However, authors of autofictional/autoethnographic texts, who often suffer from tensions between "I" and "ego", do not simply try to inscribe their marginalised identities on dominant discourses. They seek to recreate the multiple and fragmented identifications with different societies and the experiences of both pleasant and painful nature in order to understand the "truth" of their self and to make sense of their place in the world. In this respect, autofiction/autoethnography provides authors with a "third space"[20] where they renegotiate their multiple subjectivities produced as a result of connections and disconnections to various locations and societies. This book focuses on autofiction/autoethnography by multi-ethnic writers who have links with multiple spaces and cultures which ascribe them distinct identities. It is argued that in tune with the postmodern/postcolonial conceptions of self and society, multi-ethnic authors of creative autoethnography embark on a quest to discover something "true" about their selfhood by writing texts which deal with locations fracturing and destabilising subjectivity. Their journeys back into ethnic roots reveal the anti-essentialist notion that people or groups can possess different subjectivities in different situations. It is also maintained that autoethnographies adopt a fluid approach to thinking about the concepts of memory, belonging and the self. Lack of narrative linearity and fragmentary writing characterising autoethnographic texts not only emulate the poststructuralist understanding of memory's workings, but also represent the fractures and instabilities of a multi-ethnic subjectivity. Autoethnographic crossings over the boundaries between autobiography and ethnography, the personal and the collective disrupt the fixed and unifying Western categories of race, nation and ethnicity, and open up space for multi-ethnic authors to express their unbelonging to a singular identity and space. By writing the split and multiplicity of the self, multi-ethnic authors of autoethnography reject the essentialist assumptions of Western historicism which has homogenised colonial subjects and confined them into stereotypes. They take up a counter position in line with the postcolonial considerations of subjectivity and community marked by heterogeneity, hybridity and plurality.

---

20 According to Homi Bhabha (1994), the "third space" is a mode of articulation which does not merely reflect but engenders new possibilities of cultural meaning. It is an interruptive, interrogative, and enunciative space that questions established categories of culture and identity, and enables new positions to emerge. Therefore, it is an ambivalent site where cultural representations have no primordial unity or fixity (p. 211).

Chapter 3 Multiethnicity as an In-between Cultural Position

Conceptualisation of Multiethnicity

This chapter aims to discuss the concept of multiethnicity as an in-between cultural position so as to establish its connections to autofiction and other developments it has led to, such as autoethnography and autotheory. To this end, it is crucial to overview various approaches to ethnicity, before attempting to scrutinise its engagement with multiplicity. The OED defines the current usage of *ethnicity*, first recorded in 1953, as referring to "ethnic character or peculiarity". *Ethnic*, in turn, is defined as "pertaining to or having common racial, cultural, religious, or linguistic characteristics, esp. designating a racial or other group within a larger system; hence (US colloq.), foreign, exotic." In *Rethinking Ethnicity* (1997), Richard Jenkins formulates the term on the basis of Max Weber's *Economy and Society* (1922/1978), in which Weber differentiated between ethnicity and what he calls "anthropological type" (i.e., race). Jenkins remarks that Weber not only defined ethnicity as a belief in a common descent, he also stressed its predominantly political nature. In Weber's view, the belief in common ancestry is the result of collective political action; people come to see themselves as belonging together as a consequence of acting together. Collective interests do not simply reflect perceived similarities and differences between people; however, the active pursuit of common interests encourages ethnic identification (p. 10). In *Ethnicity* (2010), Steve Fenton thinks of ethnicity, primarily, as referring to social identities – typically "descent" and "cultural difference" – deployed under certain conditions. As a further step, he considers ethnicity as referring to the social construction of descent and culture, and the implications of classification systems built around them (p. 3). As Tabish Khair (2017) puts it, right at the start "ethnicity" was and is situated between two stools: biological and political (p. 213).

Having a great deal of common ground with the terms "race" and "nation", "ethnicity" has inevitably been entangled with racial arguments, particularly, the white supremacist proposition which held that white peoples had destiny to rule over or even supersede and eliminate lower races, and that race mixing was dangerous. As Edward Said points out in *Orientalism* (1978), the political power and hegemony of the West turned many European perspectives into the main and at times the only definitive truth about non-European places, ideas, histories, customs, or peoples. Accordingly, for over many centuries, the "black" as a racial or ethnic category had been homogenised and ascribed only negative connotations within Manichean dualism that postulated an absolute division between "the West" and "the Rest". The identity of the black subject was hence negated as Other, primitive, and even un-human. With the development of postmodern politics and the collapse of master narratives of the Western Enlightenment, however, the idea that assumed identities to be fixed, coherent and stable has been replaced by the experience of doubt and uncertainty. The fragmentation of traditional sources of authority and identity has weakened the sense of belonging to singular collective spaces, such as "class" and "community". In line with the poststructuralist thesis, social identities have been recognised as constructed in language in order to serve certain political projects. As such, the conceptions of race, ethnicity, and culture have been reckoned as discursive products that are made "real" within matrices of power relations. The racial, ethnic, and social categories have been understood to be limited to express the complexities of modern individuals. Besides, these supposedly "pure" and "irreducible" categories have been revealed to accommodate members that differ remarkably from one another, depending on a wide range of factors including gender, sexuality, work, class status, geography and historical circumstances. Within a context informed by postmodern, poststructuralist and postcolonial developments, multi-ethnic paradigm emerges as an ambivalent condition that is unclosed, constantly changing, embodying diversities, and disrupting hegemonic relationship between "dominant" and "minority" cultural positions. For the purpose of theorising multiethnicity within the context of Britain, this book will be grounded on the works of prominent Black British figures who have considered ethnicity from a non-essentialist and pluralist stance, such as Stuart Hall, Hanif Kureishi and Paul Gilroy.

End of Essential Identities

In "New Ethnicities" (1988/1996), Stuart Hall declares "the end of the innocent notion of the essential black subject", and calls for the recognition that the category "black" is composed of diverse subject positions, social experiences, and cultural identities. Since the term was coined as a way of referencing the common experience of racism and marginalisation in Britain, suffered by a variety of groups and communities with different histories and ethnic identities, Hall emphasises the "black" to be essentially a politically and culturally constructed category which cannot be grounded in a set of fixed racial descriptions (p. 444–445). Contrary to their negative and stereotypical representations within discursive spaces of the English society, Hall stresses black subjects not to be unified or stabilised by a natural essence. In line with the view that regimes of representation in a culture constitute, rather than reflect the reality, he argues that the black experience in Britain is simplified, stereotyped, and marginalised as a result of specific political and cultural practices that regulate and normalise discourses positioning the black as an inferior racial category. With the assertion of the end of essential identities, Hall contends that there are not fixed "selves" which people adopt based on their race, and that issues of race are always crossed and recrossed by other categories such as class, gender, sexuality, and ethnicity. Accordingly, he suggests a new politics of representation that considers individual differences, and contests the conventional meaning of the term "ethnicity".

Hall (1988/1996) observes that ethnicity as a closed, exclusive national identity results in racism which operates by constructing symbolic boundaries between racial categories, and by attempting to naturalise the difference between belongingness and otherness typically through a binary system of representation (p. 446). In order to decouple it from nationalism and racism, Hall urges on construction of a new conception of ethnicity; a new cultural politics which engages rather than suppresses differences, and which depends partially on cultural construction of new ethnic identities (p. 447). This new understanding of ethnicity acknowledges the role of history, language and culture in construction of the subject, and the positionality of all discourses. Thus, Hall conceives the splitting of the notion of ethnicity between the dominant view which connects it to nation and race on the one hand, and the beginning of a new conception of ethnicity of the margins on the other. The latter stands for a recognition that every individual speaks from a particular place, out of a particular history, experience, or culture without being contained by that position. Unlike the former in which the hegemonic ethnicity of "Englishness" is constructed through marginalisation of non-white individuals, the new politics of ethnicity is predicated on diversity and difference. It is tied to a positive understanding of margin marked by negotiation, production and change. The pluralist notion of ethnicity counters the homogenous conception of Englishness, giving way to contestation over the meaning of being "British" (p. 447).

In "Cultural Identity and Diaspora" (1990), too, Hall calls attention to individual differences transcending racial and ethnic categories. He suggests that there are at least two ways of thinking about "cultural identity". The first position defines it in terms of one, shared culture, a sort of collective one true self, hiding inside the many other. It is held in common by people with a shared history and ancestry. It provides with stable, unchanging and continuous frames of reference and meaning beneath the shifting divisions of a particular cultural history. It traces back the origins of descendants and considers historical experiences of ancestors as a shared truth (p. 223). This position is relevant to the hegemonic understanding of national identity. In Britain, narratives of Englishness, Welshness, and Scottishness often take this form. Ancestry, in particular, has begun to play a significant role as white Britons have found themselves confronted by increasing numbers of British born citizens of Asian, African, and mixed descent (Weedon, 2008, p. 20). The second view of cultural identity recognises that notwithstanding many points of similarity, there are also critical points of difference, which constitutes "what we really are" or rather, due to the intervention of history, "what we have become". Cultural identity, in this second position, is a matter of "becoming" as well as of "being". Cultural identities have histories, yet like everything that is historical, they undergo constant transformation. Far from being fixed in some essentialised past, they are subject to the continuous play of history, culture and power. Rather than securing one's sense of being, they point to the different ways an individual positions himself or herself within history. Cultural identity is therefore not an essence but a positioning (Hall, 1990, p. 225–226). In regard to the black identity, Hall acknowledges the oneness in the black diaspora tracing back to the African heritage, which has a unifying effect on the black experience. However, he also recognises the differences within the diaspora resulting from the destructive nature of the transatlantic slave trade. His conception of cultural identity thus expresses both unity and internal distinctness.

The juxtaposition of "black" and "British" problematises immediately the assumptions of the essentialist view of identities because it conceives the British identity as a white Anglo-Saxon one. Considering Hall's conception of cultural identity, however, it is possible to argue that Britishness can involve being black with ancestors from Africa. Like the black identity, the meanings of other ethnic identities including Britishness are unclosed and determined by historical circumstances. In this regard, being black British would be clearly different from being black African or black American despite the common heritage connecting the black population in different parts of the world. Hall's anti-essentialist position stresses that identity and difference are inextricably knitted together. Cultural identity is organised around points of similarity as well as of difference. Being never finished or completed, it is subject to continual change. In this book, the discussions of multiethnicity and its relevance to autofiction are largely built on Hall's pluralist politics of ethnicity and anti-essentialist view of cultural identity engaging differences. It is argued that autofiction is a useful arena for exploring multi-ethnic experiences because autofiction's stylistic and thematic transgressions help authors to express the tendencies of multiethnicity to disrupt and cross over the preestablished racial, national, ethnic, and cultural boundaries. As autofiction embodies contradictory elements from dissimilar literary forms, being open to accommodate diversities, multi-ethnic position is characterised by mixing or juxtaposition of various dimensions from distinct identities. As a result, autofictional writing with its blurred borders provides space for articulation of plurality of ethnicities constituting the individuals who inhabit multiple spaces. Autofiction is argued to be a "third space" where multi-ethnic authors can negotiate their identities, their plural "selves". In this respect, autofiction is considered as a productive space that can contribute to construction of new ethnicities and a new politics of representation. Autofiction's constant vacillation between the fictional and factual realms manifests, in a sense, multi-ethnic subjects' experience of straddling across different communities; therefore, autofiction can provide greater possibilities than traditional autobiography for conveying life stories of authors who do not fit in fixed categories. As autofiction and autoethnography cross the borders between the self and the community, the personal and collective histories, they enable multi-ethnic authors to highlight individual differences subsumed under homogenising ethnic categories, as well as intricate connections between various histories that intersect in their fragmented and hybrid subjectivities. Autofiction and autoethnography with their propensity to contain variances and contradictions, allow authors with multi-ethnic heritage to explore different facets of their selfhood in relation to multiple overlapping historical narratives.

Reformulation of "Englishness" and "Blackness"

Being a mixed-race author with a Pakistani father and an English mother, Hanif Kureishi has been greatly influential in transforming monocultural definitions of British national identity. Having felt displaced both in Britain and Pakistan as a result of an identity politics based on homogeneous conceptions of nationality and ethnicity, Kureishi is impelled to forge a new sense of belonging that reconciles differences. Refusing to consider the idea of nation in monolithic terms, he commits to illustrate diverse ways of membership of any community. In this respect, as Sara Upstone (2015) points out, Kureishi's works can be considered as fictional counterpart to Stuart Hall's writing on the end of the essential black subject (p. 128). As Hall articulates the possibility of being both black and British, Kureishi deconstructs fixed ethnic identities by creating complex, racially and/or culturally hybrid characters who challenge stereotypical representations, while simultaneously he explores different forms of being British.

Kureishi conveys that neither cultural nor national identity is organic; however, hegemonic discourses of identity and practices of social institutions may operate to make it appear so.

In *The Buddha of Suburbia* (1990/2009), Kureishi portrays the situation in which genetically and culturally hybrid individuals with Asian or African heritage have the right to be British, but the British society fails to recognise them as the members of it. The mixed-race protagonist of the novel, Karim, points to the denial and discrimination which individuals with dual heritage are subject to, declaring: "We were supposed to be English, but to the English we were always wogs and nigs and Pakis and the rest of it" (p. 53). Regardless of which culture they identify with, ethnic minorities and mixed-race subjects have been ordained to stereotyped steadiness of an essential authenticity in which they were expected to play out roles designated for them. In a theatrical play, for instance, Karim is asked to mimic an authentic Indian as inscribed in the minds of the Westerners. He is made to demonstrate "the white truth", in other words, the white stereotype of the black immigrant, which Karim performs for the sake of popularity and prosperity in his acting career. Similarly, Karim's Indian father, Haroon, reinvents himself as the exotic Other, the Buddha of the title despite being a Muslim. He performs the exotic Indian, as stereotyped by the society, to move out of suburbs and to lead a more upper-middle class life. Both examples suggest that rather than being ruled by a natural essence, racialised subjects are pressured by the dominant culture to perform stereotypes and at times to manipulate them to survive. In this respect, Nick Bentley (2003) indicates the ambivalence in stereotypical representations of race by making a distinction between two types of addressees. He observes that performing the collective black immigrant identity, as formed through the perspective of the dominant culture in Britain, can be empowering for the black addressee on some occasions. Subordinate black subjects may choose to act in conformity with stereotypes as a way of celebrating their cultural difference. On the other hand, for an addressee belonging to dominant white culture, performance of stereotypes would only reproduce them. For Bentley, the fact that significances of stereotypes differ from one social group to another reveals the specificity of the cultural understanding, which contradicts the claims for universality and essentialism of racial identities (p. 43). Both Kureishi and Bentley are concerned with illustrating that the validity of stereotypes is undermined when they are reproduced individually, and not by the whole community. Moreover, they suggest that performance of stereotypes does not ensue from a natural essence; they are sometimes performed situationally and strategically.

Racial stereotypes certainly limit the possibilities of the self, and trap minorities within singular, reductive identities, which leads to their oppression and marginalisation within the dominant culture. In his essay "Rainbow Sign" (1986), Kureishi gives accounts of racism and discrimination that he experienced as a mixed-race teenager in Britain and of his struggles to transcend the essentialist black identity imposed on him by the society. He emphasises that racializing and denigrating discourses, like British politician and minister Duncan Sandys' speech in 1967[21], caused him to hate and deny his Pakistani roots. Like Karim in *The Buddha of Suburbia* (1990/2009), Kureishi describes himself as embarrassed and anxious of being identified with the "loathed aliens...the Pakis" (p. 28). However, after having travelled to Pakistan and discovered how much he was affected by both British and Asian cultures, like Karim, he understands racism not to be a personal problem but based on unreasonable doctrines of the society. As a result, he is able to assert confidently, "I wasn't a misfit; I could join the elements of myself together. It was the others, they wanted you to embody within yourself their ambivalence" (p. 27-28). In line with Stuart Hall's pluralist conception of identity, Kureishi, at the end of the essay, suggests that the situation of racism in Britain could be changed only with reformulation of the concepts of Englishness and nationhood. He declares,

> It is the British, the white British, who have to learn that being British isn't what it was. Now it is a more complex thing, involving new elements. So, there must be a fresh way of seeing Britain and the choices it faces: and a new way of being British after all this time. (p. 38)

Kureishi maintains that the histories of Britain and its colonies are intermixed; they have always been parts of each other, and that as a result of the colonial legacy, Britain will not stop being a multi-ethnic society. It is the white British who will have to adapt to the changes. He believes that this could be realised only by a new conception of Englishness that would acknowledge the coexistence of several cultures, races and ways of thinking in Britain, and the possibility of cultural hybridisation, such as being black and British simultaneously.

In *The Buddha of Suburbia* (1990/2009), Kureishi's multi-ethnic characters are radically deconstructive presences that disrupt all the racial and cultural

---

21   In his speech, in 1967, Duncan Sandys said, "The breeding of millions of half-caste children would merely produce a generation of misfits and create national tensions" (Kureishi, 1986, p. 11). Similarly, MP Enoch Powell stated in 1968 that being English and being black were fundamentally incompatible, representing ethnic minorities as being alien to British identity because of the colour of their skin (p. 11).

assumptions of a society obsessed with clear cut definitions of identity. Their racial and/or cultural hybridity allows them to overpass the forces that try to confine them within borders of fixed categories of ethnic belonging. Multiplicities contained in these characters are illustrated by their adopting, to various extents, aspects of both British and Asian cultures. For example, Karim is presented as feeling "English while cycling and enjoying his tea or acting like a hooligan after watching a football match with Uncle Ted and Indian while savouring the delicious food cooked by his aunt Jeeta" (p. 43). Like Stuart Hall who argues for a conception of cultural identity that engages differences, Kureishi allows his characters to embrace their diversity and actualise different versions of what it means to be British. Accordingly, the multi-ethnic central character in *The Black Album* (1995), Shahid, being stuck between two completely different worlds of Englishness and Indianness, decides not to have any limits in building his own identity, and contemplates,

> How could anyone confine themselves to one system or creed? Why should they feel they had to? There was no fixed self; surely our several selves melted and mutated daily? There had to be innumerable ways of being in the world. (p. 274)

In addition to his argument that there are diverse ways of being British, Kureishi emphasises subjectivity to be a shifting entity. As Stuart Hall (1990) points out that identity is never an accomplished fact, but always in process, constantly being transformed by one's experiences (p. 222), Kureishi portrays subjectivity of his characters as evolving. Karim and Shahid, for example, move from ambivalence to acceptance of influences of the British and Asian cultures on their selfhood. Thus, they become representatives of Hall's new ethnicities that engage differences, and manifest Kureishi's multicultural and hybrid vision of Britain. The book considers that as autofiction disrupts clear cut categorisation of literary forms, and promotes a genre that incorporates diverse writing styles, multiethnicity transgresses the established boundaries, requiring reformulation of conventional categories of identification. Through autofictional strategies, multi-ethnic authors are able to discover or invent their own way of being without constraints imposed on them by traditional Western forms and doctrines. Hybridity of autofiction allows multi-ethnic authors to express their experiences of cultural hybridisation beyond limiting discursive practices of the West. Based around Kureishi's thinking of a more comprehensive British identity, which recognises the fractural structure of both black and British communities, the book will be focused on autofictional works by authors whose diverse ethnic backgrounds challenge the notion of homogenous Britishness and Blackness.

"The Black Atlantic": Hybrid Identities

In *There Ain't no Black in the Union Jack* (1987), Paul Gilroy observes that the politics of race in Britain is based on the conceptions of national belonging and homogeneity that blurs the distinction between race and nation. Through the mechanisms of inclusion and exclusion, it specifies who legitimately belongs to and who is banished from the national community, depending on skin colour and place of origin. As a result, both Asians and Blacks are considered as incompatible with authentic forms of Englishness, and denied national membership. Moreover, their presence is constructed as a threat to the idea of a homogenous, white Britain. In line with the contentions of Hall and Kureishi, Gilroy opposes to identification of race or culture with nation that is grounded on the notion of racial or cultural "purity". He argues culture not to "develop along ethnically absolute lines, but in complex, dynamic patterns of syncretism" in which new forms of being black or English emerge (p. 13). His conception of the black Atlantic is therefore an attempt to change the paradigm of cultural identity from a nationalist and essentialist one to a more "rhizomorphic" one. In order to speak of a more fluid and historically contingent form of identity, Gilroy (1993) employs the trope of the ship on the black Atlantic which he regards as the image of "a living, micro-cultural, micro-political system in motion" (p. 4). It signifies people moving through cultures and nations that will forever destabilise identities. The ship illustrates that self is not in a fixed position, but in shifting places.

Making the black people who suffered from the Atlantic slave trade the emblem of his notion of diasporic subjects, Gilroy (1993) conceives the black Atlantic as a transnational and intercultural space which exceeds the borders of nation states. He maintains that the displacement or movement of black people across the Atlantic produced new hybridised cultures because the transatlantic slave trade involved not only a commodity exchange but also a cultural exchange, a circulation of ideas. Hence, this historical occurrence necessitates a new way of theorising identity, separated from nationhood and race, and instead associated with the notions of "creolisation, metissage, mestizaje, and hybridity" (p. 2). The new concept of cultural identity that Gilroy thinks of transcends racial discourse, and foregrounds multiplicity, instability, and mutability of subjectivity. Because the black people in the West have been influenced by the European culture as a result of the movements across the Atlantic, Gilroy propounds that their condition can be described by du Boisian "double consciousness"; the recognition of their connection to the land of their birth and their ethnic political constituency that have been completely transformed. For black Britons, therefore, European and black identities are not mutually exclusive. Their black British experience is distinguished by doubleness and cultural intermixture. This perspective affirms the pluralistic understanding of identity that confronts ethnic absolutism, and considers blackness "as an open signifier", that is, black people share a common African heritage, yet they are divided by a variety of factors such as class, sexuality, age, ethnicity, economics, and political consciousness (p. 32).

For Gilroy, the African diaspora provides a model for a new way of considering identity and identification. In his understanding, the idea of diaspora problematises the conventional notions of fixed borders and rooted belonging. As he puts it, the diasporic condition "disrupts the fundamental power of territory to determine identity by breaking the simple sequence of explanatory links between place, location, and consciousness" (Gilroy, 2000, p. 123). Dismantling established connections between land and identity, diaspora proves to be of antinational positioning. As a result, the concept of diaspora becomes useful in directing views on identity towards contingency, indeterminacy, and conflict. As opposed to the notion of identity as a finished production, Gilroy suggests it to be defined by temporary linkages and shifting networks that enable "new understandings of self, sameness, and solidarity" (p. 128). Transforming the perceptions of both space and identity, these unsteady relations create "new possibilities and new pleasures" (p. 129). Diaspora is hence conceived as bringing along mutable forms of being that require redefinition of identity to incorporate motion and variation.

The autofictional/autoethnographic idea of journey into one's ethnic roots and deep realities of the self can be reconsidered in the light of Paul Gilroy's notion of the black Atlantic journey that fractures the unified sense of selfhood and produces culturally hybrid subjects. This book argues that transgressive tendencies and in-betweenness of autofiction enables representation of instability and hybridity of diasporic subjectivity. As diaspora creates new possibilities of personhood, autofiction with its emphasis on plurality of the self allows multi-ethnic authors to explore and invent multiple versions of themselves. Moreover, autofictional blurring of boundaries creates potential for communication of a transnational cultural history as Gilroy envisions. As a strategy of countering the dominant ideas of fixed borders and categories of race, nation and ethnicity, autofiction permits multi-ethnic authors to assert their subjectivity into mainstream history. Autofiction enables these authors to negotiate their own sense of self and belonging, and to escape hegemony of dominant culture's representations. By means of its non-linear and non-chronological narrative strategies, autofiction can capture multi-ethnic authors' fragmented sense of history.

The book uses Gilroy's concept of the black Atlantic to examine the transnational journeys that Black British authors embark on, with the aim of discovering their ethnic origins, during which their subjectivity becomes transformed and culturally diversified. As Gilroy considers cultural identities as "routed" rather than "rooted", these authors' multifaceted subjectivities are illustrated to be unconstrained by boundaries of nations or other established categories. In line with Gilroy's aim of placing national identities within a wider "webbed network" of interactions between the local and the global, and Stuart Hall's similar consideration of cultural identities on collective and individual levels, Black British authors are argued to portray identities that are constituted by entangled histories and cultures. As Gilroy attempts to exceed the limitations of nationalist thinking without discarding the specificity of localised cultural forms, Black British authors are observed to engage with transnational possibilities of being and to unclose heterogeneities contained in notions of Blackness and Britishness with emphasis on regional particularities of both identities. For Gilroy, these gestures across national and cultural boundaries bring along "double consciousness" which helps negotiation of being both European and Black. In like manner, autofictional narratives of Black British authors present processes of reconciling their Blackness and Britishness, and of embracing the multiplicity of ethnicities that constitute their subjectivity. In contrast to racist, nationalist or ethnically absolutist discourses which represent Black and British identities as mutually exclusive, Gilroy points to the possibility of occupying a distinct space between the two. Along the same line, drawing on the in-betweenness and ambivalence of autofiction, Black British authors are argued to profess their multiethnicity as locating them in an in-between and hybridised cultural position. Thus, autofiction and multiethnicity as counter-modern conceptions are united in the act of transgression, the state of multiplicity and in-betweenness, and the preoccupation with fluidity and unpredictability. When considered that multi-ethnic writers do not fit in preestablished biracialised social contexts, autofiction with its uncertain literary position becomes a useful form for narratives of multi-ethnic experiences. Hanif Kureishi and Stuart Hall who have been influential in theorisation of multiethnicity, narrated their own multi-ethnic experiences in the works that can be labelled as autofiction/autoethnography and autotheory. For the purpose of strengthening theoretically the links between multiethnicity and autofiction, the book will first examine autotheory, and discuss how Kureishi's and Hall's works are relevant to autofiction, autoethnography, and autotheory.

Autotheory and Multiethnicity

Autotheory describes the works of literature, writing and criticism that integrate autobiography with theory and philosophy, such as Chris Kraus' *I Love*

Dick (1997/2006), Claudia Rankine's *Citizen* (2014), and Maggie Nelson's *The Argonauts* (2015). Like autofiction, autotheory blends autobiography with fiction, yet it is distinguished by a significant essayistic, theoretical and/or philosophical dimension. Autotheory is therefore a mode of writing that employs literary techniques and subjective narrativity in its engagement with theoretical/philosophical discourse. Works of autotheory are simultaneously personal disclosures of life experiences, and theoretical/philosophical treatments of universal subjects such as identity, existence, ethics, aesthetics, politics, and the problems of literary representation itself. Along the same lines of autofiction's claims for representing the self sincerely, autotheory recognises the contingency and social/linguistic constructedness of the self, and yet insists on the "reality" and value of lived experience. On the other hand, Ralph Clare (2020) makes a distinction between autofiction and autotheory, observing that autofiction emphasises the personal inwardly without any didactic or activist propensity, whereas autotheory explores and expands the notion of the self via theory, with the consideration of the individual within a larger, collective politics (p. 90). All in all, autotheory, like autofiction, is both a reaction to and a result of poststructuralist ideas around subject formation, textual authority, and intertextuality.

Autotheoretical fusion of the personal, private, and/or confessional with the theoretical/philosophical is a critique against the poststructuralist reduction of self to a pure textuality that creates a meaning of impersonality in line with the deconstruction of the subject and the authorial authority. By means of such intermixture, autotheory reasserts the value of embodied experience in contemporary critical discourse. In addition, autotheory's emphasis on the "auto", the subject, is understood as an attempt to underscore the relevance of theory to one's immediate, everyday life. In this respect, Clare (2020) regards autotheory as a response to critical theory's institutionalisation and supposed "death" ensuing from the recent accusations that theory has become detached from life (p. 90). As an effort to consider theory in a more practical and pragmatic perspective, autotheory treats it as an inseparable part of life by establishing relations between theoretical/philosophical thoughts and lived experiences of persons. When doing so, autotheory, like autofiction, transgresses genre conventions and disciplinary boundaries. Personal narratives interwoven with philosophy and criticism loosen the definition of theory and put in question its authority. Shifts between different modalities of thinking and examining the world, between the personal and the theoretical, create distinct ways of knowing and analysing, which are held to be of equal significance, rather than placed in a hierarchy. Thus, autotheoretical crossovers between the autobiographical and the theoretical defy the authority of dominant discourses, and interrogate who is entitled to theorise. In that way, autotheory opens up the practice of theorising to individuals who have been marginalised and excluded from the domain of theory. While the specificity of personal experiences helps the autotheorist avoid the problem of essentialism around identity politics, autotheory presents the self as enmeshed in lives of others, history and power relations (Young, 1997, p. 69). Accordingly, autotheory explores and interrogates the subjective construction of the self as well as the self's positionality within a broader frame of power and politics. Because autotheory transcends the boundaries around genre, around identity, and around ways of knowing, it provides a field for marginalised individuals, particularly those who are gendered and racialised, to explore their personal experiences through theory, and situate themselves within mainstream narratives and histories that have silenced or ignored them.

Lauren Fournier (2021) contends autotheory to be particularly a feminist practice, considering that theory has been strictly a masculine realm in the Western male-centric academic culture of scholarship. She notes that personal experiences, feelings and bodies have been coded as female and excluded from discourse of knowledge. In contrast, autotheory acknowledges one's physicality and lived experiences as materials among others like theory (p. 54). Interrogating the politics of access and power around the production of theory, Fournier suggests autotheory as a means of reinscribing what constitutes acceptable knowledge, with its incorporation of the subjective, embodied experience (p. 35). The autotheorist switches between the self and theory, employing the personal experience of living in the physical world as the ground for developing theoretical views and contentions. In other words, materials of the autotheorist's life become a catalyst or framework for thinking about aesthetics, ethics, social and political issues. Besides, as autotheorists shuttle between their personal experiences and theoretical reasoning, they engage in processes of gathering knowledge about themselves and their place in the world, in similar fashion to autoethnography (p. 32). The practice of autotheory involves active and ongoing attempts to understand and interrogate the self and one's life within a social, cultural and political context. Like autoethnography, autotheory with its transgressive tendencies and emphasis on the personal, produces counter discourses against the hegemony of socio-political forces that attempt to impose the knowledge and identities serving the interests and reinforcing the authority of those in power.

Similarly, autotheory can be argued to provide space for multi-ethnic and racialised individuals to explore their personal experiences through theory and resist hegemonic ideologies that have precluded them from producing knowledge and authorship. Restoring forms of knowledge, language, and culture that have been suppressed by the West, indigenous autotheoretical practices present possibilities of decolonising theory and broadening perspectives on issues of discussion such as self, knowledge, place and nation. As a result, like autofiction and autoethnography, autotheory becomes a site of subjective truth, difference, and comprehension. The act of engaging with theory in autobiographical narrative enables the autotheorist not only to understand better his or her experience in the world but also to provide insight gained from that experience into topics that concern other people. In that way, autotheory opens itself to transtextual relationships across stories, histories and texts of reflection (Fournier, 2021, p. 163). Practitioners of autotheory incorporate writings of others which resonate their experience, and they propose critical thoughts or theories based on the evidence provided from lives of their own and others. The fact that autotheorists draw on intertextuality to understand themselves and their lives in relation to other people is an attempt to uncover shared experience and connection. When seeking to relate his or her experience to the ones theorised by others, the autotheorist is shown to have a desire for belonging and solidarity (p. 215). Like autoethnography that blurs the dividing lines between the personal and the collective, autotheory can be considered as engendering both individualist and collectivist worldviews. In place of delimiting categories and distinctions, autotheory provides a way of understanding the self and the world around the self, and hence, how individual experiences are tied to collective subjects of consideration such as philosophy, ethics, aesthetics, politics, history and identity.

Hanif Kureishi's My Ear at His Heart

In *My Ear at His Heart* (2004), Hanif Kureishi narrativizes his ambivalent relationship with his father, Rafiushan Kureishi, upon his death, reconstructing the past that traces back to his father's childhood in India, and examining what impacts his paternal legacy had on the formation of the writer's selfhood. For this aim, Kureishi reads his father's three unpublished novels autobiographically, goes through documentary materials, and draws on his own memory of the past which he acknowledges to be imperfect and full of gaps. At the outset of the book, he states clearly that a great deal of what he claims to know is grounded on supposition and fantasy: "this free-form work of mine is probably closer to fiction than I would like to think. But this research, I hope, will take me much further" (p. 16). Although his father insisted his books to be fiction, Hanif Kureishi identifies in them significant resemblances to his father's actual life. Therefore, he treats his father's books as autobiographical materials that usher the author back into the past while bearing in mind that they provide fictionalised versions of the reality. Documentary sources like photographs are, as Kureishi states, "silent", and require the beholder to make predictions about the context in which they were taken (p. 16). As for memory, it presents a disorganised and disconnected picture of the past that necessitates imagination to interfere and to fill in gaps. As a result of the unreliable nature of the instruments that the author employs for illuminating the past, Kureishi interweaves lived experiences and imagination into his narrative of family history and life story. The autofictional strategy of transgressing the boundaries between fact and fiction enables Kureishi to move beyond traditional autobiography, and to include in his life writing imaginaries and fantasies that complement referential fragments. It allows the author to embrace not only memory and documents, but also fiction as a valid ground for his transgenerational exploration. Importantly, autofictional/autoethnographic modes of writing provide insights into Kureishi's multi-ethnic heritage in that they help the author to inquire into his transculturation in connection with the collective experience of immigration, and to pursue his ethnic roots in both real and imagined spaces. While Kureishi gives first-hand accounts of his life in Britain and the impacts of British culture on who he has become, he imagines India and Pakistan through others' stories that shed light on unknown aspects of his subjectivity. Kureishi's intertwining of fact and fiction, hence, proves to be helpful to grasp a better understanding of himself, his relations to ancestors and places, and their influences on his selfhood.

Kureishi's autofictional/autoethnographic narrative develops around both his own and his father's memories of the past which are impaired yet capable of yielding significant meanings in regard to the "real" nature of self and life. For this reason, as authors of autofiction typically utilise psychoanalytical techniques to examine their memories and to unveil the deep truths embedded in them, Kureishi pens *My Ear at His Heart* (2004) as the part of a psychoanalytical process in which he searches retrospectively for himself and his position in history. In an interview, Kureishi indicates: "Psychoanalysis is [...] like literature in its deepest sense: this is where we think about who we are" (2014, as cited in Athanasiades, 2016). Then, he expresses that he has come to realisation of the complexity of his relationship with his father through such an introspective therapy (Athanasiades, 2016, p. 29). In *My Ear at His Heart*, Kureishi conveys some of these moments of psychoanalytical revelation. For example, when reading his father's accounts of childhood, Hanif Kureishi discovers that his father acquired a powerful envy of his sibling, Omar, and a competitive attitude as a result of Colonel Kureishi's harsh treatment of Rafiushan Kureishi. Hanif Kurishi's perusal of his father's stories evokes his own childhood memories in which his father wanted Kureishi to be successful but feared of him becoming too powerful or rivalrous, and therefore, he often made Kureishi feel humiliated and have breakdowns. Contemplating on such moments of tension between his father and himself, Kureishi realises that he has developed a liking for disruptive moments in works of art as a consequence of his strained relationship with his father (p. 52). As authors of autofiction narrate their life both in order to remember the past and to uncover something hidden about their self, Kureishi is often amazed by what he discovers about himself while writing, which he explicates with a quote from St. Augustine, "In writing this book I have learned many things I did not know" (p. 115). For revelation of the truths that are not accessible to the conscious mind, Kureishi proclaims to write with suspended reason without knowing what sort of book he is creating, but spinning "his words out of his words, stories out of other stories" (p. 115). He inscribes his memories and reflections as they occur to him similar to the way in which mind functions. He produces psychic patterns with digressions and diversions, which results in a form of writing that is disordered and fragmented like any mind. His autofictional mode of narration and direct statement of a preference for stream of consciousness technique demonstrate his consideration of the unconscious contents of memory as a crucial source of self-knowledge, regardless of their involvement with imagination and fiction.

Autofiction and autoethnography characteristically require the author to embark on a metaphorical and/or physical journey in order to search for hidden truths of the self, embedded in memories of various kinds of life experiences such as trauma, or to trace the impacts of social communities and collective experiences on one's identity. *My Ear at His Heart* (2004) consists of a psychic journey into the author's unconscious mind and an imaginary journey through his father's stories into the ancestral past and spaces of origin like India and Pakistan. Being born to British and Pakistani parents, Kureishi reads and writes in order to make sense of his multi-ethnic position in the world, and to discover the ways in which his dual heritage shapes his subjectivity. Inhabiting a liminal space between Britain and Pakistan, Kureishi is beset with cultural and ethnic conflicts. His travelling through memories that are related to his own and his father's pasts in two distinct countries is therefore an attempt to locate himself in an appropriate territory, constructing a sense of belonging. In line with the observation that autofiction and autoethnography propound the possibility of occupying concurrently multiple spaces, the realms of both fact and fiction, of both the individual and the collective, Kureishi suggests a notion of "home" that encompasses plural spatial and cultural territories, having discovered that his subjectivity is incontestably tied to both his "lived England" and "imagined India". That way, he challenges conventional ways of thinking about belonging.

Colliding with the views that consider concepts of "nation" and "ethnicity" as stable and uniform constructs, Kureishi loosens the boundaries pertaining to his sense of belonging, and enables multi-ethnic subjects like himself to avoid being defined by rigid categories. As the fictional element in autofiction functions to weaken the constraints of traditional autobiography, it permits individuals with dual heritage to dictate their own terms for belonging. As a result, a new kind of identity emerges that challenges dichotomies such as either/or, and that comprises multiplicities and transformations. In the manner that the Black Atlantic journey, defined by Gilroy, destabilises and fractures identity by bringing different cultures in contact, the real and fictional movements between the spaces of India and Britain, as experienced by Kureishi and his ancestors, lead to formation of new composite kinds of identities. Inasmuch as transnational and transcultural movements undermine monolithic conceptions of self, Kureishi's exploration and inscription of his multiethnicity through autofictional strategies point to the possibility of new understandings of "Britishness" that is, as Athanasiades (2016) articulates, infused by imagination and personal histories (p. 30). The autofictional fusion of imagination and reality enables Kureishi to construct his own British identity, exploring and creating possibilities of the self. Thus, he incites reconsideration of Britishness as a more comprehensive and heterogenous conception in which it is recognised that each individual is unique and determined by their memories of past and imaginaries.

Autofiction's ambivalent positioning between fact and fiction permits Kureishi to emphasise the idea that fiction is indispensable part of self. This view is relevant particularly to multi-ethnic subjects like Kureishi when they lack the knowledge of spaces to which they are connected by means of their roots. They are compelled to imagine homelands through memories and stories of others, which are themselves always interwoven with fantasies. Such situation of uncertainty and unknowability about one's relations to the ancestral past and spaces underlines the elusive and polyvalent identities, and yet it has a power to liberate the self from political and social constraints (Athanasiades, 2016, p. 36). Rather than knowing for certain, imagining about historical events of the past provides insight into the subject's unconscious desires, and therefore, approximates closer to the reality of self. Kureishi draws attention to the self-revelatory potential of autofictional writing of his life with the question "Will I be different in the end?" posed at the beginning of his journey through his and his father's memories, which also affirms the perception of selfhood as being in process and constantly changing with every new experience. In addition to the split of subject between imagining and imagined selves, Kureishi reasserts the inextricable relationship between self and fiction with the realisation that "there are real people and the phantoms we mix with them. [...] I thought I was one thing but really I'm another" (p. 156). In order to argue for plurality of the self that is constructed both individually and socially, Kureishi relies on autotheoretical strategy of reflecting and identifying with others. As he recognises that much of philosophy emanates from minds rather than selves, which prevents him from relating to its ideas, Kureishi breaks down the boundaries between the autobiographical and the philosophical for exploring and expressing the multifaceted nature of his subjectivity, both real and fictional, and for revealing the ways in which he is composed of others. For instance, incorporating Freudian ideas of the unconscious and split subjectivity, Kureishi proclaims to be writing in order to understand the dark parts of his selfhood. He investigates "the forbidden" not only through writing but also reading others' works, which leads him to realise the discrepancy between the self his father devised for Kureishi and the self Kureishi has experienced. After reading about the sense of liberation that John Stuart Mill attained upon his father's death, with whom he had a tense relationship, Kureishi begins to question if he were really the person his own father thought and wanted him to be. He continues to reflect further on his subjectivity, reading Jean-Paul Sartre's autobiography *Words* where Sartre expresses his loathing for his childhood, and Philip Roth's novel *The Ghostwriter* which depicts conflicting relationship between the protagonist and his father, based on Roth's own lived experiences. Kureishi's meditations, through philosophy and literature, on himself and his relationship with his father reveal the self of his own to be broken and fragmented.

Autofictional, autoethnographic, and autotheoretical modes of narration in Kureishi's life writing transgress textual limits, and challenge the idea of a unified text, which reflects the fractured nature of the process of the author's construction of "home" and identity. While the border-crossing character of these hybrid genres enables creation of a multi-layered space that is appropriate for exploration and expression of Kureishi's multi-ethnic heritage, the intertwining of literary and lived selves generates novel ways of understanding and representation of his plural identity. In contradistinction to the dominant discourses of fixed categorisation of race, nation, and ethnicity, by the help of these textual strategies, Kureishi is able to discover and negotiate different facets of himself, and to illustrate the conception of Britishness to be a complex entity that can no longer be considered as singular. He states that fragmented subjectivities in today's world of transnationalism and transculturation urge for reconsideration of all established categories from social to literary fields.

Stuart Hall's Familiar Stranger

Stuart Hall's *Familiar Stranger: A Life Between Two Islands* (2017) is an example of autotheory in which the author merges his memories with theory and literature in an attempt to discover what his subjectivity consists of and where he belongs to. It is a personal exploration of the inseparable links between his life and his ideas. While he gives an account of his lived experiences, at the same time, he interrogates how they have impacted on the formation of his socialist mindset and anti-essentialist perspective on identity. As autotheory describes processes of gathering knowledge about the self and his or her positionality within a broader frame of power and politics, Hall inserts his autobiography into the history of Jamaica entangled with British colonialism and investigates how the historical and political conditions of his existence have influenced his self-hood. Rather than a strict recounting of Hall's life, *Familiar Stranger* is organised around entwining liminalities; it narrativizes the space between Jamaica and England, Jamaica's internal social and racial split, his life and ideas, and private and collective histories. It is therefore simultaneously personal, theoretical and historical. Despite its loose chronological order, the book is composed of thematically grouped reflections that shift between self-narration, theoretical reasonings, and historical accounts. That way, Hall points to the impossibility of delimiting such categories as life, theory, and history.

Hall's autotheoretical life writing traces back to the history of his ancestors who were uprooted from Africa and transplanted in the Caribbean, and to his own childhood in Jamaica where he experienced alienation from his family and the Westernised middle class of Jamaican society after observing the dire living conditions of the poor and rural Jamaican folk. He describes the colonialisation of his people and dispossession of their native culture by considering works of postcolonial theorists like Frantz Fanon. He reflects on how the coloniser establish a political and cultural hegemony and impose a particular subject position on Jamaicans by referring to the theories of Antonio Gramsci, Michel Foucault, and Roland Barthes. Feeling deprived of a sense of belonging, he examines his own out-of-placeness by identifying with Edward Said and W.E.B Du Bois. Having been acquainted with European texts and culture at school and set off to the continent for his university education, Hall arrives in Britain with the expectation of finding a "home"; however, he defines the whole experience as pulling him into the position of a "familiar stranger". His dislocation from the structures of Englishness coupled with his ambivalent relationship with Jamaicanness force him into a liminal space of unbelonging. In order to make sense of his colonial/diasporic self and place in the world, Hall recognises that he has to confront his

African and Caribbean pasts. Therefore, he writes his life in the hope that he unearths some of the relations between him and the societies which he has been dislodged from yet still connected to. Accordingly, *Familiar Stranger* includes a number of journeys which Hall embarks on, from Jamaica to England, from England to African and Caribbean histories, from colonial childhood to a pre-eminent postcolonial manhood, from literature to politics.

In accordance with autofictional, autoethnographic, and autotheoretical writing's emphasis on the unreliable nature of memory, Stuart Hall (2017) declares, at the beginning of his narration of the past, that his memory is "fitful, episodic, unreliable and no doubt fanciful" (p. 9). He acknowledges that the stories he narrates inescapably involve errors of chronology or facticity, and yet they provide invaluable insight into deep realities of his subjectivity and origins of his ideas. The childhood memories which Hall focuses on are remarkably pertinent to social divisions in Jamaica based on differences of class, wealth, colour and education. Accordingly, he enunciates coexistence of two distinct Jamaicas; on the one hand, the Jamaica of the poor, rural, black masses, and on the other hand, Hall's own social location, creolised Westernised brown middle class that is conscious of its role as an intermediary formation between the world of the white colonisers and the one inhabited by underprivileged multitudes. His being witness to the exploitation of poor Jamaicans, class discrimination and consequent labour rebellions leads Hall to become disenchanted with and alienated from the wealthier middle class aspiring for social recognition and privileges. In such a society torn between conflicted economic and cultural orientations, Hall feels a kind of internal exile, wondering where he fundamentally belongs to, which marks the onset of his fragmented sense of being. Through his readings about Freud's psychoanalysis, Hall comes to the conclusion that the colonial history of enslavement and exploitation has psychic impacts on all Jamaicans like himself. The chaos of colonial arrangement in Jamaica is reflected in the disorder inside its people. He observes that the colonial rule has been a traumatic experience for Jamaicans who are racialised, oppressed, and dispossessed, which is manifested in psychic pathologies. In this respect, he holds his sister's neurotic disorder to be a result of this colonial culture in which Westernised Jamaicans fantasise themselves as being recognised by the whites, but in fact they are victims of an unconscious and destructive structure of misrecognition (p. 60). Because of the intricate relations between the interior and exterior worlds of colonised subjects, Hall is impelled to employ a form of writing where he does not have to make a distinction between the "objective" and the "subjective" aspects of social processes, and where he is able to express his inner conflicts in relation to larger history of colonialism. For him, domains of the social and the psychoanalytic are intimately intertwined, regardless of differences in their rules or modalities of being (p. 59). When Hall transgresses the boundaries between the personal and collective histories, he alleges that the social and psychic afflictions which accompanied his upbringing are not specific to his own life but experienced by all Jamaicans. They are displaced from Africa, disinherited from their native culture, and transported to a place where they do not have control over history. Therefore, Hall underlines the importance of examining his own life in connection with others' experiences, which is enabled by autotheory's disruption of boundaries and categories, and its embracing of stories of others as a form of countering hegemonic historical narratives.

Stuart Hall's personal and professional life has been concerned with the politics of who colonials think they are and where they belong. Referring to Frantz Fanon's descriptions of the colonial experience, Hall (2017) points out that colonialised societies and individuals have been irreversibly reshaped, their native legacies have been destroyed, and they have been impelled into a contradictory state of alienation which Fanon formulated as "black skin, white masks". As a result, Hall notes that colonialism has "othered" the subjugated people to themselves and rendered impossible positive identifications within the coloniser's rhetoric. In line with Michel Foucault's arguments on the role of discourse in subject formation, Hall indicates that "colonial" as a state of being has been imposed upon Jamaicans, framing their existence and subjecting them to the coloniser's discourse (p. 21). As Roland Barthes unveiled the processes of naturalisation of dominant culture's beliefs and perceptions in regard to the dominated, Hall emphasises that colonialist ideology has worked to normalise Jamaicans' subjugated position and to make it appear to be given by nature (p. 105). While Hall acknowledges the colonial system to have indelibly impacted on his subjectivity, he proclaims that his identity has been formed more by resistance to the colonial circumstances upon disenchantment with the social structure of Jamaica under the British colonial rule. He asserts the ambivalence of his selfhood with the articulation that "I was framed by and against the colonial" (p. 22). Hall conceives identity as being constantly constructed across various intersecting and conflicting discourses. Therefore, instead of completely negating the legacy of the colonial system, he seeks to find a way of coming to terms with what cannot be disavowed. Being aware of his "double consciousness", as W.E.B Du Bois defines it, Hall stresses having experienced life in Jamaica as divided into unequal but entangled halves. When he settles in England, Hall similarly embraces a diasporic identity, recognising that his Jamaican past is indispensable to his present self in the imperial metropole. He explains the "diasporic" as a state of double inscription and multiple belongings (p. 144). Accordingly, Hall professes that he has belonged to both Jamaica and England, at different times of his life, in different ways, yet not positioned fully within either of them. As a result of his diasporic experience, he has not stayed fundamentally the same, but not totally different either. Hall's enunciation of a self as containing multiple cultures or ethnicities points to the idea that one can belong to more than one world.

Autotheory's concurrent belonging to distinct categories of writing – autobiography and theory/fiction – makes it an apt form for Hall to convey his realisation that he does not have to choose between the viewpoints of colony and metropole. A third space where both can coexist is possible like the autotheoretical hybrid literary space that brings diverse genres together, illustrating the artificiality and fragility of dividing borders. In order to explain the multiplicities embodied by his life, Hall incorporates into his self-narration not only theoretical arguments but also literary works. His acquaintance with modernism, particularly, through T.S Eliot's *The Waste Land* and James Joyce's *Ulysses*, helps him understand the ambivalent state of his subjectivity, and the possibility of another world that is removed from the diktats of the colonial order with its strict categories and claims for absolute knowledge. When Hall reads Eliot's poem, he feels that he is somehow deprived of the knowledge to make sense of the contemporary world although he is well educated in British history, literature, manners, norms, and ideals. Regardless of the difficulty of the poem and its challenges to comprehension, Hall remarks it to have opened doors into new sensibilities. Rather than being interested in the idea of modernity as referring to the Enlightenment principles of "rationality", "progress", and "disinterested knowledge", he is inspired by the fact that new currents of thought were emerging and transforming the intellectual world to which writers and artists responded with creative and experimental forms. Hall understands modern rhythms as striving to enunciate a new emotionally charged and cognitively challenging contemporary consciousness, reflecting the trauma and social crisis of Western society as a consequence of the World War I. Similarly, the unconventional composition of *Ulysses* induces Hall to interrogate the circumstances that led Joyce to produce it, and ask if his experimentation with language was linked to the fact that he was Irish, and if Irishness and cosmopolitanism were mutually exclusive for him. Identifying with Joyce, Hall is stimulated to consider the Caribbean as mise en scène for an odyssey. His reading modern works hence makes Hall think about new possibilities of being beyond the colonial rationale, and incites him to confront his past to understand himself better. As he sets off to Britain with a desire to see the broader picture within which he is articulated as a colonial subject, Hall feels the need to embark on a metaphorical journey into the Caribbean culture and its relations with Britain and Africa. He supposes that an understanding of the complex negotiations of creolisation and the rise of a distinct culture in the Caribbean, modulated with the histories of slavery and colonialism can illuminate his relationship to this formation and provide answers to the questions about his identity and belonging. Autotheory as a means of searching for the self through theoretical and literary materials becomes a useful tool for Hall both to discover and to express his connections to various cultures, experimenting with narrative form to accommodate the intricate nature of multi-ethnic colonial and diasporic selfhood.

Emphasising the impacts of journeys, movements, and cultural contacts on the formation of his subjectivity through autotheoretical hybridity, Hall suggests that it is "routes" rather than "roots" that determine one's identity. Multi-ethnic position of individuals constituted by varied cultures, histories, and languages goes beyond the reductive boundaries of conventional identity politics. Multiethnicity transforms, reconstructs, problematises and pluralises identities, challenging the essentialist view that assumes the self as whole, integral, and static. Against the monolithic consideration of identity, Hall embraces colonial and diasporic ambivalence typical of contemporary world by which numerous cultural formations coexist and interconnect. As a result of his own positionality within complex interrelations between Britain, the Caribbean, and Africa, he acknowledges to contain plural identities. Despite not belonging wholly to any of these spaces, he realises that his subjectivity has been shaped by each. Because his multi-ethnic self does not fit neatly into singular and unified narratives of identification, he urges for creation of new narrative forms to capture the complexity and plurality of selfhood. His autotheoretical exploration of his multifaceted self is an attempt to place his existence within a framework, combining the psychic dynamics of his inner life and the social discursive, subjective emotional attachments and objective socio-historical location (p. 170). Autotheory's transgression of the boundaries between the personal and the collective, self and others, autobiography and theory/literature creates potential for new understandings of identity and representation of multiethnicity which exceeds the limitations of fixed categories of race, nation, and ethnicity. Autotheory's propensity to occupy multiple textual spaces and resistance against categorisation allows Hall to treat identity as plural and never achieving finality. Considering identity as the means for becoming, Hall assumes his autotheoretical narrative to capture the self in transience, and proclaims his work never to reach its final destination even if he adds finis to the final page (p. 63). Autotheory's shifting modality thus corresponds to Hall's view of identity as a constantly shifting process of positioning and identifications, which is never singular, complete, or reaches finished state of being despite the part of one's self remains essentially the same across time. Hall's reconciliation of contradictory elements which constitute identity – unchanging and inconstant aspects – is reflected in autotheory's merging and juxtaposition of conflicting modalities.

Autofiction/Autoethnography by Multi-ethnic Black British Women Authors

Traditional autobiography foregrounds the Enlightenment views of subjectivity as articulated by white European men, and therefore, notoriously excludes women and people of colour from expressing their subjectivities in the ways they experience them. Because the genre stresses the individual as a supreme and unique being, it leaves out of consideration the externally imposed cultural identities of women and other oppressed groups. The emphasis on individualism as the precondition for autobiography hinders historically marginalised authors from entering the canons of autobiography (Friedman, 1988, p. 75). Since the late 1980s, feminist critics have expanded the study of autobiography, challenging the male criteria for construction of autobiographical texts. Scholars such as Sidonie Smith (1987) and Liz Stanley (1992) note that as women's stories have been often silenced in a patriarchal culture and androcentric genre, women have turned to fiction to produce the fragmented female self in contradistinction to the whole, coherent, and autonomous male subject. As Leigh Gilmore (1994) recapitulates the argument, women have produced discontinuous self-representation which has served to shatter the discourses that were previously assumed to be whole. They have enunciated the female ego as having flexible boundaries, disrupting masculinist definitions of truth, identity, and genre (p. 45). Strategies of fictionalisation and fragmentation in autobiographical writing thus allow women authors to confront the ways in which they have been represented by men, and to give a voice to their experiences of the self and the world fractured by gendered power relations.

In the light of feminist critique of autobiography and female practice of self-narration, Myra Bloom (2019) considers women's autofiction as an "autobiographic" tactic (p. 12).[22] Women practitioners of autofiction transgress the boundaries between autobiography and fiction to diagnose and denounce the constraints imposed on female creators in a male-dominated society.

---

22 In *Autobiographics* (1994), Leigh Gilmore uses the term "autobiographics" to describe innovative writing forms that shift the practice of autobiography from grand narratives dominated by the Western white men to the fragmented subjectivities (p. 5).

Concerning themselves with female authorship and the social structures that impede it, women authors of autofiction target masculine categories, both literary and societal, and the hierarchies established among them. In opposition to exclusory tendencies of autobiography, women's autofiction aims to create spaces of inclusion. According to Hywel Dix (2018), when engaging with autofictional practice of self-narration, many female authors deliberately veer away from the established schools of critical thought such as deconstruction, poststructuralism, and even from feminism (p. 10). The poststructuralist assumptions have certainly benefited women writers in deconstructing masculinist hierarchies and other structures that have excluded women. They have helped recognition of the female subject as constituted culturally and politically by texts rather than a particular governing "essence". The poststructuralist approaches to subjectivity have contributed to the formulation of female self as fragmented, divided, and discursively positioned. However, the poststructuralist reduction of the subject to textuality has meant silencing the voices of women authors who had not yet achieved critical recognition for expression of female subjectivity (Anderson, 2011, p. 184). The death of the subject and the author has raised the danger of obviating the possibilities for women to write in their name after having long been denied expression of female subjectivity and experiences. As Nicole Ward Jouve (1991) puts it, women first must have a self before they can afford to deconstruct it (p. 7).

From the poststructuralist viewpoint, all autobiography is necessarily fictive. Autobiographical selves are created through the process of writing which cannot produce the real selves because of the inherently nonreferential nature of all signs. The corporeal subject himself/herself is constructed through acquisition of symbolic systems like language and discourse, which splits the self between the "real" and the "symbolic" in Lacanian terms. Women writers of autofiction maintain that cultural representation of women leads to alienation because they cannot recognise themselves in the constructed images. As a result, women develop a dual-consciousness of self; the self as culturally defined and the self as different from cultural prescription (Friedman, 1988, p. 76). In their perspective, the autofictional self is not a mere play of words on the page detached from the referentiality. Nor does the female sense of alienation come from creation of the self in language. Alienation and fragmentation resulting from historically imposed images of the female self-stimulate women's autofictional self-narration, which serves to interrupt male representation of female subjectivity. The development of women's autofictional practice has been greatly influenced by feminist critical theories such as Helen Cixous's exploration of gendered and hierarchal binary oppositions structuring the Western culture and her proposal of subversive female writing (écriture feminine) that comes from the female body; Julia Kristeva's positioning woman outside discourse, in a "feminine imaginary" that escapes the dualism of the masculine subject and disrupts men's speech; Luce Irigaray's embracement of a pluralistic epistemology that defies modernist dualisms. They all have critiqued cultural creation of the concept "woman" as subordinated to men, emphasised the female subjectivity as different from the male, promoted models of dispersed and decentred selfhood, and encouraged transgressive modes of female writing to intervene in male discourse. Although the aims of female authors in writing autofictional texts are allied with feminist endeavours, racialised women's autofiction runs counter to feminism due to the latter's tendency to privilege a certain definition of "woman", that is, white heterosexual middle-class women. In Western feminism, "woman" becomes a monolithic category which emphasises the difference between men and women, but overlooks the difference between women. Because it fails to consider adequately the multiple ways in which identities are shaped by issues of race, ethnicity, and culture, women of colour protest against the dominance of white, middle-class women, and draw attention to the possibilities within the category "woman" such as African-American women, Chicanas, Asian-American women, Black British women, etc. As Dix (2018) sees autofiction as providing more freedom to experiment with the expression of subjectivity outside the parameters of critical schools, autofictional writing can be argued to be liberating for racialised women to assert their difference.

The book focuses on autofiction by multi-ethnic women of colour for their experience of "double-invisibility" in the West because of both their race and gender. Not only are black women marginalised by white men's ethnocentric and androcentric discourses and forms of writing, like autobiography, but they are also excluded from white women's Eurocentric theoretical work of feminism. Considering that voices of black women have been suppressed by patriarchal structures and the essentialising view of "woman" in Western feminism, multi-ethnic women of colour have not had sufficient opportunity to examine their racialised and gendered subjectivity. Autofiction provides space for these individuals to articulate their experiences outside constraining paradigms. Because the concept of "black women" is comprehensive of diverse races, nations, cultures, and ethnicities, this book is restricted to black British women authors of autofiction, by whom categories of "black", "British", and "woman" are treated as problematic social constructs. In this regard, Hazel V. Carby (1982/1997) emphasises concepts of race and gender to have little coherence given the fact that "herstories" of black women in Britain are numerous and varied (p. 45). She also remarks that the gender of black women is constructed differently from the white femininity because of racism which they are subject to (p. 46). Carby thus points to the heterogeneities and differences contained in the notions "black" and "woman". Along the same line, Heidi Safia Mirza (1997) interrogates the hegemonic conception of Britishness as referring to the white and excluding black women. She enunciates that the construction of a national British identity based on white ethnicity invents "truths" about one's belonging according to physical features, and leaves out the possibility of being both black and British as a contradiction. On the other hand, Mirza asserts that black women occupy a critical in-between space that overlaps the margins of race and gender discourse, a space that resists definition and the essentialist notion of homogeneous black womanhood. She accentuates the potential of this space of dislocation to produce "other ways of knowing" that challenge the normative discourse (p. 4–5). Similarly, Sara Ahmed (1997) points to the impossibility of the racialised and gendered subject's being addressed through a singular name, such as "British" or "woman". Through the adjoining of plural signifiers in "Black woman", one can argue the subject to be assigned into different, divisive and contradictory positions by various relations of power such as gender and race. The collision between relations of address constitutes the instability of subjects. Therefore, the "Black woman" as a subject position is not a fixation, but a story of difference and movement. (p. 155). Its meaning is continuously negotiated and renegotiated through diverse discourses. In addition, Ahmed underlines the internal divisions within the signifier "the Black woman" that encompasses distinct ethnicities and cultures. "Black women" provides a temporary and partial identification in that as a heterogenous concept, it does not resolve the "traumatic lack of belonging" (p. 163). She emphasises the "Black women" and "Black woman" not to be foundational categories. They partially position and fix subjects, which entails phantasy and misrecognition (p. 164). As these black British feminist critics describe "Black woman" as a site of heterogeneity, contradiction, and ambivalence, women of colour can be made visible through personal discourse like autofiction which occupies an in-between space and allows transgression of normative categories. Blurring the dividing lines between embodied experience and imagination, between the psychic and the social, autofiction can reveal temporary, unstable, and antagonistic nature of identifications.

Through the works studied in this book, it is argued that autofiction allows multi-ethnic black British women authors to consider the ways in which they have been constructed and represented by dominant discourses in society, and conversely, to narrate their own personal experiences. The fluidity of the genre allows each author to negotiate her individual subjectivity in the face of preconceptions formed by complex relations of power. This enables the authors to define their own specific lives beyond the constraints of imposed collective identity. Contrary to homogenising, fixed categories of identification, indeterminate character of autofiction allows the authors to represent themselves in multiple positions as well as to construct alternative versions of subjectivity. As a result, it becomes evident that there are a number of close connections between multi-ethnic identity and the literary form. Autofiction, transcending the boundaries between autobiography and fiction, destabilises the meaning of subjectivity in literal form, and creates a new space where dominant assumptions of race and ethnicity are deconstructed, and new hybrid identities come into being. Multi-ethnic black British women authors make use of autofictional strategies in order to interrogate unifying conceptions. Drawing on autofiction's ambivalence and resistance to categorisation, they problematise monolithic perceptions of not only race and ethnicity, but also gender. They emphasise gender to be intersecting with various other factors such as race, nationality, ethnicity, and culture, which results in different experiences of what it is to be a woman. Multi-ethnic black British women authors' predilection towards autofictional mode of self-narration can be understood as an indication of their refusal of being labelled and categorised. This rejection is reflected in their treatment of racial, national, ethnic, gender, and sexual identities as being neither homogeneous or stable. Their engagement with autofiction's transgressive possibilities can be considered as a desire to be freed from political and theoretical discourses which suppress their individual differences.

The book postulates a parallelism between autofiction's generic plurality and multi-ethnic identity on the first level, heterogeneity of categories "black", "British", and "woman" on the second level. Autofiction's potential to represent multiple and fractured subjectivities is discussed in relation to personal narratives of multi-ethnic identity, such as Guyanese – Welsh author Charlotte Williams' *Sugar and Slate* (2002), Nigerian – Scottish author Jackie Kay's *Red Dust Road* (2010), and Nigerian – English author Bernardine Evaristo's *Lara* (1997/2009), with a particular focus on the distinctions within "Blackness" and "Britishness" as illustrated by the diversity of the authors' cultural inheritances. While all of these three authors rely on autofictional/ autoethnographic fusions of fact and fiction, of the subjective and the collective in order to explore their own racial and ethnic hybridity, they portray unique journeys into writing the self and different engagements with race and ethnicity. Far from expressing a uniform experience of being "black British woman", all three authors recount their multiethnicity and ambivalence on their own terms. Therefore, the sense of fractured self characterising autofiction appears in distinct manners in the authors' articulation of hybrid identities. All in all, autofictional strategies such as generic hybridity, pluralised "I", and structural fragmentation prove to be useful for representation of unstable and plural subject positioning. Autofiction's in-betweenness and incorporation of contradictory elements mirror the multiethnic experience of inhabiting multiple spaces, and enable multi-ethnic women authors to define themselves outside the given boundaries. The ways in which autofiction and multiethnicity interrelate yield culturally hybrid fresh perspectives on subjectivity, authorship, writing, history and memory.

Chapter 4 Charlotte Williams's *Sugar and Slate* (2002)

In the preface to *Sugar and Slate* (2002), Charlotte Williams highlights the ambivalence that predominated her childhood in Wales as a result of her mixed-race heritage and the dislocation that she felt in regard to her identity, belonging, and position in the world by virtue of constraining and exclusory nature of existing categories of identification that fail to accommodate differences. She writes,

> I grew up in a small Welsh town amongst people with pale faces, feeling that somehow to be half Welsh and half Afro-Caribbean was always to be half of something but never quite anything whole at all. I grew up in a world of mixed messages about belonging, about home and about identity. (Williams, 2002, para. 1)

The fact that Williams is deprived of the sense of a unified and coherent self, characteristic of traditional autobiographical subject, and that she is situated in a liminal space intersected by multiple, and most of time oppositional, histories and cultures qualify autofiction as an appropriate literary form for narrating complexities of her selfhood and life. As autofiction straddles the realms of fact and fiction, never belonging completely to either side, the author is impelled into a state of oscillation between fixed legitimate identities that deny her full membership. Similar to the way autofiction's generic hybridity resists categorisation, the duality of Williams' racial and ethnic heritage collides with the conventional notion of a singular identity. In line with autofiction's representation of a metaphorical and/or real journey to uncover the "truths" of the self through writing, Williams narrativizes her physical journeys to Guyana, to her fatherland, in search for her roots to understand in what ways she is connected to the pasts of her ancestors, and to attain a somewhat stable sense of the self. Her travels across the Atlantic convey meanings that are more than an ethnographic investigation. They enable Williams to recognise certain aspects of her subjectivity that have been "dormant", "undernourished", and "denied" (p. 104), which creates significant changes in her understandings of identity and ethnicity. As such, her life writing becomes a project that provides "an account of a confrontation" with herself and "the ideas of Wales and Welshness" (para 2). She is led to question monolithic perceptions of the self and ethnicity. Drawing on the uncertainty created by autofiction's interrogation of the strict separation between fact and fiction, Williams disavows homogeneity of cultural identities. Autofiction's capacity to bring together seemingly contradictory elements allows her to inscribe reconciliation of her blackness and Welshness that are held to be mutually exclusive in the politics of identity based on white ethnicity. As a result, her self-narration becomes a story of numerous contradictions constituting the reality of her selfhood and life, "of Welshness and otherness, of roots and rootlessness, of marriage, connection and disconnection, of going away and of going home" (para 3).

In *Sugar and Slate* (2002), Charlotte Williams interweaves episodes of her childhood with recollection of her journeys to Africa, Guyana and Wales, in each of which she spent a different period of her life. Her acts of travel and experiences of these places provide the referential material for her autofiction, yet the processes of remembering and transcribing them are interfered by her imagination. Besides, the author often relies on the potentials of fiction in her exploration of histories pertaining to various places and of the ways in which past events shape her identity today. As the borders between the factual and the fictional are constantly transgressed, Williams's life experiences are placed within histories of different geographical locations, which blurs the dividing line between subjective and objective modalities of narration. Blending of distinct genres, such as memoir, poetry, fiction and history, stylistically reflects the author's mixed-race heritage in that both are marked by crossings of established categories and divisions. Subversion of generic conventions enables the author to evade representing a narrowly defined self, and instead to produce a complex textual subject that manifests the ambivalence and fragmentation of her multi-ethnic subjectivity.

Autofictional strategies of transgressing boundaries, disrupting and hybridising categories allow Williams to imagine alternative ways of being and belonging outside acknowledged forms of identity which fall short in defining her multi-ethnicity. Autofiction's liberation from literary constraints provides the author with a space for articulation of the historically invisible experience of being black and Welsh, and the "truths" about straddling the cultural worlds of Africa, the Caribbean, Wales and Britain. The range of generic forms incorporated in her autofictional work is accordingly as diverse as her racial and ethnic backgrounds. In this respect, the practice of autoethnography, which is concerned with exploring multi-layered connections between people and places, permits Williams to represent her identity as destabilised and fractured by multiple locations. She illustrates that one can identify and disidentify with different places and societies over time, which attests to the unstable and fluid nature of the self that cannot be fixated by certain categories. Interrogating thus cultural signifiers that are used to define "belonging", Williams expands spaces of identification to explore and to represent the multiplicity of identities she possesses. Autoethnographic investigation of individual life stories in relation to collective histories enables the author to uncover her ties to various cultures which are themselves proven to be interrelated with one another within the complex networks structuring the whole world. As a result, autoethnographic examination of her life mediates Williams to inscribe the black experience onto the Welsh history and to excavate Welsh traces in the international locations which she is linked to.

Her interweaving of the histories of the black and the Welsh unsettles further monolithic politics of ethnicity and identity. Although her book is stylistically divided into three sections with the names of distinct geographies – "Africa", "Guyana" and "Wales" –, memories and histories narrated in each are not restricted to a single place. In "Africa", Williams includes parts of her childhood in Wales. "Guyana" details some of her experiences in Britain. "Wales" entails an account of her brief return to Guyana. Crossings of borders, as exemplified by all sections, depict in a way disjointed functioning of memory as well as artificiality of geographical and other divisions for multi-ethnic individuals who are connected to more than one location and culture. In the context of multiethnicity, it becomes impossible to isolate one place from another in that it is always tainted with meanings and experiences acquired in other places. The non-linearity of narration serves the author both to imagine subjective significances of remembered places, and to destabilise fixed notions of territory, boundaries and belonging, creating a new space that is capable of accommodating her multiple identities.

Entwinement of Individual and Collective Memories

Charlotte Williams's narration of her life is marked by the blurring of dividing lines between personal experiences and collective histories which are conveyed through imagined and yet illuminating interrelations. Therefore, her text involves repeated shifts between the intimate and interpersonal frames of stories provided by domains of family, neighbours, school, domestic and social lives, and the broader geopolitical frames of colonial histories and power relations. While retracing her own story of a black Atlantic family life, Williams also registers voices and experiences of silenced subjects of the colonial past. She examines their stories in order to make sense of the ambivalence of her own existence constituted by the conflicting influences of multiple cultures. In turn, through her experiences of displacement and marginalisation, she sheds lights on the realities of colonial enslavement, immigration and cultural dispossession of those who were victimised by imperial powers. Although Williams has to resort, at times, to imagination and contemplate possibilities in her recreation of the historical pasts, to which her access is not unproblematic, her literary undertaking indicates the story of one's life to be closely entangled with those of others who belong both to the present and the past. The fact that she incorporates in her narrative a variety of documents, writings, letters, testimonies by other people suggests that stories of the self both inform and are informed by lives of others. As a result of the acts of crossing the boundaries between the individual and the collective memories, the self and others, referentiality and imagination, the author both articulates her own black Welsh subjectivity and allows other forgotten black Welsh subjects in history to speak for themselves, challenging the hegemonic accounts that have disregarded their experiences.

Williams' recollection of her individual memories hints significantly at the subjective factors involved in determining what is to be remembered in line with the contemporary views of memory that emphasise its highly selective nature. Her childhood travel to Sudan with her mother, which situates the author at the beginning of the book in a movement that continues up to the final page, is understood to be a profound event in her life, carved in her memory by the help of powerful feelings reached through the organs of senses. While remembering the scene of the voyage by ship, she thinks that she can still smell the wet tarpaulin which was used to put up a temporal canvas swimming pool on the deck. She recalls everything in the ship to have tasted like salty sea water, and that the sound of engines lulled her to sleep at night (Williams, 2002, p. 6). The sensory details in her description of the sea journey suggest senses to play a crucial role in making moments of the past linger in memory. The moments imbued with sensations and feelings in her life accordingly constitutes the materials of what she can remember, which are retrieved in a loose and disconnected manner. Williams declares, "Only pieces of these moments come to me now, pieces that shaped me. The memories don't fall out in nice neat lines [...]" (p. 6). She acknowledges that there are gaps between remembered episodes of the past that she narrates, and yet they are significant moments in her life inasmuch as they have influenced who she has become, in other words, they have had direct impacts on her identity. Therefore, albeit they are flawed and fragmentary, her memories are still of great value for the understanding of her selfhood. In the text, the author remembers the moments of the past largely through associations between meanings of the past occurrences for her without apparent linkages among them as autofictional mode of writing requires suspension of reason for the revelation of memories freely to provide insight into the truths of the unconscious mind. For instance, while Williams reflects on her mother's inner drive to move away from the claustrophobic state of her life in Wales that urges her to travel to Africa, the author concludes her mother to fit rightly in "a place between somewhere and elsewhere" (p. 7), which leads the reader to another memory in which the author experiences being in a similar limbo state while waiting in transit at Piarco Airport in Trinidad. Again, that reminds her of another moment at which she watched a television programme about a man who was trapped "in the-transit no-man's land of Schiphol airport" because he was not accepted by any country (p. 7). The process of recollection that starts with the memory of travel to Sudan with her mother unfolds towards contemplation of in-between spaces and experiences of unbelonging, which are proven to be closely connected to her multi-ethnic subjectivity.

As Williams (2002) illustrates that the workings of memory, with all its gaps, through associations reveal meanings in regard to one's self and life, she embraces the potentials of imagination in making sense of parts of one's identity. In consideration of Katie Alice's, her mother's willingness to leave Wales for Africa and her identification with the African spirit, in a section of the Africa story entitled "Afternoon Dreaming", the author watches her mother sleeping in the heat of Africa and imagines a series of scenes of oppressive childhood and life that she might have experienced in Wales and motivated her to break boundaries by marrying a black man and crossing the sea to Africa. Even though Williams states that she has not been told about the stories of her mother, she thinks she can read them on Katie Alice's face and hear them when her mother calls out in her sleep (p. 16). The author's fantasying about her mother's past is an attempt to apprehend the reasons laying behind her independent and defiant nature and, by extension, the influences it has had on her own subjectivity. Autofictional strategies Williams employs in her treatment of memory reliant on senses, associations and imagination serve for the creation of liminal spaces or states, such as the ones between sea and land, sleep and waking, or the conscious and unconscious minds. That way, the author allows her act of narration to unveil deeper truths about her selfhood, and at the same time, to mirror her racial, ethnic and cultural in-betweenness. In Africa where she lived for some time together with both of her parents, Williams portrays her identity as influenced by the inner struggles of the two. Therefore, it becomes necessary for her to examine their life experiences along with her own. In this respect, Williams imagines the young Katie Alice as residing at the orphanage in Wales and sympathising with black children in Africa since they both were brought up with the teachings of Christianity and often mistreated (p. 19). Moreover, readers learn that after having left the orphanage, Katie Alice recurrently experienced racism in England, in the way black people did, for being Welsh. Her Welshness, like black skin, marked out her difference. As a result, she has developed a sense of Welsh pride, and a defiant and independent attitude, which Williams indicates to have become part of her subjectivity too. The author's own inclination for defiance and freedom is manifested in her childhood when she performed with her sisters all the mischiefs that her parents told them not to do. In regard to one of their habitual misbehaviours that involves leaving the security of the compound in Khartoum and roaming free outside it, she articulates, "We had to break the boundary like Ma" (p. 21). Katie Alice's unruliness is thus shown to yield impacts that shape the author's own sense of self.

In like manner, Charlotte Williams (2002) includes in her narrative her father's life story to explore the ways their subjectivities are connected to one another. She portrays his inner struggle as resulting from his experience of Du Boisian double consciousness. Based on her childhood memories of his father and references to his autobiographical novel *Other Leopards*, readers learn Dennis Williams to be culturally divided between Africa and Britain. Relying on the story of his book, a fictional source, Williams envisages her father as feeling like his body is inhabited by two different men: Lionel who is the educated and civilised one, and Lobo who is the savage. This state of "twoness" derives from the aggregation of his African heritage and British education. Lionel that he considers as the outcome of the latter is constrained by the Western logic and caught up in ways of thinking and representing himself which are not natural to him because he has adopted them later without having any previous historical or cultural links to them. On the other hand, Lobo that he associates with the African spirit is "free, wild, authentic" (p. 20). Dennis Williams' life is marked by the struggle against his desire to be Lobo, but then, his Westernised mind robs him of his true natural spirit. He is hence split between two conflicting selves that are not yet reconciled. His acquired European thinking and manners suppress his African free spirit, yet Lobo continues to lurk in his soul, tormenting him. As a child, Charlotte Williams often witnesses to Lionel in his father when he gives her instructions to avoid acting like a savage, such as "Behave yourself child. Don't go jumping about like a monkey", "Keep your tail cool, girl", "Keep your mouth quiet" (p. 21). His father's fear of turning a savage and his repeated warnings against it contribute Charlotte to be alienated from and disidentify with Africans. In one episode of childhood, she remembers climbing a tree and feeling wild and boundless, having the sensation that nothing stands between her and natural wildness. She feels the threatening power of nature in her. She and nature become one. Markedly, she disassociates herself from the savages that his father identifies with the untamed and uncivilised Africans. She makes a clear distinction between herself and Africans with the words, "I thought his savage meant to be African. We weren't Africans. Weren't we saved as Ma had said?" (p. 23). The episode captures the influences of the psychic states and conflicts of her parents on Williams's childhood self who is represented as unbounded and unruly like her mother, and yet shunning from becoming the savage that his father fights against. When Williams turns to the examination of her life at older ages, it becomes noticeable that her father's inner struggles and sense of split identity between Lionel and Lobo surge in herself. In Wales where she is exposed to only negative and stereotypical images of Africans, and therefore, estranged further from her African heritage, like her father who strived to suppress Lobo in himself, Charlotte Williams is induced to dismiss or cover up her associations with Africa, which she tells to "pop up again and again like a shadow" (p. 4). Similar to her father's struggles, Williams experiences difficulties in reconciling with her African roots. On the other hand, not feeling entirely comfortable with her Welshness either, as a result of exclusionary and ethno-centric identity politics in Wales, she begins to long for finding out Lobo, the free African spirit in herself during her trips to her fatherland. As Charlotte Williams presumes all dislocated individuals to face with the problem of reaching a reconciliation between Lionel and Lobo in themselves (p. 20), the autofictional narrative of her life is an exploration and representation of her own experience of racial and cultural in-betweenness which splits her subjectivity and of her strivings to come to terms with her different selves, comparable to Lionel and Lobo. Given that autofiction allows authors to explore and imagine different versions of themselves, Williams investigates the plurality of her European and African identities and conceives of possible ways of being that embodies her multiethnicity.

In Africa, both Katie Alice's defiant Welsh spirit and Dennis Williams' restrained Victorian demeanour shape the author's selfhood and her cultural memory. In Llandudno, a small town in the north of Wales, where her father is mostly absent and there is not a black community that she can be a part of, Williams (2002) is ascribed an "essential" collective black identity as invented by the Western discourses, and she is denied Welsh identity on the ground of her skin colour. In a way, she is dispossessed of the self-formed by influences of her parents in Africa and positioned within the dominant regimes of representations that conflict with her own sense of selfhood. In Wales, she encounters racialised and stereotyped statements and treatments on everyday basis, which makes her embarrassed with and resentful of her African heritage, and tempts her to conceal her difference (p. 38). As Williams narrates her experiences of racism, she points to the fact that many English words have racist connotations. The word Africa, "darkie, monkey, black, and any word that started with 'nig' or that sounded even vaguely like 'coon' or 'wog'" (p. 43) or banana immediately cause her to feel ashamed with herself and her African origins. She is constantly exposed to negative images of black people in songs, commercial products, books, on TV and in speeches of people even when they have no racist intentions; for example, when they ask questions such as "Are you that colour all over?", "Can't tell when you're dirty can we?", "You don't have to wash so often I suppose?", "People like you don't blush do they? I mean, there's no point." (p. 49). Because there is no recognition for blackness in conventional conception of Welshness, Williams describes her and other black Welsh individuals' position in the society as "highly invisible and punishingly visible" at the same time (p. 49). They are not only ignored and excluded from social structures, but also constantly marked out and reminded of their difference. The sense of ambivalence created around their presence and identity in Wales results in self- denial, doubt, and alienation. Being interpellated into the hegemonic assumptions of white superiority and black inferiority, the author indicates that they would renounce and deny themselves for the white acceptance (p. 50). As Franz Fanon (1961/1963) argued that when one learns to evaluate oneself from the perspectives and values of the coloniser, a sense of inferiority derives from the internalisation of the coloniser's knowledge, Williams illustrates that the Western logic both constructs black people as different from the British and the Welsh, and subjects them to that knowledge, leading black individuals to internalise cultural significations of the constructions of blackness and whiteness. Accordingly, black subjects in Britain often become loathful of anything associated with Africa about themselves and impelled to act white for acceptance. In line with Fanon's delineation of the psychological condition of self-alienation resulting from the internalisation of the coloniser's perspective, Williams portrays the profound psychic impacts of the processes in which she learns to evaluate her black body and African heritage based on the values of the dominant ideology, and she begins to despise every part of herself that does not measure up to the white ideals. Her subjectivity becomes divided between the reality of her African origins and the internalised white perceptions of black people. As a result of the inferiority attendant on such self-division, Williams no longer knows who she is or what she is (p. 51). It becomes impossible for her to talk about a unified and coherent self or belonging associated with traditional autobiography. Her subjectivity is fractured by the fact that the representations of the Symbolic order are imposed on the Real nature of the self in Lacanian terms, rendering her as a fissured and occult being that cannot be entirely understood and defined.

The ambivalence and alienation characterising the author's experience of the self-apply also to her gender identity. Internalising the white standards of femininity, Williams (2002) is alienated from her gender from an early age on, which she expresses with the words, "I was struggling on the margins of femininity already [...]. I knew that I was something other than a little girl like the rest of them but I didn't know quite what" (p. 42). A sense of uncertainty surrounds her gender identity when she learns the discrepancy between the female beauty standards, as defined by the white majority, and her black physical features. She is not only estranged from her own femininity and impelled to make changes in her appearance to comply with the white ideals of female gender, like hot combing her hair to give an English shape, but also fractured by stereotypical white assumptions of black female, considered often as "promiscuous, sexual and wild" (p. 70), which do not correspond to the way she experiences her femaleness. Thus, rather than representing the reality, the dominant discourses construct the black subjectivity and black femininity, which causes a fragmented sense of being in black individuals in Britain, divided between the self as experienced and the self as represented. In a similar vein, Williams highlights the doubleness of her life in Wales, split into private and public spheres. In public, she puts on a mask and performs white normalities in order to fit in the society, and at home, she feels free to be herself (p. 47). When her selfhood, gender, and life are marked by uncertainties, the author is compelled to write about possibilities, rather than giving only factual accounts of her experiences. Besides, she is driven to investigate the unconscious and repressed truths in regard to herself, which are formed as a result of the imposition of cultural representations on the self, and to narrate psychic conflicts both to make sense of her subjectivity and to provide a more "truthful" representation of her being and life.

In conventional understandings of ethnicity, having a black skin automatically categories one as belonging to African culture; however, Williams (2002) recounts her ambivalent relationship with Africa in her novel. Because of the absence of her father or a black community in Llandudno, the author is largely deprived of the knowledge of African ways of life. Having no sense of a shared history and culture, Williams lacks the means of identifying with Africans. At home, she is surrounded with the artifacts of Africa, yet they are disconnected from their cultural meanings for her. As a result, she is positioned in a situation where she both belongs to Africa and does not. She emphasises that when one is dispossessed of the history and culture that racial roots assign, he or she has to invent his/her identity in his/her way (p. 47). Accordingly, not having the knowledge she needs to make sense of her African heritage in Wales, the author professes to have invented her identity without knowing how much of it is universal and how much of it is particular to her (p. 49). The idea that fiction is necessarily a part of the self for historyless individuals is reiterated when Williams attempts, in various sections of her book, to excavate the collective memories of African slaves, immigrants, and missionaries. For the author, there is a particular type of remembering that is enacted by retracing the steps of one's forefathers. She asserts their memories to have been imprinted on the physical sites. By returning to these places, one enters the coded site of the memory where the past is replayed as a part of the present (p. 130). The processes of recreation of the past rely principally on fragments of documented events as well as on imagination. Nonetheless, they unveil significant meanings that help one to understand truths about the self by imagining or inventing connections between oneself and the collective experiences of the ancestors. The reconstruction of the past events and one's imagined links to them enable him or her to locate the self within history, which provides a sense of collective identity and guides towards a deeper understanding of who he or she is.

One such instance is exemplified when Williams (2002) retraces the collective memories of black people in Wales in order to establish connections between herself and the others who shared her in-between position in the past. She notes that when diasporic people do not have a collective historical event which they refer to, they invent one to define their presence in the adopted country (p. 26). By the same need for feeling as the part of a community, Williams is urged to unearth the historical events that are connected to her black Welsh identity, which involves acts of imagination and invention. In this respect, the author narrates her visit to the graves of the Congo boys, two brothers who were brought from the Congo to Wales by the Reverend Williams Hughes in 1885, and who were trained as Christian missionisers to be returned to the Congo. Their history has long been forgotten, and yet it comes out to hold great significance for Williams inasmuch as it helps her to understand her position within history and to make sense of herself in the present. In his diaries, the Reverend provides stereotypical descriptions of Africans and the boys, such as the ones that associate them with superstitions and witchcraft. Also, the Reverend's writings about the Congo boys and other historical accounts of their life prove to be full of gaps, which compels Williams to complete their stories by speculating and imagining the possibilities as to what might have occurred. Nevertheless, through the surviving documents, she figuratively returns to Llandudno of 1885 and imagines their lives in Wales. Her reconstruction of the history of the Congo boys brings along a new vision in regard to her identity. She reads that the Africans in Wales advocated the voice of the African despite acquiring the ability to speak impeccable English, and that the Reverend too preferred to pray in Welsh. Thus, they encouraged the congregation to pray in their own language and to protect their culture against the English domination. Much as speaking Welsh was forbidden in schools and those who spoke it were punished, the Africans provided the idea that English was not the only valid language (p. 33).

Williams identifies with the Congo boys' experiences of dislocation, of exposure to the racialised images of black men created through Bible culture, and of being treated as a curiosity. More importantly, the story of the Congo boys allows her to see a commonality between the Welsh and the African despite the prevalent representations of the two as inherently opposite and incompatible. That is, both Welsh and African people and their cultures have been suppressed by the hegemony of the English. In spite of their differences and incongruities, Williams is awakened to the idea that Wales and Africa can be brought together through shared historical events and to the possibility of a cohabitation of their cultural values. Drawing on autofiction's stylistic capacity of reconciling seemingly opposite narrative forms, Williams's self-narration offers thematically a reconciliation between assumedly incompatible cultures and ethnicities of Wales and Africa. She realises that blackness and Welshness are not absolutely antagonistic as they have been represented. In the way autofiction blurs the dividing lines between fact and fiction, Williams's work therefore problematises the demarcations between conventional ethnicities.

Charlotte Williams (2002) historicises herself by including the story of the black people in Wales in her autobiographical narrative, which becomes an account of her individual and collective selves. Autofictional/autoethnographic transgression of narrative forms enables her to examine her inner conflicts in relation to a larger history. While Williams investigates meanings of the fragments of past events for her subjectivity, she also ascribes individual meanings to these events. As a result, she imagines and situates herself within a shared cultural history. However, in line with autofiction's emphasis on divergence between the "remembering I" and the "remembered I" because of the inextricable links between the autobiographical and the fictional, Williams underlines a split between "the self that looks" and "the self that is looked at" in her inquiries into the history of black people in Wales by virtue her double consciousness. She is bent on uncovering her connections to Africa, yet she looks at "an Africa with the eyes of Wales" (p. 33). She acknowledges that she is both a part of the story of the Congo boys but also apart from it. She experiences herself both as the knowing subject and the object of knowledge. Occupying thus two positions simultaneously as a result of her multiethnicity, Williams avoids enunciating a unified and universalised history of the black. She knows that she has links to the stories of Africans, but she also recognises her individual differences, which repudiates essentialising ethnicities in compliance with Stuart Hall's reformulation of cultural identity and Paul Gilroy's conception of the Black Atlantic.

"Travelling Across Worlds of Thinking"

In *Sugar and Slate* (2002), Charlotte Williams uses the autofictional/ autoethnographic trope of a journey in a number of ways, which is stylistically reflected in the non-linear form of narrative structure. Repetitive temporal shifts between the past and the present experiences, and constant back and forward movements between the memories and stories of Sudan, Guyana and Wales represent the border crossings of the author's travels, which are argued to mirror her multi-ethnic identity. Besides, the fragmentary recounting of her journeys undercuts the teleological path of conventional narratives of quest that move towards a single destination. In accordance with the disjointed narrative structure of the text, Williams's physical and symbolic journeys do not follow lines of progression that lead to an ending or closure. As autofiction and autoethnography assume that the author's journey for discovery of the truths of the self continues even after the final page of his or her work, travel in Williams's narrative is represented as a continuous activity that never reaches a final point. Accordingly, her book opens with a childhood memory of journey on a ship to Sudan with her mother, and it ends with the memory of a flight back to Wales from Guyana in her adulthood. As autofiction and autoethnography are concerned with representation of the author's quest for the hidden psychic and collectively shared realities of the self, Williams's work conveys a particular relationship between movement, place and subjectivity (Edwards, 2010, p. 156). Her physical journeys to the geographical spaces that are linked to her ethnicities enable her to confront with her inner conflicts, to realise the unknown aspects of her self, and to discover the multiplicities constituting her selfhood. Significantly, her self-narration is an exploration of multiple identities that are not only mediated by her journeys but also created during these movements. Therefore, Williams conceives the self not as a static, unchanging phenomenon ruled by an essence, but as the one that undergoes changes perpetually with every new experience and cultural contacts. Accordingly, her quest for the self, her movements and discoveries of truths about her subjectivity are never finalised.

Williams's urge to travel to Guyana, back to Wales, and the sites of historical events is a response to her inner conflicts about her identity and belonging, and to larger socio-historical issues. She travels to each place in the hope of attaining a better sense of orientation and clearer knowledge as to who she is and where she belongs, seeking to uncover the connections that bound her to the collective experiences of the communities in these locations. Because the rift that she experiences in her subjectivity is fundamentally a result of the histories of colonialism and the power relations involved in them, she portrays her personal world as intricately linked to the collective worlds. As such, the true understanding of her self relies on an autoethnographic research for her positionality within history and how her subjectivity is shaped by the complex relations among spaces, histories and cultures. Through the autofictional/ autoethnographic concept of journey into the realities of the self, Williams illustrates that travel in the present can construct imagined links to the past, which in return can provide insights into one's being. Accordingly, the author's narration of her journeys foregrounds the self's relations to the collective histories, newly gained self-awareness about her identity, and fresh perceptions of belonging and ethnicity outside their conventional definitions.

Autofictional/autoethnographic strategy of enriching the facts with the potentials of imagination enables Williams to visualise and to portray her personal movements as connected to the collective movements of the black subjects in history, such as the transatlantic slave trade and the migrations following the dismantling of the colonial system. Even her highly individualised travel from Wales to Sudan with her mother is considered in relation to The Middle Passage by which millions of enslaved Africans were transported to the Americas to be worked in sugar plantations. In this respect, Williams (2002) recounts her visits to the excavation sites in Sudan together with her father who joins in the archaeological activities of digging out relics in some of the ancient provinces, and examining and interpreting the sacred figures of the old communities. Denis Williams, for his lifetime work on African art, studies the techniques that were used in the creation of these effigies, trying to understand the images and their meanings. As the African proverb "A thing is always itself and more than itself" suggests that objects are more than their materiality, the relics are treated as symbols of worlds of meaning and representations of the ancient ways of life. Therefore, Charlotte Williams and her father are figuratively taken on a journey through "tales of war, tales of love, of fertility and prosperity and more" (p. 90). The digging also guides them to the answer for a question that preoccupies Denis greatly. He wonders what it could be that prevailed on the Africans to sell their fellowmen into slavery. The fabric of the metal artifacts holds the key to the understanding of the transatlantic slave trade. Charlotte Williams comprehends iron to have been abundantly used in the ancient African communities. The smiths provided the tools for farming and hunting, weapons for war, and the metal effigies and figures representing the deities, which the ancient Africans made offerings to and used as the medium of communication in rituals. However, when the need for iron grew and the local smelting centres could not meet the demand, the Africans started to trade the iron of Europe which was brought to Africa in trade cargoes from Brymbo, Bersham, Shotton, Merthyr in Wales (p. 91). The iron trade along the route between Wales and Africa, which Charlotte as a child traverses with her mother, later became entangled with the slave trade when the sugar industry in the West India grew and the need for manpower increased. By selling their brothers into slavery for labour on the West Indian sugar plantations, the Africans could acquire the iron that they needed.

Williams's paternal ancestors were among those Africans who were transported to the West Indies to work on the sugar plantations where they experienced oppression under the colonial system of exploitation. Although the histories of the African slaves are different from Williams's life stories, on her trip to Guyana, Williams (2002) hears the unrecorded stories of the African slaves from the local Guyanese, and realises that she shares their experiences of dislocation, cultural dispossession and ambivalence of identity, such as "Christianised African" developing out of the contact between African and colonial cultures. Similarly, despite the fact that the author accentuates his father's movement to Britain to be different from the history of the Windrush migrations, she concludes herself to be still tied to that history in certain ways, identifying with the rootlessness of the immigrants as well as their experiences of racism and exclusion in the British society because of skin colour. Charlotte Williams's own and familial movements that are imagined to be connected to the historical collective movements bring about an awareness about her multi-ethnic subjectivity. As Francesca Rhydderch (2003) argues, Williams's work represents a figurative journey that is the author's "journey of self-awareness", her movement towards "an understanding of her cultural identity as a mixed race Welsh Guyanese writer" (p. 4). Narrativizing her journeys to Africa, Guyana and back to Wales, Williams (2002) portrays her negotiations between multiple places, histories and communities. During her travels, the ways in which her multi-ethnic identity is tied to different geographies and their cultures are both uncovered and also created by the force of imagination. Thus, Williams illustrates her identity as "in process", as a matter of "becoming" rather than "being", which Stuart Hall (1990) articulates to result from the continuous play of history, culture and power (p. 226). As Williams interacts with the cultures of different geographical places, her self is reshaped, reconstructed and repositioned within history. In line with Paul Gilroy's conception of a more fluid and historically contingent cultural identity that is transformed by cultural contacts, Williams portrays her subjectivity as continuously shifting and hybridised when crossing the geographical and cultural borders of countries, which generates new perceptions of "home" and "belonging".

Having travelled to the geographical sites which she is connected to by her multi-ethnic heritage, Williams (2002) understands that "home" is not a fixed and singular place where she can simply return and belong to. Rather, she comes to recognise that "home" is the movement found both in her individual journeys and in the collective histories of her ancestors. Therefore, her childhood voyage to Africa is not a return, but a "relocation", which suggests a sense of temporary settlement and taking up abode. "Home" as a fleeting concept is constituted during the ceaseless shifts defining her life that are inextricable from the collective movements in the history of Africans. As Gilroy's conception of the Black Atlantic emphasises cultural identity to be formed and reformed through the exchange of values and ideas over the course of journeys across various geographies and cultures, Williams indicates her identity to be conceived in the process of travelling through the triangle of Africa, Guyana and Wales, and cultural interactions among these locations. She explains her understanding of the concepts of "home" and "belonging" with the words,

> So Ma and Dad became lovers, eventually married and moved on. That's how we began to learn about movement. It was movement that was home. Home was not a particular place for us in the very early years. Home was Ma. We arrived in exile; into a state of relocation that was both hers and his. And the journeys were more than physical journeys. They were travels across worlds of thinking, across generations of movements. These boat stories and seascapes, I now know, are part of a collective memory lying buried below the immediate moment. (p. 11)

Williams's journeys are more than physical movements as in the paradigm of the Black Atlantic. They are travels also through diverse perceptions of life and ideas, as well as an imagined collective of African diaspora consciousness (Edwards, 2010, p. 159). Each journey connects her to the historical movements of her African ancestors through shared experiences of displacement, disintegration and dissemination across continents. At the same time, her subjectivity is constantly transformed and reconstructed in unique ways through her individual experiences of places and cultures. When Williams (2002) travels to Guyana for the first time, and meets at the Piarco airport the Rasta man who wears a shirt with the map of Africa imprinted on it, she knows that there is a common history that bounds her and him together, but she is also convinced that their journeys are different from each other. His Africa is not the same as hers (p. 15). As Stuart Hall (1990) argues cultural identity to be constructed by both a shared collective history and individual experiences, Williams depicts the black identity as connected to the historical transatlantic journeys, and yet as subject to variations depending on individual journeys. Both personal and collective motions are marked by border crossings. The stories and histories of movement that Williams recounts communicate the processes of cultural hybridisation and multiplication, as a result of which discursively constructed boundaries between nations and cultures are blurred, and the conventional notions of homogenous, singular "identity" and "belonging" evaporate. The essentialist discourses of race, ethnicity, and identity that place people in strict categories are dismantled to incorporate motions and variations. Discussing "identity" as a mutable entity, and "home" as being in transit, Williams gives a voice to rootless histories and selves. She illustrates that for the individuals who inhabit multiple spaces, "belonging" is not located in a particular static place or in a certain category of identification. Rather, movement and mutability define their selves and provide them the sense of "at-home-ness".

Blurring of the Borders Around Britishness, Welshness and Blackness

Drawing on the autofictional/autoethnographic strategy of blurring the boundaries between factual and fictional literary genres, between personal and collective narratives, between self and others, Charlotte Williams (2002) interrogates the fixed categories of ethnicity, and imagines alternative ways of defining ethnic identities. She blends her own experiences of ethnicity with her imagination of those of her parents in order to argue that essentialist understandings of ethnic and cultural identity are intrinsically flawed and groundless. In her reconstruction of the past of her parents, Williams imagines the times when her West Indian father and Welsh mother lived in London which both experienced as a place of unbelonging. As Sam Selvon depicts in his novel *The Lonely Londoners* (1956), the Windrush migrants to the "motherland" in the 1950s were not welcomed and were frequently subjected to racism and discrimination. They were considered as strangers and inferior others who were feared to be invading Britain. Although Denis Williams's English education and cultural capital contradict with the Western assumptions of the black ethnicity that homogenise people with African origins as savage and uncivilised, he does not escape from facing regularly racist treatments and prejudices in the English society. In like manner, Charlotte Williams represents Katie Alice as otherised by the English for being Welsh. The author accentuates that despite having white ethnicity, the Welsh were marginalised and treated in the same way as the non-white population. She points out, for example, that when the Welsh and Irish girls came to London for work, they could find accommodation only in the lodging houses that were willing to admit also the coloured people (p. 10). Kristi Bohata (2004) predicates that the "civilising mission" of the British Empire in its colonial activities finds an expression within Britain itself too (p. 9). The English marginalised the Welsh, stereotyping them as backward people who were in need of the enlightening influences of the English language. As the imperial forces held indigenous languages and cultures in Africa to be inferior and that Africans needed to be deprived of them, the Welsh language was viewed as an impediment to the "civilising" project of the Empire. Therefore, the 16th century colonial policies in Ireland and Wales aimed to undermine their native languages and cultures (p. 18). At schools, Welsh children were forbidden to speak their own language, which contributed to the Welsh sense of self-alienation, inferiority and ambivalence in the personality as a result of internalisation of negative British perceptions and constructions of the Welsh (p. 24). Drawing parallels between Wales under the English hegemony and the British colonies, Bohata propounds the psychological analysis of the colonial situation to be useful in understanding the Welsh experience (p. 24).

Charlotte Williams (2002) accordingly presents Welshness as a minority identity as a consequence of the processes of othering by the English. Like the black subjects in Britain, Williams' white mother experiences discrimination when she is dismissed from nursing in an English hospital because her lack of English is considered to be backwardness and incompetence (p. 20). Katie Alice often feels like an outsider during her stay in London, perceiving herself as "the real dark stranger" (p. 10) whereas her husband with his education under the British in the West Indies proves to be more English than her. Williams therefore illustrates that monolithic definitions of ethnic identities such as Britishness and blackness do not represent accurately her parents' experiences of ethnicity. Her mother reveals greater aspects of being "different" despite being white and British. Whiteness does not guarantee her the English identity. In this respect, Williams (2010) argues Britain to have never been mono-cultural nor mononational. She writes that the "old minorities" of the UK – the Welsh, the Scottish, and the Irish – pose a challenge to the assumed homogeneity of Britain (p. 50). In *Sugar and Slate* (2002), therefore, Williams represents Welshness as disrupting the imagined uniformity of Britishness. Besides, she portrays the fallacy of the homogeneous notion of blackness through her father's hybridised identity resulting from his upbringing in Guyana and schooling in English. As Denis Williams does not fit in the black identity designated by the Western thought, he unsettles the notion of white Britishness with his black skin and British ways of thinking and manners.

As Charlotte Williams (2002) describes the ambivalence of her own identity and the feeling of unbelonging in Wales with the line "I wasn't black, I wasn't white" in the poem titled "S'cuse Me" (p. 74), she travels to Guyana in the expectation of finding a sense of belonging in her father's country. However, in Guyana too, she is seen as "different" by various groups. Being the wife of a British man,

Malcolm, among the privileged white expatriate society in Guyana, Williams is often reminded of her skin colour, which leads her to feel excluded from that circle. Moreover, being unfamiliar with the ways of life in Guyana, Williams feels mostly awkward and very British in her interactions with the natives. Because her British upbringing collides with the Guyanese views of the world, she is unable to feel as a part of the Guyanese society either. Considering ethnicity in Western terms as divided into separate, pure categories, Williams attempts to distance herself from anything that is white and to reclaim her Guyanese national. However, she is repeatedly reminded that she is a mulatto and from somewhere else. Her relationship with Olive, her colleague at work reveals that there is a colour hierarchy in Guyana, a difference between Negro women and the coloured, insiders and outsiders. Even though their African ancestors had a shared culture and both the black and the coloured are joined at one point, she cannot overcome the white imposed colonial hierarchy, which makes it difficult for her to belong. She explains her strivings to belong and failures with the words,

> I wanted to go native, to make the place [Guyana] my own. But belonging can't just be plucked off a tree like a juicy mango. History and attachment don't just flow into your body like the deep breathes of warm ait…that part of your identity can't automatically fit you like the "I love Guyana" tee-shirt you can buy anywhere on Main Street. Still, I tried. (p. 149)

Charlotte Williams (2002) is connected to Guyana by means of family and heritage, and yet she also shares complex forms of social allegiance to other places, pasts and cultures which she cannot simply do away with. The question she poses to the Rasta Man at the Piarco Airport, "Do you think we can ever really return?" (p. 153) hence finds an answer in line with Stuart Hall's assertion of the plurality of cultural identity, Paul Gilroy's conception of the black Atlantic, Homi Bhaba's notion of cultural hybridity. As she gets in contact with different locations, histories and cultures, her subjectivity becomes fractured and hybridised, which conventional categories of identity remain deficient in defining. Williams comes to the recognition that she is intimately linked both to the coloniser and the colonised. She occupies an ambivalent position in history where her efforts to "put back into Guyana what colonialism had taken out" (p. 126) by working for an aid agency, and her affiliations with the coloniser's history, culture and social status are all melded into one another. Monolithic terms fail to provide her with a sense of orientation. She moves between parallel worlds, between the realms of the white and the black (p. 134). She straddles parallel lives, holding the white privilege and trying to live like the black (p. 135). While narrating her life, Williams' blending of factual stories with the imagined ones, shifting between personal and collective memories, blurring the dividing lines between the self and others serve to reflect her racial, ethnic and cultural in-betweenness and ambivalence. Autofictional/autoethnographic transgression of the boundaries allows her to inscribe her dual heritage and exceeding of the fixed categories of identification. Her unbelonging is illuminated through autofiction's/ autoethnography's constant movements between and blending of assumedly opposite narrative forms, such as memoir, fiction, prose, poetry and history, as well as through contemporary theories of multiethnicity that foreground the plurality of any culture in contradistinction to singularity and purity of cultural identity. Williams's experience of Guyana awakens her to the idea that mother country is erroneously identified as a single and static place and that it provides only an imaginary sense of belonging, suppressing the differences within it. Like the UK, she finds out that there is not one unified Guyana. She cannot find belonging in Guyana because it is divided by race, colour and class. There are deep splits between Indo- and Afro-Guyanese, between the black and coloured Guyanese, between the poor and the élite class with their British education. There is not one way of being Guyanese,

> I had been chasing the idea of a Guyanese-ness…until I changed my perception of what it was to be Welsh or what it was to be Guyanese, or both, I would never feel the satisfaction of belonging…I would have to accept my role as the spectre at the feast and stay in my limbo, in transit at Piarco airport, somewhere and nowhere at all. (p. 184)

Charlotte Williams (2002) realises that she has to transform conventional understanding of ethnicity and pre-existing categories because they disregard the multiethnic position of in-betweenness and inhabitation of plural spaces. Therefore, as Hanif Kureishi (2011) urges for a new way of being British that embodies differences, Williams imagines new ways of being Guyanese and Welsh. In *Race and Ethnicity in a Welfare Society* (2010), Williams writes that the essentialist politics of identity and cultural inscriptions cast Welshness as whiteness (p. 54). Besides, one cannot be Welsh unless they speak Welsh even though many people in Wales had to stop speaking the language under the English hegemony. The definition of Welshness based on a linguistic affiliation makes those who were forbidden to speak Welsh outsiders in their own country (p. 85). The conventional understandings of national identity therefore causes the author to be doubly excluded from Welshness by her colour and by her inability to speak the language. However, through the broadened perspective gained in Guyana, where she realises how she has been interpellated into the dominant discourses and understands cultural identity to be hybrid, Williams (2002) rediscovers Wales in her novel, paying attention to its variances and incongruities rather than seeing it as a unified and coherent whole (p. 167). Accordingly, she describes Wales as a country of contradictions, and argues the Welsh identity to be complex, plural and paradoxical,

> There is the north Welsh Wales they call it and a very different South connected only in name. The Welsh and the English, the Welsh speaking and the English speaking, the proper Welsh and the not so proper Welsh, the insiders and the outsiders, the Italians, the Poles, the Irish, the Asians and the Africans and the likes of us all fighting amongst ourselves for the right to call ourselves Welsh and most of us losing out to some particular idea about who belongs and who doesn't. How would we ever make sense of it? (p. 169)

The postmodernist and postcolonial visualising of Wales as divided, fragmented, and characterised by plurality and diversity allows Charlotte Williams (2002) to argue the conventional perceptions of nation and ethnicity as constraining and exclusionary cultural constructs. Because Wales as described in nationalist discourses denies her membership, she decides to reconstruct Wales in a way that contains her multiethnicity. She relocates herself within Wales by uncovering the ties between her dual-heritage position and the multiplicities of the country. Accordingly, she indicates both herself and Wales to be "mixed up" (p. 169). Furthermore, Williams emphasises that both she and the country of her birth have experienced marginalisation, and that they are linked to the West Indies in different ways. Then she lays bare the similarities and shared connections between Wales and the West Indies in order to assert that they do not inherently exclude each other. She perceives Wales and the West Indies to be historically interrelated on various occasions, particularly through the experiences of English oppression. She imagines the histories of both countries as intertwined and marked by struggles over freedom and identity, which eliminates the supposedly conflicting aspects between the two (p. 176). Thus, Williams sets forth the possibility of "a non-mutually exclusive Welsh and the West Indian position" which leads towards new understandings of ethnic identities.

In line with autofictional/autoethnographic strategy of border crossing to problematise conventional categories and, by extension, systems of thought, Charlotte Williams (2003) articulates that she aimed to "achieve a blend of art and politics" in order to create space for inscribing herself back to Wales (p. 30). Autofictional/ autoethnographic fusion of seemingly conflicting elements enables Williams to insert her black Welsh identity in history and nation, and to assert against monolithic perceptions of ethnicity that she is not half of anything. Reconciling blackness and Welshness, she challenges the hegemonic versions of ethnicities which are defined on the basis of skin colour or place of origin.

Drawing on the hybridity of autofiction/ autoethnography, Williams melds a variety of narrative forms as well as cultural perspectives for her project of making space for black Welsh identity. Homi Bhaba (1994) describes the potential of hybridity as achieving what the dominant discourse denies. It enunciates the difference within cultures, and enables interrogation of the concepts of identity, subjectivity and belonging. Accordingly, autofictional/ autoethnographic hybridity that involves border crossings permits Williams to argue that identities, like boundaries, are not innate but culturally and politically constructed. They are unstable, shifting and defiant. She illustrates that a continual process of border crossing provides multiple points of identification. Consistent with autofiction's ambivalent position, through such liminalities as "an in-between spectrality" or "a sense of limbo" (p. 184), Williams evades essentialist descriptions of identity. Her constant movements between spaces and cultures open up the concepts of subjectivity and belonging to differences. In this regard, she describes her long journey as the one that involves "grappling with the landscapes [...], changing them and redefining them, of corrupting the pure" (p. 191). She accentuates that one inherits fragments of a traditional culture, yet they do not remain the same eternally. They are reformulated and reinvented along one's individual journey, which renders it impossible to treat ethnic and cultural identities as pure, singular, essential concepts.

"Sugar and Slate": Entangled Histories of the West Indies and Wales

Charlotte Williams's physical movements between Wales, Africa and Guyana prove to be travels also through a variety of subject positions, which points to the notion of identity as multiple and shifting. The facts that she is the ostracised black girl in Wales and the privileged expat in Guyana reveal the intricate relations between identity, place and power. Rather than innate factors, one's identity is discursively constructed on the basis of political, economic or cultural structures. Therefore, while Williams is otherised in the Welsh society as a result of the assumptions of white supremacy, she is given access to privileges in Guyana on the ground of her affiliation with the white British expats and of her higher position in the colonial colour hierarchy with her mulatto skin tone. Williams (2002) illustrates that one is assigned to distinct subject positions in different societies depending on their own power dynamics. She challenges the essentialist view of identity and its binaristic depictions of the white and the black, of the coloniser and the colonised by unveiling the contradictions within national, historical, and cultural narratives, as well as by representing her adoption of a wide range of identities that at times conflict with one another. In this respect, she portrays herself as a tourist, an expatriate, an immigrant, an exile, a displaced person, and eventually a confident Welsh and Guyanese (Edwards, 2010, p. 158). Autofiction's potential to embody multiplicity of the subject, such as the referential self, the textual self, the unconscious self, the imagined selves provides Williams with the language and the literary form to represent her fractured and pluralistic identity. Autofiction's generic diversity creates a pluralistic space to examine and depict the multiple aspects of her self beyond the constraints of conventional categories. Furthermore, autofictional/autoethnographic blurring of the generic boundaries allows the author to challenge the discursively constructed borders between the West Indies and Wales with regard to nation, ethnicity and culture, and to foreground the connections that bind the two together. As autofiction/ autoethnography blends seemingly opposite elements to offer new possibilities that exceed traditional conceptions, Williams (2002) represents the histories of the West Indies and Wales as intertwined, and experiments with the possibility of a multi ethnic black and Welsh identity that is marked by reconciliation of cultural differences. Thus, she argues against the presumption of an absolute division or incongruity between the histories and cultures of the West Indies and Wales, calling attention to the shared historical experiences.

As Charlotte Williams (2002) juxtaposes the West Indies and Wales in the title of her work through the metonyms of "sugar" and "slate", she contests the binaristic discourses that set them in opposition to one another. Guyana, her father's country, is a place of sugar which holds substantially significant meanings. Since sugar became a major commodity that spurred colonial activities and thus exploitation of African slaves, it has played a crucial role in determining the history and shaping the perceptions of the region. Bethesda in North Wales, her mother's birthplace, is a town with slate quarrying industries. Therefore, Williams uses the slate as the signifier of a Welsh community that is marked by a tension between slate miners and slate masters within, and that is in conflict with the English for being nonconformist under their hegemony. As opposed to the narratives that accentuate discrepancies and incongruities between the coloniser and the colonised, the white and the black, Williams blurs the dividing lines between the places of "sugar" and "slate". She brings to the fore the experiences that unite the Welsh and the West Indians, and explores the possibilities that emerge from the encounter of their differences. She points to the convergence of Wales and the West Indies, on the familial level, through her description of the relationship between Denis and Katie Alice that is defined by the harmony of their minds and ethnicities: "He loved the rhythms and poetry of her thoughts. Her ideas fell together like jazz, the blue notes resonating across the staves with their own logic, defying the predictable sequences and the rudimentary facts" (p. 9). Williams recognises Katie Alice's rebellious Welsh thinking within the patterns of music genres of African origins. Her thoughts dissenting from the English rationale are attuned to the polyrhythms of jazz and the unexpected interference of the blue notes that clash with the conventional pitches in a musical composition. Through the union of her parents, Williams portrays Welshness and Guyaneseness as forming a harmony in their divergence from the straightforwardness of English perceptions of culture and ethnicity.

Williams (2002) brings together "sugar" and "slate", on historical level, by focussing attention on both the Welsh and the West Indian experiences of English oppression and cultural dispossession. Although there is a need for recognition that Wales and the West Indies differ in terms of their distinct styles and scales of historical suffering, Williams's consideration of their histories alongside one another provokes the questions of cultural crossover and resistance which the stylistics of autofiction can mirror with its hybridity and opposition to the conventional categorisation of literary forms. In order to highlight the parallels between the pasts of Wales and the West Indies, the author makes a comparison between the English policies for repression of the Welsh and African languages. In Wales, school children were forced to carry around their necks the "Welsh Nots"[23] when they spoke their own mother tongue as the token of a shameful act. In the West Indies, the enslaved Africans were separated from others who spoke their language in order to prevent them from communication and formation of a community (Donnell, 2008, p. 10). The silence that was forcefully imposed both on the Welsh and the West Indians finds an expression in Williams' work where she articulates their suffering as well as their resistance to the English cultural authority. When Charlotte Williams visits a church with Olive in Guyana, she learns from her the stories about the Anglicised Africans that are not recorded in the official history. Olive recounts the Africans' embrace of Christianity as an act of resistance, which is, for instance, not presented in the slave museum on Liverpool Dock (Williams, 2002, p. 127). Contrary to the conventional historical narratives that are based on logic and binary between the powerful and the powerless, Williams finds out that the African slaves had a paradoxical relationship with Christianity. The Anglicisation was a part of the process of colonialism, and it plundered the indigenous rituals and traditions; however, the slaves also

---

23   The Welsh Nots were wooden boards with the inscription of 'Welsh Not' or the initials 'WN'. They were designed to be worn around the neck to shame Welsh children from speaking Welsh in in the late 19th and early 20th century (Evans, 2002).

found solidarity and freedom in it. Christianity reprieved them from hard work on sugar plantations. Because the slaves did not work on Sundays, they went to church which became a place of union, meeting, solidarity against the planter (p. 127). Christianity dispossessed the African slaves of their native culture, yet at the same time, it provided them with freedom. Church came to signify both "the seat of colonialisation" and "the seat of revolution" against the plantocracy (p. 129). Therefore, Williams notes the alliance between missionary work and slavery to be full of contradictions. Slavery and missionary do not form a binary, or colonialism and missionary do not serve the same ends. There are ambivalent relationships among slavery, missionary and colonialism. The slaves were treated differently by the missionaries and the planters who themselves continually came into conflict with one another. Through the autofictional/autoethnographic strategy of blurring the boundary between historical and individual accounts, Williams's investigation into the past unveils the contradictions and ambivalences within the historical narratives of colonialism, which brings along a new perspective focused on the ties between seemingly antagonistic forces, as opposed to the West's binaristic thinking.

Charlotte Williams represents the history of slavery as entangled with the history of Wales in complex ways that the binary of the coloniser and the colonised fails to explain. She indicates that figures like Richard Pennant[24], later Lord Penrhyn, who made profits from the West Indian sugar plantations built slate industries in Wales, which resulted in slateocracy based on the exploitation of slate workers (p. 175). Because Wales is divided by various factors such as class, contrary to homogenising national narratives, the connections between "sugar" and "slate" are not simply a matter of the binaristic relationship between the coloniser and the colonised. The recognition of differences within a nation allows Williams to perceive that although certain Welsh subjects had colonial interests in the West Indies, and the expansion of the transatlantic slave trade had direct impacts on the expansion of Welsh slate industries, the exploitation of Welsh miners brings them in alignment with the enslaved Africans in the West Indies. The shared experiences of suffering and resistance against the oppressors create

---

24 Richard Pennant (1737–1808) was a Welsh slave owner and anti-abolitionist MP who made a fortune from sugar plantations in the West Indies worked by hundreds of slaves in the 18th century. When he returned to the North Wales, he developed a slate quarry and industry on a massive scale, and invested substantially in the Penrhyn estate using the profits generated by the sugar. He opposed to the arguments for abolition that he claimed would lead to an economic disaster ("The Welsh slave owner and anti-abolitionist MP Richard Pennant", 2015).

bonds between the Welsh and the West Indians that exceed the racial, national, ethnic, and cultural boundaries. Williams points to the facts that the Welsh slate miners staged the longest strike in British history[25], and that Bethesda supported the abolition movement and anti-apartheid (p. 173–175), which affirms the Welsh empathy with the enslaved Africans' suffering and their spirit of resistance. Accentuating thus the conflicting relations within the national narrative of Wales, Williams challenges the prevailing story of slate masters that sets Wales against the West Indies, and asserts a different viewpoint that considers Wales as linked to the West Indies in a less antagonistic way. Her recovery of the slate workers of Bethesda as historical victims, rather than agents of colonial exploitation, generates a sense of solidarity between the Welsh and West Indian bodies that are connected by suffering and resistance (Donnell, 2008, p. 17–18). Their common struggles against the oppressors bring along the possibility of mutual understanding and a positive relationship between the white Welsh and the black West Indian communities. Williams's focus on contradictions and paradoxical circumstances within history leads her to question the authority of the dominant narratives and to create a space for the stories of the powerless, which eventually provides insight into the intricate connections between Wales and the West Indies.

Coming to the realisation of the complexity of the ties that bind Wales and the West Indies together, Charlotte Williams (2002) finds it impossible to dissociate herself from any of their histories. Her slate memories and her sugar memories are forged together (p. 175). She comes to terms with her ambivalent position within the triangle of Wales, Africa and the West Indies, and with the multiethnic formation of her identity through her recognition of the contradictions and paradoxical relations within history and nation that unsettle the dominant narratives. She is awakened to the idea that one's identity can consist of seemingly opposing elements, which gives her confidence to assert that "I'm Welsh and I'm black" (p. 178). Her autoethnographic investigation into history and autofictional journey into her subjectivity guide her towards hybridity of cultures and plurality of the self. As a result, she is reconciled with the African "Lobo" and the Western "Lionel" parts of herself. Williams draws on autofiction's transgression of established literary categories to renegotiate the conventional notion of ethnic identity as determined by race and ties to place of origin. By disclosing the

---

25 Known as "The Great Strike of Penrhyn", the miners at the Penrhyn Slate Quarry, located near Bethesda, went on a strike on 22 November 1900 that lasted three years until 1903. It became the longest dispute in British industrial history (Crump, 2013).

historical and cultural crossovers of the boundaries between different geographies, she advances the possibility for different forms of subjectivity. Through the autoethnographic strategy of blurring the dividing lines between the personal and collective histories, Williams examines her life in relation to the experiences of other marginalised individuals and social groups. Her imaginative exploration of shared histories creates a new space for living differently outside the one that is defined by the powerful. Williams illustrates that autofiction and autoethnography can help to challenge monolithic perceptions of ethnicity and stereotypical representations of ethnic others. Their transgressive and hybrid nature open up the prospect for considering identity as a complex process that is shaped by cultural differences, individual experiences, and narratives of shared history.

Chapter 5 Jackie Kay's *Red Dust Road* (2010)

Born to a black Nigerian father and a white Scottish mother from the Highlands, and adopted by white Glaswegian working class parents, Jackie Kay makes use of autofictional strategies in *Red Dust Road* (2010) to recount and explore her experiences of adoption and multiethnicity. Because her biological and adopting parents are tied to diverse geographies, ethnicities, cultures, political positions, and social classes, Kay inevitably acquires a multi-layered identity as a mixed-race adoptee and inhabits multiple spaces of belonging, which conventional autobiography remains too limited to provide a truthful representation of. Autofiction's hybrid form and its ambiguous position within literary categorisation enable the author to portray what it means to be "adopted" and "bi-racial" in the Scottish society that is predominantly accepted as white. Being dislocated from both familial and national home, Kay's life journey is significantly marked by a continuous quest for the self through tracing of her biological parents and by struggles to reconcile her dual heritage that is seen as mutually exclusive from the West's monolithic and binaristic viewpoints of nation, ethnicity and culture. Blurring of boundaries and juxtaposition of seemingly contradictory elements in autofiction make it an apt form for narration of the liminalities that the author occupies and the multiplicities that she embodies.

As Doubrovskian autofiction is compared to the talking cure of psychoanalysis to confront inner realities of the self and to come to terms with them, Petra Tournay-Theodotou (2014) regards Kay's transformation of her traumatic memory of "unbelonging" into narrative as a "therapeutic re-enactment" by which the author not only recovers psychologically but also recovers the lived experiences through narrative articulation (p. 16) in line with the practice of autofictional writing that serves as a medium for remembering the past occurrences. Furthermore, as the author of autofiction aims to uncover the unconscious "truths" about the self through the act of narration, in an interview conducted in 1997, Kay states overtly that narrative practice allows her to explore different parts of herself (Gish, 2004, p. 176). Her work, therefore, does not simply convey the veracity of her life. Rather, it manifests the author's engagement with the ambiguities of the self. Moreover, as Hywel Dix (2017) and Tim Parks (2018) emphasise that authors of autofiction constantly cross over the boundaries between fact and fiction in order to discover the possibilities that the authorial subject might consist of, Kay often fuses referential events of the past with her imagination of other probabilities that could have been lived if she were not adopted, which she considers as constituting the reality of her subjectivity. Hence, Kay's project of self-narration is an attempt to explore who she is and to define her identity on her own terms.

In her interview with Richard Dyer, Jackie Kay calls attention to the power relations involved in construction of one's identity, criticising the hegemony of the white heterosexual man that is held to be the same as the author of conventional autobiography. She declares,

> It is liberating to define yourself if you're the one that's doing the defining but when other people are constantly doing the defining and when all they ever do is define the Other in society, the black person, the gay person, the woman, they assume the white heterosexual man is the norm and everybody else deviates from that. (Dyker, 2004, p. 238)

Since Kay perceives the subject "I" of autobiography as occupying a privileged position in the society to categorise people and to establish hierarchical relations among them, she is compelled to experiment with a distinct language and literary form for inscription of her black, Scottish, woman and lesbian identities that are marginalised by the white heterosexual man. By interrogating the dividing lines between the literary categories of autobiography and fiction, Kay confounds the conventional categories of race, ethnicity, nationality, and sexuality, and she complicates the straightforward processes of determining one's identity to the political ends. In this sense, autofiction's disruption of pre-existing categories allows the author to define her identity by herself. Rejecting the white heterosexual man's singular and exclusionary perspectives on the self and the literary forms invented by him that are as constraining as his ideologies, Kay demonstrates the empowerment of "doing the defining" through the freedom and myriad possibilities offered by autofiction.

As opposed to the linearity of life story in autobiography, in *Red Dust Road* (2010), Jackie Kay creates a fragmented chronology. The book begins with her meeting with her Nigerian father Jonathan in a hotel in Abuja in 2003, by which readers learn later that she had already contacted and met her biological mother Elizabeth in Milton Keynes, England. Kay's tracings of her biological parents are interspersed with her memories of growing up with her adoptive parents John and Helen in Scotland, her experiences of racism, and her fantasies about her origins and birth parents. There are constant shifts between various locations, periods of time and episodes of the past. Tournay-Theodotou (2014) accentuates that this lack of linearity in Kay's work not only emulates the working of memory, but also it captures the fractures and instabilities of a diasporic subjectivity (p. 16). The author's fissured self is mirrored also in continual alternation between factual and imaginative stories of her life. Kay suffuses the narration of referential experiences with fantasies, pointing to the uncertainties that pervade her life. Personal history and fiction play complementary role in her work particularly by virtue of the fact that she has grown up without the knowledge of her biological parents, Nigeria, and Africans. The ways she is connected to them are a mystery to her and inevitably left to her imagination. In her interview with Nancy K. Gish (2004), Kay expresses that all people contain seeming opposites in themselves in a lot of different ways, yet adopted people tend to hold even more for the reason that "the past is unknown to them" (p. 175). She expounds that for adoptees, "the past is constantly open to dreams, imagination, fantasy, and interpretation. [...] the possibilities for the adopted people to constantly re-invent themselves are endless" (p. 175). Kay obtains from the stories told by her adopting parents and documentary records only small pieces of information about her birth parents and their past. She proceeds to imagine what she does not know so as to complete her history of origin. As a result, fiction and fantasy necessarily become a significant part of her self.

Straddling the realms of fact and fiction, autofiction provides individuals like Kay, who are dispossessed of their history, with a space to represent their life and subjectivity that are intricately interwoven with imagination, unlike autobiography which requires the author to place value only on verifiable facts. Moreover, autofiction enables exploration of contradictions that surround the lives of people who inhabit liminal spaces. In respect to her adoption, for example, Kay contemplates on the questions such as "How can somebody be your mother and not be your mother?", "How can somebody be real and not be real?". Autofiction's embodiment of seeming opposites permits Kay to bring forward these questions that she maintains to be at the heart of what it means to be adopted (Gish, 2004, p. 174). In addition, autofiction's transgression of boundaries provokes Kay to question the fixed and stable notions of race, nation and ethnicity, leading her to renegotiate her blackness and Scottishness and to conceive a black Scottish identity that can accommodate her dual heritage without incongruity. Both her adoption and multiethnicity impel Kay to deliberate over the possibilities of having other fates and lives. Her book, therefore, constantly examines the idea of "the road not taken", in other words, the other possible lives and futures that she could have had if she were not adopted or if she had moved to Nigeria with her biological father. All such fantasies about leading other possible lives constitute the selfhood of the author when the self is considered in the modern sense as a complex entity formed by conscious thoughts, unconscious desires, and fantasies. Kay draws on the potentials of autofiction to recover both lost family and collective histories, to redefine identities, and to create a space of belonging for herself.

Story of Adoption and Dual Heritage Interwoven with Fantasy

In an article for *The Guardian*, Jackie Kay (2021) lays a significant emphasis on the intricate relations between life and fiction as she depicts in *Red Dust Road* (2010) that narrativizes her story of adoption and experience of being mixed-race in Scotland. She expresses the convergence of her life and fiction with the words: "It's difficult when your writing infiltrates your life and vice versa, difficult to work out what actually happened and what didn't. Your imaginative life is your reality". Kay reiterates the idea that fantasies are a part of one's life to such an extent that the distinction between the referential and the imagined becomes problematic. Recognising the role of the imaginative capacity in formation of one's perceptions of reality, the author readily embraces her fantasies as integral to the truth of her life. In her work, Kay treats imagination as a critical source of meaning for her life particularly because she lacks knowledge about her birth parents and connections to Africa. She resorts to imagination to complete the gaps in her story of origins, which ends up becoming the reality for her. Kay persistently interrogates what is defined as "real" or "unreal", and offers a subjective kind of reality. As Linda Anderson (2011) explains, when Helen Kay reveals to Jackie at the age of seven that she is not her real mother and that she is adopted, upon Jackie's realisation of her difference from her mother, what the young Jackie has accepted as the "real" dissolves (p. 121). She is left with only uncertainties and fragments in regard to her past, which obliges her to rely on imagination so as to make sense of her self and position in the world.

Conventional understandings of identity determine who one really is in connection with the genes of their biological parents. Kay's rudimentary knowledge of her "real" parents, and therefore of her own self, is hinted at the beginning of her book with the statement "I have been told they [Elizabeth and Jonathan] met in 1961 in the dance hall in Aberdeen" (Kay, 2010, p. 3). Kay can know about her birth parents to the extent other people know about them. The second-hand accounts of the lives of Elizabeth and Jonathan are not only limited and filled with gaps, but also often impaired by the failings of memory of those who perform the act of remembering. On one occasion, when Jackie asks Helen why she did not tell her before the story of receiving a cardigan knitted by Elizabeth for her, Helen replies: "Probably just forgot. Maybe I've even made it up. Maybe I thought she should have knitted you something. You get all mixed up with what's truth and what's not" (p. 27). Helen's response suggests that one's imaginings can feel quite true and even replace referential facts. It is not always possible to decide definitively where the real ends and the imaginative starts. Facts and fantasies are inextricably tangled together in human mind, which autofiction is concerned with representing through the blurring of the dividing lines between factual and fictional literary forms. Along similar lines, the stories about Jack's birth, invented by her adoptive parents as a consolation for her lack of a narrative of origin, become inseparable from what Jackie comes to perceive as the truth of her selfhood. Helen conjures up Jackie's birth father as an African chief and evokes the possibility that Jackie might be an African princess (p. 41). Based on such surmises, Jackie as a child pictures herself in traditional African clothes and imagines a "red-dust road" in the landscape of Africa (p. 42), which is later revealed to have lingered in her mind, surfacing on her trip to the ancestral town in Nigeria as an adult. Whether fantasies match with reality or not, the author illustrates that they are as valuable as verifiable facts in that they become a part of one's understanding of his or her self. Helen's other contrived story about Jackie's African father recounts that he had to leave for Nigeria because he was *betrothed* to another woman (p. 42). The story helps Jackie to believe that she was not an unwanted child by her birth parents, or that her adoption was not directly linked to broader issues such as politics and racism. Her convictions about her origins, regardless of how deluding they are, provide a positive self-affirmation and impact on the way she develops an identity. As such, Kay accentuates fantasies to be inseparable from the ways in which one understands the self and life. In a similar manner that she inherits genes of her biological parents, Kay acquires a creative capacity for story-telling from her adoptive parents, which serves a significant function in the formation of her selfhood. By imagining a lost past among its obscurity and inventing stories to make up for its fragmentary composition, she embraces and celebrates the potentials of fiction, imagination and narrative in construction of memory and identity (Fox, 2015, p. 290). Mythmaking about her origins proves to be a crucial part of how Kay understands her past and self primarily because, as she puts it, "if you are black and brought up in white country, then in a sense all you have is myth" (Page, 2010). Since she is deprived of the knowledge about her birth parents and ancestral past, and otherised because of her dark skin colour by a society that associates Britishness with whiteness, she is driven into the realm of myths and imagination. Not only does the white society promote stereotypical assumptions in regard to black people which are essentially mythical, but also the absence of a shared ancestral heritage compels Kay to invent myths that can elucidate her position in the world. The ambiguities and uncertainties surrounding Kay's existence necessitate her to rely on fiction to attain a sense of orientation, which becomes constitutive of her reality.

Before meeting her African father in person, Jackie Kay imagines him based on the images of the black people that are available to her, such as Sidney Poitier, Nelson Mandela, Martin Luther King, and Cassius Clay. In the way that she imagines her father, she fantasies about Africa in order to invent a heritage for herself. Along the same line, she dreams about her natural mother; first as Shirley Bassey and then as somebody else after learning that she was white and a nurse. The fact that she has to modify her fantasies in accordance with every newly acquired information about her parents and their past, implicates that her conception of "truth" is subject to constant change. Accordingly, her story of adoption never reaches an end point. It continually undergoes transformation. As the "reality" of her life changes, the knowledge of her own self alters too, which renders it impossible to assume a static adoptee identity. Because her story of adoption has neither a unity nor an ending, and her state of being as an "adoptee" is predominated by feelings of ambivalence and incompleteness, Kay is urged to employ a mode of self-narration that is freed from the constraints of autobiography. Fictional element in autofiction allows her to reconstruct the past, to explore the ways she is connected to her natural parents, to understand what their pasts mean for her present self, and to represent her subjectivity and life with all their ambiguities. Because her understanding of the self depends greatly on imagination and probabilities, she expresses her adoption story to seem like there is "something made up about it" (Kay, 2010, p. 29). It feels to her like "the story of a fictional character" (p. 134). Autofiction's hybrid form comprising fact and fiction corresponds to Kay's life story that is a mixture of real and unreal. Autofictional self that embodies both the referential and fictional selves of the author is capable of reproducing Kay's subjectivity constituted by elements pertaining to the domains of both the factual and fictional, which she explicates with the words: "Being adopted is like having a double life. […] You live in two worlds at once; your imaginary one and the so-called real one" (Kay, 2021).

Kay's self-narration illustrates that reality and imagination may collide; however, they do not cancel out one another. Rather, they open up new potentials. Contrasting with Kay's visions of her birth parents, Elizabeth comes out to be a fragile woman with mental-health problems and Jonathan appears to be only five foot one, which gets Jackie shocked when she meets him. On the other hand, the encounters with her biological parents awaken her to different perceptions of identity. She comes to recognise that biological relations alone do not suffice to explain who one really is. One can find himself or herself through the gaps in their story and workings of imagination. Fragmentary knowledge of one's existence leads him or her to a continual search for the self. For Kay, it is this act of perpetual quest, connecting with people and places, that creates identity. "The trail of finding" (Kay, 2010, p. 146), not what stands at the end of it, enables revelations about one's self, which inevitably involves imagination of possible versions of the person on quest. Kay articulates her conception of identity with the words:

> You cannot find yourself in two strangers who happen to share your genes. You are made already, though you don't properly know it, you are made up from a mixture of myth and gene. You are part fable, part porridge. (p. 47)

In this regard, Jackie Kay's efforts for making contact with her biological parents so as to find out about the past and her origins result largely in frustration. Neither of her parents is able to provide fulfilling answers to the questions in her mind. Her access to the past and the "authentic" knowledge of her self remains problematic due to issues with memory. Having married to different people with children and dedicated themselves to spirituality, both Jonathan and Elizabeth now consider the existence of Jackie as embarrassing evidence of their sinful past. Therefore, rather than demystifying her beginning for Jackie, they prefer to conceal it, rejecting and voluntarily trying to forget the past. When Kay meets Jonathan in Abuja, Nigeria for the first time in 2003, instead of having an opportunity to express her yearnings to hear about his life in Britain, how he met her mother, what he felt about her birth, and why he left for Nigeria, Jackie has to endure through Jonathan's frenzied performance of a religious sermon to cleanse himself of his past sin. He tells Jackie that he is "born again", and now he is a pure man, repenting of his previous self and life. He proclaims, "You are my before; this is my after. You are my sin, now I lead this life" (p. 10). Far from providing the story of Jackie's birth, Jonathan can offer only a chance to cleanse her of the sin of her birth. As Dix (2018) points out, Kay's meeting with her natural father does not help her for authentication of her African heritage and black identity. Her tracing of biological ties does not enable her to better understand and locate herself within neat categories of identification (p. 96). Because Jonathan's rebirth disconnects him from the past, Kay is barred from obtaining somewhat more certain knowledge of her beginning. Identically, the author is disappointed by her meeting with Elizabeth, who is equally reluctant to remember the past. Instead of communicating the past memories that could illuminate parts of her self disguised from her consciousness, Elizabeth's stories digress from the topics that interest Jackie. She writes, "I want to interrupt and ask her things, but I don't have the heart" (Kay, 2010, p. 64). Elizabeth remains an enigma to Jackie. She cannot find out anything relatable or learn what she wants to know about. Furthermore, in one of their following meetings, Jackie realises that Elizabeth has been having problems with her memory as a result of dementia, which makes the past even more inaccessible to the author (p. 75).

Kay treats memory as a flawed and flimsy entity which one cannot rely on for truthfulness of past events. Elizabeth keeps forgetting not only the moments of the past but also of the present. Jonathan can barely remember anything about Elizabeth even when he is willing to talk about the past. Not surprisingly, Jonathan and Elizabeth end up giving different accounts of the past. For instance, Kay notes that Jonathan says he met Elizabeth when she came to hear him play while Elizabeth says they met in a ballroom in Aberdeen (Kay, 2010, p. 97). Being unable to attain the knowledge of the past through the meetings with her birth parents, Kay decides to trace their footsteps in the places where they lived and to search through the written documents about them that are available. In hope of finding some hints to their past, she visits the Douglas Hotel in Aberdeen. In the ballroom where they are said to have met, the author realises the potential of a good imagination to provide redemption. She visualises her parents as dancing who seem like illusions in her head, like fictional characters in a novel (p. 149). She pictures them as walking down the streets of Old Aberdeen. They stop "at the crossroads between the old High Street and Market Street, between fact and fiction" (p. 151). With the help of imagination, she reconstructs the past of her birth parents that is partly factual and partly fictional. Elizabeth and Jonathan "move in and out of reality" (p. 151). Similarly, Kay pays a visit to Aberdeen University where Jonathan studied agriculture. There she examines his father's documents in the student achieves and tries to picture his life, bringing little pieces of information together. Although she holds in her hand only fragments of facts, she finds tiny details to illuminate, "like the sparkle in the stone", the past (p. 138). Next, Kay takes a trip to Nairn, a small town in Highlands where Elizabeth was born. Based on her aunts' accounts of Elizabeth's life, Jackie imagines about her mother's past days in the Scottish countryside (p. 161). As Jackie perceives Elizabeth's Alzheimer to have led her to be more open and more truthful, seeing that dementia picks out pieces of truth and presents them in new ways (p. 86), she demonstrates that what can still be remembered, what is left over from the past are capable of conveying important meanings. The uncertainty of the reality knot together with fiction incites Jackie to keep delving into the past and to find out about herself during the process. Her second journey to Nigeria, after having met Jonathan, is prompted by an unfulfilled desire for the knowledge of the past, which is shown to be quite revelatory about the conception of identity. Exchanging stories in her ancestral village with friends, relatives, and natives who still pay regard to the ancient African culture and customs, Jackie discovers her connections to the Nigerian land. Their stories of indigenous ways of life and thinking provide her with what she has been seeking out. It is through narrative relation and story-telling that her identity becomes woven, just as the stories of her adoptive parents have contributed to her understanding of the self. Her life gets intertwined with the lives of others. Her story intersects with others' stories, which is never finalised. She realises that as long as she continues to search for herself, her identity keeps evolving. The gaps in her story filled with fiction, therefore, prove to hold potential for the evolvement of self. She illustrates that memory, narration and identity are constitutive of one another.

"Red Dust Road": Journey to the Interior

Despite being rejected by Jonathan who wishes to keep Jackie as a secret from his family and not to see her again because she reminds him of his sinful past, the author decides to travel to Nigeria for the second time: "I still want to see the village he came from, to one day visit the east of Nigeria, Igbo land" (Kay, 2010, p. 143). In defiance of her father's determination to exclude her from the Igbo family and to curtail her links with his land, Kay undertakes the journey with the belief that she will "feel some connection with the place" (p. 169). Her desire to explore the ancestral earth arises from a profound personal need to quench the "all-consuming insatiable appetite for self-knowledge" (p. 47). As Doubrovskian autofiction compares the act of narration to a kind of a journey to the interior to explore and discover the unknown parts of the self, to attain a deeper self-understanding, Kay takes both a physical and metaphorical journey to Africa, motivated principally by the urge for determining the place of the continent in her life and personality. Doubrovsky maintains the self to be largely inaccessible due to the splitting of ego between the conscious and the unconscious, and therefore, he ventures to engage with the hidden realms of his being through the journey of language. In a similar vein, Kay feels obliged to grapple with the ambiguities of her selfhood. She explicates her imperfect knowledge of the self with the words: "Part of me came from Africa, part of me was foreign to myself, strange to myself" (p. 38). Like Doubrovsky, Kay points to the part of her self that remains dark and obscure, which she enunciates to result from her adoption and racial hybridity. Being cut off from Africa when she has been adopted by white parents and raised in a white society, her journey back to the ancestral land signifies an attempt to unveil the ways her subjectivity is still connected to her place of origin, and to come to the terms with her dual heritage.

When Jackie meets her father for the first time in Abuja, she asks him to give her an Igbo name, following the Igbo tradition of baptizing an Igbo child with an Igbo name. Not showing much interest in this ancient tradition of his Igbo culture, Jonathan offers Jackie two names, of which she is to choose the one she likes to have. They are *Ijeoma* and *Obiama* with the meanings "good journey" and "kind heart", respectively (Kay, 2010, p. 107). Thinking about her good journeys from Manchester to Abuja, from Enugu to Aberdeen, she chooses to be named as Ijeoma. Getting an Igbo name shows her desire to find a connection with Igboland, to affirm her black identity. Furthermore, the meaning of the name she chooses suggests an idea of identity interlinked with movement. As Paul Gilroy's concept of the Black Atlantic holds identity to be shaped and reshaped through one's journeys to different locations and cultural exchange with different people, Kay portrays her journey to the ancestral town and her contact with the locals as awakening her to multiplicities of her identity. Her quest for the self in Igboland is shown to have profound impacts on her understanding of who she is. Her reconnection with her fatherland and its people enables her to view herself from a new perspective outside the one imposed by the white, which conveys identity to be a shifting conception. In this respect, Lisa Sheppard (2018) observes Kay's choice of "good journey" to denote the passage from a static and restrictive perspective of identity to a more fluid relationship between the self and the societies to which one belongs (p. 97). Kay represents her identity as evolving from a stage where she feels excluded from Scottishness and confined in stereotypes to another stage where she discovers that she belongs both to Africa and Scotland. She illustrates this process to be enacted by her travels through the places of origin where she hears stories of others. These stories help her identify with her roots and see herself as exceeding the conventional Scottish and black identities. In this sense, her identity is created through her movements across the continents and storytelling, pointing to the fictional element in her subjectivity. As Doubrovskian autofiction suggests that the act of narration enables the writer to recreate constantly his or her identity, Jackie Kay shows her identity to be woven endlessly through narratives of both her own and of people who she comes in contact with.

The close relations between Jackie Kay's travels and her identity are eminent in the title of her self-narration, *Red Dust Road*. The road not only refers to the African landscape but also symbolises her life's journey (Tournay-Theodottou, 2014, p. 17). Memories collected during Kay's physical movements and her journey of life shape who she is and her perception of reality, which she attempts to capture initially in the "Mull" chapter. Shortly after the episode of her getting the name "good journey", the author sets out to narrativize a number of family trips with her adopting parents to various places, starting with the one to the island of Mull in Scotland. It is immediately noticed that their travels are laden with subjective memories and experiences of these locations. Each place signifies particular life moments which are remembered not without difficulties. Because of the flawed nature of human memory, she and her parents hold at times different versions of the past. In this regard, Kay remarks Helen and John to "remember slightly different things" (Kay, 2010, p. 117). Sometimes while Jackie and her mother remember certain moments in the past, John forgets them entirely: "I don't remember that! [...] I don't remember that at all!" (p. 119), or sometimes while John can recall some past incidents clearly, Jackie fails to do so: "I don't remember you doing that. I do, your mother was upset" (p. 120). Nevertheless, Kay accentuates that the acts of remembering and recounting the stories of past moments reinforce and strengthen the authenticity of parts of their lives and beings because for them, the past is brought forward into their future (p. 122). Their past experiences impact on who they become in the future. In contrast, Jonathan and Elizabeth either voluntarily or involuntarily forget the past, denying certain parts of their selves, or who they once were. As a result, Kay argues one's memories in their life journey to contribute to the formation of their identity. Journey, memory and narrative relation are suggested to play significant roles in construction of the self.

In the book, Kay first imagines the "red dust road" based on the stories of Africa, and then she encounters it on her journey to the ancestral town, Nzagha in Ukpor, which points to a moment of her life when imagination and reality merge with one another: "The whole time I've been in Nigeria, I've never come across a red-dust road exactly like the one in my imagination until I come to my village" (Kay, 2010, p. 213). She feels a strong sense of affinity with the colours and the landscape. It feels like home to her (p. 213). When Kay takes off her shoes to touch the red earth on bare feet, she feels as if the images of her footprints have already been present in the road even before she has walked on it. For Sheppard (2018), this strange sense of recognition suggests that "African identity has always a part of her but now she is journeying towards a greater understanding of it" (p. 97–98). The red dust road becomes an emblem of her long path to self-knowledge as well as self-acceptance (Forna, 2010). Her journey to interior is yet not the one that comes to an endpoint. She arrived in his biological father's ancestral town, being led by the red dust road; however, her journey does not stop there. She continues with her quest for the understanding of her self by travelling to other places and talking to old Igbo people and her Nigerian friend, Kachi's relatives who tell her about Igbo cultures and customs. Their stories help her explore the ways in which she is connected to the Igbo land. Her experiences of reconnecting with her people in Africa lead her to conceive identity as a fluid and shifting entity. As long as she travels and shares stories with people and communities, she continues to find out something new about herself, achieving never the complete knowledge of it (p. 47). As Doubrovsky stresses that even after writing hundreds of pages about one's self, he or she still remains largely unknown, and that the quest for the self generates only an endless deferral of the object, Kay points out that "There will be always missing pieces" in one's knowledge of his or her self (p. 47). Her quest for the self, hence, does not have a destination. In this respect, the "road" in the title signals to a continuing journey toward her self-understanding. In accordance with Paul Gilroy's concept of the Black Atlantic that incorporates in identity motion and variance, and with Stuart Hall's assumption of identity as "in process", Kay constructs identity as an indefinite journey that is not finalised.

Kay's narrative of her journey to the interior differs sharply from autobiography's teleological story of Man that necessitates a fixed ending. The author of autobiography is expected to have achieved the ultimate goals in his life and to have attained a solid and stable sense of his subjectivity, by which he is entitled to pen the story of his life. On the other hand, Kay's journey of life, defined by a quest for and deferral of the knowledge of the self, is a continuous one which disrupts teleology. Therefore, Kay represents her identity and her life most accurately through unchronological narration of her memories and abrupt shifts between places and time periods. Besides, unlike autobiography that focuses on the life of the author as a unique individual, Kay's life story is portrayed as always entangled with others' lives and their stories. The autofictional form, characterised by lack of chronology and blurring of dividing boundaries, enables Kay to represent the liminality of the space she inhabits between Scotland and Nigeria, to explore the multiplicity of her self and the impossibility of reaching a coherent sense of identity that is promoted by conventional perspectives, including the one on national identity. While trying to understand her own individual story, Kay is led to inquire into it within a larger narrative. As a result, her search for the knowledge of her personal history brings to light the enmeshed histories of Britain and Nigeria. Her quest for the self therefore entails transgression of the dividing lines between the individual and the social domains as well as defiance of the demarcation of national borders.

Dislocation from Personal and National Home

Autofiction's ambivalent position between the factual and the fictional modes of writing provides Jackie Kay with an apt form and language to express the feeling of "unbelonging" that pervades her life in several ways as a result of her adoption and dual heritage. As Pamela Fox (2015) points out, Kay feels dislocated not only from a personal home but also a national one, inhabiting an in-between space between her biological and adoptive parents, and between Scotland and Nigeria (p. 280). On the personal level, Kay is positioned between two families that possess completely opposite values and frames of mind, which problematises the question of who her "real" parents are. Although she recognises her genes and roots to tie her undeniably to her biological parents, she has difficulty in identifying with their social and cultural world. On the other hand, while Kay's physical appearance marks her out as different from her adoptive parents, she shares their ideological perspectives and mind-sets. As opposed to the socialist and nonconformist stands of Helen and John, the religious commitments of Elizabeth and Jonathan cause Jackie to face rejection from her natural parents, which contributes further to her sense of dislocation. As a Mormon[26], Elizabeth embraces the belief that "adopted people cry out to be adopted while they are still in the womb" (Kay, 2010, p. 3). That belief helps Elizabeth absolve herself of the blame for giving her daughter up for adoption and implicate to Jackie herself. Elizabeth's religion also leads her to consider Jackie's birth as illegitimate, and therefore, to shy away from revealing Jackie to her family. Similarly, Jonathan's religious rebirth impels him to view the birth of Jackie outside marriage as a sin of his former self, of which he thinks he is cleansed now, and to keep her as secret from her Nigerian siblings and relatives. It becomes clear that Jackie cannot belong fully to either of her two families in the conventional sense which places emphasis particularly on roots and genetic relations in determining one's identity.

Kay's personal history of "unbelonging" is not detached from the larger histories of Scotland and Nigeria. As Miasol Eguíbar-Holgado (2018) observes, Scotland has practised "a form of closed, exclusionist nationalism" as a consequence of its concern with gaining autonomy from England (p. 170). Promoting a distinctive and homogenous Scottish national identity strictly restricted to Celticity in cultural and racial terms, the Scottish society has discriminated against nonwhite ethnicities, placing them outside the norms of Scottishness. For Eguíbar-Holgado, the circumstances of Jackie Kay's adoption are closely linked to the conservative ideologies of Scotland in the 1960s, considering that it would have been difficult for her mother to raise a black child in a small narrow-minded town in the Highlands (p. 174). Scotland's monolithic perception of national identity that excludes those who do not possess Celtic attributes, and the resulting racist attitudes against these people in the society create a pressure on Elizabeth to put Jackie up for adoption. As Helen expresses overtly to Jackie, it is "because of racism in the Highlands" that her biological mother was forced

---

26 Mormons are a religious group that embrace concepts of Christianity as well as revelations made by their founder, Joseph Smith (History, 2021).

to leave her (Kay, 2010, p. 44). Similarly, Jackie's aunt Edna explains the reason for her adoption with the climate in Scotland back in the sixties when people did not approve of having babies with black men (p. 156). Because miscegenation has been considered as a threat to the purity of monolithic Scottish ethnicity, and therefore, despised by a great majority of the public, Jackie's birth raises concern in Elizabeth's family who decide keeping her would not be right at that time. Along similar lines, Jackie's personal history of dislocation is understood to be related to the history of Nigeria in complex ways. First, Kay perceives Johnathan's rejection of her to be a result of the intricate ties between the British colonial rule of Nigeria and Christian missionaries from the mid-nineteenth century until 1960 when Nigeria became independent. She recognises Christianity to have taken away his father's native African culture and interpellated him into the West's religious doctrines including the ones that define her birth outside marriage as illegitimate (p. 6). Next, Kay maintains his natural father's lack of paternal recognition to be linked to the Nigerian Civil War between 1967 and 1970 after the country's independence. Jonathan explains the impacts of the Biafran war[27] with the words: "It wiped us out. It took everything. All the photographic history, all the other family documents were completely lost during Biafra, everything personal" (p. 145). Because Jonathan has lost the memory of the past, Kay understands that she is cut off from his past self, which damages their father-daughter relationship today in that along with the memories of the past, Jonathan loses his Igbo spirit of acknowledging somebody from his blood. In her book, therefore, Kay is concerned not only with exploring her own personal history, but also with the histories of the people and places she is connected to, which are proven to be all intimately interrelated.

Jackie Kay's adoption and dual heritage impel her to occupy a space between reality and fantasy, between the real and imagined worlds. Accordingly, she names the two of the chapters in her book as "Reality Scotland" and "Fantasy Nigeria". The former recounts Kay's experiences of exclusion and marginalisation in Scotland as a black adoptee woman. The latter presents Kay's imagination of her fatherland as an attempt to invent a heritage that may provide her with a sense of belonging. In the author's another book, *Trumpet* (1998), the main character, a black jazz musician, Joss Moody claims: "Every black person has a fantasy Africa

---

27 The Nigerian Civil War is also called as the Nigerian–Biafran War or the Biafran War, for it was fought between Nigeria and the Republic of Biafra that seceded from Nigeria in in 1967 due to political, economic, ethnic, cultural and religious tensions (Backhouse, 2022).

[…]. Black British people, black Americans, Black Caribbeans, they all have a fantasy Africa. It is all in the head" (p. 34). In *Sugar and Slate* (2002), Charlotte Williams states that diasporic people invent a collective history of their roots to define their identity and to attain somewhat a feeling of orientation in the space between their adopted country and homeland (p. 26). Identically, in *Red Dust Road* (2010), Kay enunciates that black people who are displaced and deprived of history, like herself and his adopted brother, fantasy about Africa and create stories about their past which turn into a kind of heritance for them (p. 199). As such, Kay invents her own Africa and the story of her origin to feel like a part of a community.

Although Kay's Scottish roots undeniably entitle her to Scottishness, the normative national identity, which associates Scottish ethnicity with whiteness, denies the author belonging to Scotland. Her black body is seen as a signifier that collides with the conventional definitions of Scottishness. In this respect, Kay portrays a number of disturbing scenes of racial abuse and discrimination as she has suffered at different stages of life in Scotland, which she indicates to result from "an irrational fear and hatred of black people" (Kay, 2010, p. 191). At school, she is exposed to partial and biased information about Africa and African people. She is made to learn the stereotypical assumptions of the West that considers Africa as a whole, homogeneous mass, and that imagines it as a place of primitive, superstitious, irrational and wild savages (p. 39). Such epistemic violence makes it difficult for Jackie to embrace her African heritage, and causes self-alienation and inferiority complex in her as Fanon describes in *Black Skin, White Masks* (1952), from which she incorporates in her self-narration an entire passage (p. 40). Furthermore, the question "where are you from?" which is constantly asked her despite her Scottish accent, makes Jackie feel, in a more sophisticated way, that she does not belong to Scotland because of her skin colour (p. 192–3). For many people in Scotland, her blackness and her Scottish roots create a contradiction, and therefore, she is considered as an outsider.

Being unable to belong fully to Scotland because of repetitive racist discourses and treatments, and reading about similar experiences of black authors such as Audre Lorde, Alice Walker, Toni Morrison, and Ralph Ellison, Jackie Kay decides to explore her African heritage in her own way, hoping to find a space of belonging and self-affirmation. Her attempts to belong to Nigeria in the Western sense of being positioned in one particular static "home" are, however, largely frustrated. First, her natural father refuses to acknowledge her and welcome her to the ancestral town and familial home. Then she is immediately marked out as a white person by Nigerian communities because of her comparatively light skin colour, and treated like a foreigner. During her visit to the market in Ukpor, Kay draws the attention of a group of Nigerians who gather around her and touch her skin because she seems white to them. They call her "Oyiba" and "Onye ocha" which she learns to be pidgin words for white people. On the other hand, Kay feels desperate to be recognised as an Igbo and to belong there. She wishes other Nigerians to see in her face that her father is an Igbo. She yearns to be accepted as one of them. She even resents her white roots, feeling an urge "to sit out in the broad bold sun for hours till my skin fucking toughens up" (Kay, 2010, p. 216). Contrary to her aspirations to affirm her black identity and relationship with Nigeria, Kay's blackness is called into question. Whereas she is considered as too dark to be accepted as a Scottish in Scotland, she realises that she is too white to be recognised as an Igbo (Forna, 2010). This is a significant moment of revelation for Kay in that she understands any notion of essential identity to be a false conviction.

The fact that the author is viewed as black in Scotland and as white in Nigeria demonstrates identity to be in fact contingent on time and place. Having failed to fit in the essential Scottish and Nigerian identities, Kay is convinced of the impossibility of an authentic and fixed identification with a particular race, ethnicity or community. Shortly before recounting her second travel to Nigeria when Kay finds out about her difference from other Nigerian people there, she states her error in assuming identities to be innate and singular with the words: "The problem was I went too far the other way, and didn't dwell on or even like being Scottish until I met the African-American poet Audre Lorde" (Kay, 2010, p. 201). Her meeting with Lorde helps her realise the need to change her monolithic perspective of identity. As a mixed-race African American who knows the racial tensions, Lorde suggests her that she does not need to make a choice between her two races, that she can embrace both at once, and that she can be both African and Scottish (p. 201). Kay's experience of being marked out as different in Nigeria reiterates the idea that she does not have to belong to a single category of identification, enabling her to understand for the first time in her life what it means having multiple ethnicities (p. 216). As a result, challenging the constraining belief that the cultural identities of Scottish and Black are mutually exclusive, Kay moves towards a pluralistic identity that combines her Scottish and African heritages. Instead of focussing on the conflicts and differences as in the Western system of thinking, she foregrounds the connections and parallels between the two. Kay remarks,

> I want to talk to old Igbo people about their customs and beliefs and how they've changed over their lifetime; and then to do the same in the Scottish Highlands and Islands. It interests me that my father is from a village in eastern Nigeria and my mother from a small town in the eastern Highlands of Scotland. (p. 217)

Kay is awakened to the idea that Scotland and Nigeria do not necessarily exclude each other, and that both Scottish and Nigerian elements can coexist in her subjectivity. As she becomes aware of the hybridity of her identity, she realises the fictional quality of borders and nationalities, which she accentuates through the consideration of shared experiences in the histories of Scotland and Nigeria. In an article in *The Guardian*, Jackie Kay (2007) highlights an overlap between the pasts of Scotland and Africa: "It's time that Scotland included the history of the plantations alongside the history of the Highland clearances." The painful experiences of both Scots and the black slaves who were cleared off their land in the past under the British control link them together. The parallels between England's dominance over Scotland and British colonialism in Africa have been pointed by several critics. Berthold Schoene (1998), for example, asserts that the events like the Highland clearances[28] carried out by the English in order to expand the sphere of their influence was a part of a "colonial enterprise" of the Empire (p. 59). Cairns Craig (1996) articulates that Scottish people were oppressed by the English not because of their skin colour but the colour of the vowels in their Scottish language (p. 12). In a similar way to the colonial repression of native African languages and cultures, the Act of Union in 1707 invalidated indigenous Scottish language and impeded Scots from expressing themselves in their mother tongue. In addition, Scotland's own traditions and cultural practices were substantially suppressed by the English. As the colonisers stereotyped Africans in derogatory terms, the English considered Celts as an inferior and barbaric race, which instigated a process of alienation within Scotland between Highlanders and Anglicized Lowlanders, resulting in the ambivalence of Scottish identity (Eguibar-Holgado, 2018, p. 168). In this regard, Nancy K. Gish (2004) points to the heterogeneity of Scottishness with the statement that "there is something in being Scottish that means English, Scottish, Highland, Lowland-all those things" (p. 181).

Contrary to the conventional definitions of national identity as uniform and homogenous, in her book, Jackie Kay gives a portrayal of Scotland that is divided by class, regional identities, and landscape. Her adoptive parents from Glasgow and her biological mother from the Highlands are not alike in their political, social and cultural positions. While Elizabeth and her family members in Nairn adopt the Christian and conservative ideologies, John and Helen, who comes from a working-class family in Lochgelly, declare themselves as

---

28　The Highland Clearances were the forcible eviction of feudal tenants from the Scottish Highlands and Islands between 1750 and 1869 (Connell, 2003, p. 43).

atheist and socialist, and they prove to dissent from orthodox views by adopting coloured children. Kay conveys further the internal diversities of Scottish people to be mirrored in Scottish landscape. During a family trip to Glen Coe in the Highlands of Scotland, she recounts her parents' amazement at the difference between the Highlands and Lowlands: "Dramatic, my dad says, Christ Almighty, what a country! Stunning, my mum says, nothing like it, our ain wee country" (Kay, 2010, p. 124). Similarly, Kay indicates the impacts of British colonialism on Nigeria through Jonathan who is dispossessed of his native African culture and spirit. Even though colonialism has worked towards the erasure of Igbo ways of living, Kay illustrates Nigeria to be culturally and politically divided. She pictures the country as split between Anglicized Nigerians like Jonathan and the indigenous Igbo people like Kachi's relatives, between those who grieve that colonialism ruined the African culture and the others who resent Nigerian independence from Britain like Pious who believe the country to be left in a chaos (p. 253).

Because neither Scotland nor Nigeria is singular or homogenous as imagined conventionally through the concept of nation, Kay is unable to belong fully to either of the countries. This is also the reason why she is grounded between acceptance and rejection in each place. As a result of their internal differences, Kay is rejected by her biological mother, yet she is accepted by her loving adoptive parents in Scotland; she is not recognised by her natural father, but she is embraced by Kachi's Igbo relatives in Nigeria. Having discerned the ways in which Scotland and Nigeria are similar to each other as opposed to the dominant discourses that always set them in opposition, Kay refuses to tie herself to one place. As Lisa Sheppard (2018) puts it, Scotland and Nigeria become different versions of "home" for her (p. 98). Drawing on the autoethnographic strategy of examining the relations between the self and society, Kay explores her connections and disconnections with both countries and realises that her subjectivity consists of diverse ethnicities contrary to the discourses that bind a person to a single space. Along these lines, in the same way that fact and fiction merge with one another in autofiction, Kay represents Scottish and Nigerian elements as blended into each other in the story of her self, pointing to an eventual reconciliation of her Scottishness and blackness. Her portrayal of multiple and fragmented identifications with different places suggests a necessity for a more fluid and flexible approach to contemplation about identity.

"Nature or Nurture": Possibility of an Afro-Scottish Identity

In *Red Dust Road* (2010), Jacky Kay represents her self in several subject positions which seem at times to contradict one another, such as an adopted child, a

Scottish woman, a black woman, a lesbian, and a mother. Considering identity to be a complex and multi-layered entity, Kay declares:

> The self is multitudes. The self is complex and often contradictory. It's all right for me, for instance, to say I'm Black and I'm Scottish; it's not a contradiction for me, although lots of people regard it as such. That is my experience; I'm Black and I'm Scottish. There is no problem with that at all. (Gish, 2004, p. 174)

Kay's self-narration is an enterprise which shows the possibility that one can contain more than a single self unlike monolithic ways of thinking about the subject. Rather than any inherent essence on its own, the self is defined by various discourses that are politically, socially and culturally structured. Being understood as a positioning, identity is constructed contingently by the circumstances of one's existence. For instance, depending on the cultural values of her birth parents and adoptive parents, Kay is positioned either as a rejected, unwanted child or as a special, "chosen" individual. Similarly, based on their distinct conceptions of the world, Kay is seen as black in Scotland and yet as white in Nigeria. The fact that she is ascribed diverse subject positions by different communities suggests that the self is far more complex than the conventional categories of identification can describe. Kay's representation of her sexual identity further problematises the conventional notion of identity that is held to be essential and unchanging. In the accounts of her earlier life, Kay reveals to have had heterosexual relationships with men although she later identifies herself as a lesbian. When she is a teenager, she gets a Nigerian boyfriend, Femi (Kay, 2010, p. 49). A year later, she gets into a lesbian relationship with Gillian (p. 58). In her late twenties, she decides to have a baby with her partner Fred D'Aguiar, and gives birth to a son, Matthew (p. 92). Later, she has a lesbian relationship with poet Carol Ann Duffy. Her experience of sexuality points to how fluid identity can be as opposed to the views that claim it to be innate and static. In regard to the changing nature of identity, Kay articulates:

> I think of identity as being a very fluid thing, and my own identity as being very fluid, as something that changes with culture and with time and with perspective. I think of it as being not at all static and not all fixed. (Gish, 2004, p. 175)

Similar to her constantly shifting sexual identity, Kay experiences her cultural and ethnic identities as evolving in the course of her journey of life that involves interactions with various communities and perspectives peculiar to them. In the earlier stages of her life, she feels unable to identify with Scottishness due to the exclusionary discourses and treatments that deny her Scottish identity on the ground of her skin colour. In like manner, she finds it difficult to recognise herself as African when all she knows about black ethnicity is the stereotypical assumptions of the West. Only after she sets out to explore on her own terms her relationships with the places and people she is connected to, she understands monolithic notions of identity to be constructs and to fall short for explaining the complex reality of her multi-ethnic subjectivity. Discerning parallels between her Scottish and African heritages in opposition to the binaristic views of them in the Western system of thought, Kay reclaims her both Scottish and black identities. Before her awareness of her multiethnicity, she strives to fit neatly in the pre-existing categories that are strictly delineated and separated from one another. After the moment of realisation of the plurality of her connections to different ethnicities, she conveys a complex portrayal of her mixed-race self, complicated with the juxtaposition or fusion of Scottish and Nigerian elements. In this regard, she represents African and Scottish landscapes as syncretic, comparing the road to Ukpor to a road in the Highlands of Scotland (Kay, 2010, p. 212). As Petra Tournay-Theodotou (2014) observes, Kay's accentuation of the redness of the road in Ukpor with the words "the red, red of it" reminds of the Scottish poet Robert Burns' poem "A Red, Red Rose" (p. 19). Later, she notices a similarity between the place where Lake Ogota meets the Urashi River in Nigeria and the rivers Dee and Don encircling the city of Aberdeen in Scotland (p. 220). On another occasion when she meets her Nigerian brother Sidney in the stadium on the way to Lagos International Airport, Kay's excitement of being recognised as his sister is reverberated in the music coming out from the stadium speakers that is "a high-life mixture of Celtic and African music" (p. 275). Her indications of historical, political, natural and cultural parallels between Scotland and Nigeria pave the way towards the acceptance of her hybrid identity.

Kay's exploration of her roots and discovery of her previously unknown connections to her places of origin bring along the question of "nature or nourish?" (Kay, 2010, p. 255) in determination of one's identity. She interrogates whether it is genes or environment that shapes who one is. At the outset of her book, Kay enunciates to have embraced the socialist and nonconformist values of her adoptive family, which creates a sharp contrast with her birth parents' conservative beliefs and morals. It is hence understood that culture and environment in which one grows up impact enormously on how he or she identifies himself/herself. On the other hand, Kay does not deny the role of genetic inheritance in formation of subjectivity. That explains the curious moments of recognition Kay experiences when seeking for her relationship with Nigeria and its people. As she arrives in her ancestral town for the first time, she feels a mysterious connection to it which she describes as "a strong sense of affinity", "a strong sense of recognition" (p. 213). Similarly, when she meets her half-brother Sidney in person and examines his facial features, she again attains a "nearly primitive" sense of "recognition" (p. 272). In another instance, she finally makes sense of her habitual obsession to read everything in signs, to wonder what things mean once she encounters with Igbo people and gets acquainted with their customs, concluding that "It is an Igbo way" (p. 246). In line with Stuart Hall's conception of cultural identity which he believes to consist of both collective experiences and individual differences, Kays depicts her identity to be connected to the ancestral heritage as well as shaped by the cultural habitat in which she has grown up. Although she is evidently tied to her roots, she is not constrained by her position within the ancestral history. Her white Scottish upbringing, particularly the values of her adoptive parents constitute an indispensable part of her self, which she defines as being "steeped in Scottish culture" and adds: "If you're brought up in a place, you get that identity very, very fixedly" (Somerville-Arjat & Wilson, 1990, p. 122). As such, based on Stuart Hall's conception of cultural identity that brings together shared heritage and cultural interactions, and on the autofictional strategy of blurring the distinction between fact and fiction, Kay dismantles the dichotomy of "nature" or "nourish", of "genes" or "environment" and proposes the possibility of an Afro-Scottish identity that consists of both parts of the binary.

Kay represents her newly acquired reconciliation of her Scottish and Nigerian heritages through *Moringa oleifera* which is a "magical tree" that has helped her to get in contact with his birth father, her Nigerian brothers and Kachi's relatives who have accepted her as a member of the Igbo community. This African tree has therefore revealed a lot about her Nigerian roots. Kachi's Uncle Nwora who is a tree-specialist like Kay's father, gives her Moringa oleifera pods to take to Scotland and plant them there. Nwora's comparison of Kay to the tree is insightful particularly for an understanding of her multi-ethnic identity. He significantly points out: "You've grown like a plant away from him, but it is still his roots. You have his face. You have his forehead" (p. 257). Although Kay has been brought up by her white Scottish adoptive parents in Scotland, she retains links with her roots in Africa. Moringa oleifera becomes a symbol of identity formation that is influenced by roots and environment, like the one that the author's self-narration presents. The African tree is uprooted from its original home in Nigeria and transplanted into the "dark, moist soil" of Scotland, which corresponds Kay's sense of African genes flourishing in her northern environment (Gagiano, 2019, p. 281). As the tree with its roots in another continent adopts to its changed environment as a part of an organic process, while maintaining her connections to her African heritage, Kay integrates naturally into the Scottish culture, with reconciliation of her two sides. Kay anticipates that the moringa tree she plants in her Scottish garden will take roots, grow, and change into a "splendid tree", which hints at an ever-changing organic life similar to the one that she has, enriched with her connections to multiple cultures. Embracing her Scottish and African heritages, Kay disrupts the singular notions of race, ethnicity, nationality, home, and self. She challenges the hegemonic views that hold blackness and Scottishness to be a contradiction. Furthermore, when she defines herself as "Scottish", she problematises the monolithic concept of Britishness in that her focus on a regional identity contradicts the assumed homogeneity of British national identity. As Hanif Kureishi (1986) urges for new forms of being British with his acknowledgement of his multi-ethnic English and Pakistani identity, Kay propounds a Black Scottish identity that enlarges the British identity as a whole.

The contemporary views of multiethnicity enable Jackie Kay to picture a multifaceted self that embodies diverse cultural elements. In like manner, autofictional form of self-narration helps her to explore and represent the self as a complex being that consists of conscious as well as imaginative thoughts. She perceives her self as constituted not only by verifiable facts but also by fantasies. Her story of adoption embroidered with her imagination of her past, biological parents, places of origin and other lives that she could have had if she had not been adopted, illustrates the ways fiction becomes a crucial part of the self. She often intersperses her narrative with reflections on what her life would have been like, had she taken "the red dust road less travelled by" (Kay, 2010, p. 274). She wonders if she would have learnt by heart the names of moringa trees, like Uncle Nwora's daughter, to please her father (p. 255), what job she might have done in Enugu, if she would have been an ethno-botanist, or if she would still have been a writer (p. 286). The autofictional act of narration allows her to ask herself questions and to imagine freely alternative fates and possibilities. In this respect, Kay proclaims that "We're all more multiple than we necessarily think we are and we all have things that we either do, or wish that we had done, and they form part of who we are as well" (Sturgeon, 2010, xii). For her, the truth of the self includes the fantasies and possibilities contained in one's being. Autofiction enables her to engage with such psychic realities, and therefore, to provide a richer version of the self. As Nicola Sturgeon (2010) articulates in her introduction to Jackie Kay's work, "Her possible past lives expand and enhance her present life" (xii).

Chapter 6 Bernardine Evaristo's *Lara* (1997/2009)

Bernardine Evaristo, born to an English mother and a Nigerian father, profits extensively from the potentials of autofictional mode of writing in her debut work *Lara* (1997/2009), in which she gives voice to the complexities and contradictions of her multi-ethnic identity. The titular character Lara does not bear the same name with the author, yet in line with Philip Gasparini's formulation of autofiction, an identitarian relationship is created between the protagonist and the writer by means of other shared aspects. For instance, like Evaristo, Lara is the fourth of eight children of an English mother with Irish and German roots, and a Nigerian father whose forebears were transported to Brazil as slaves and returned to Nigeria after emancipation. Like Evaristo, Lara was born in Eltham, grew up in Woolwich and went to school in Eltham. Moreover, the expanded version of the book reissued in 2009 features on its cover a photo of Evaristo's parents from their wedding day in London, 1955. It is known that like Lara's grandmother Edith/Peggy[29], Evaristo's own grandmother fiercely opposed to her daughter's marriage with a black man (Mixed museum, n.d.). The photographical document along with the other personal and sociocultural references to the author provide the factual basis for Evaristo's life narrative that entails at the same time deliberately fictionalised elements, such as the renaming of some of the characters. Nevertheless, Evaristo allows an easy continuity between the life stories of Lara and her own, which suggests a relationship between "fact" and "fiction", "life" and "fantasy" that is fluid and continuous, that is difficult to distinguish for certain (Kamali, 2016, p. 224). In this respect, Evaristo proclaims her book to be loosely based on her family history, defining it as "a mixture of fact and fiction", and adds,

> In one sense the skeleton of the story is based on fact, both the black and the white side, but the flesh is imagination. Some of the characters I knew personally, and some of them I didn't, so I had to rely on the memories and oral history of existing relatives to create some of the characters and to take it imaginatively from there. (Hooper, 2006, p. 4)

Due to the lack of full accessibility to the "realities" of the past, Bernardine overtly underlines her reliance on the accounts of others and her imaginative

---

29 In the 1997 version of *Lara*, Bernardine Evaristo names her maternal grandmother as Edith whose name is changed to Peggy in the 2009 version.

capacity to reconstruct her family history, which she believes will cast light on the unknown sides of her subjectivity. In the resulting fictionalised version of her origin story, the author's autofictional self Lara traces the lives of both her paternal and maternal ancestors across three continents and seven generations, and tries to understand the impacts of their experiences on her being in the present. Her journey of self-discovery is therefore marked by crossings of multiple spatial and temporal borders. As Lara travels historically back over 150 years, she traverses the moments of her father's arrival in London in the 1940s, her African ancestors' enslavement in the plantations of Brazil in the 1830s, their return to Lagos in Nigeria in the 1930s, her white ancestors' departure from Ireland because of rural hardships in the 1880s, and escape from poverty in Germany in the 1860s. As Lara explores the lives of her predecessors who have left one country for another, she comes to the realisation that the experiences of racism, unbelonging and identity crisis are not exclusive only to colonial people of African descent. Her white ancestors are revealed to have undergone similar difficulties in the process of adopting a new place as home. In this vein, Lara unveils that both white and black people who are uprooted from their native lands share histories marked by struggles for acceptance and integration, which hints at the interconnections spanning across worlds and genealogies as opposed to the assumed divides between the European and African communities.

Enabling crossover of the lines between self and others, autofictional/ autoethnographic self-narration allows Bernardine/Lara to make sense of her own personal experiences of displacement in London as a mixed-race girl/woman in relation to the pasts of her ancestors. Besides, in line with autofiction's engagement with the hidden realities of the self, Bernardine/Lara is able to explore the ways in which the historical legacies shape her subjectivity. As she travels physically and metaphorically in pursuit of the footsteps of her ancestors, she unearths the meanings of her presence, her strange dreams and mysteries of her past. In Kwame Dawes's observation (1998), she arrives at a sense that there are myths which influence her being (p. 378). The fact that Bernardine/Lara uses autofictional writing as a means of investigation into the "unknow realities" of the self who is entangled with other lives conflicts with the autonomous and all-knowing autobiographical subject. Her journeys from London to Nigeria, to Brazil with the aim of finding out about her ancestry illustrate that connecting to the roots generates new understandings of the self, and that subjectivity continues to be configured with every new experience, position and situation throughout life. Her childhood memories of difference and discrimination in London provide insight into the ways in which she is led to internalisation of the monolithic black identity imposed by the dominant power; however, her narrative also shows subject formation to be a continuous process. As Bernardine/Lara discovers the transnational pathways that intersect over the water, she appears as a site where multiplicity of racial and ethnic identities meet. In an interview, Evaristo accordingly delineates the shift in Lara's subjectivity as a progression from a "fragile sense of belonging and identity" to a state of "embracing all her selves, no longer divided but multiple" (Woolf, 2010, as cited in Toplu, 2011).

Bernardine/Lara's ever changing and multi-ethnic identity is reflected stylistically in the form of her book. Not only does she draw on the ambivalent position of autofiction between factual and fictional narrative forms, merging her referential life experiences with imagined ones, but also, she transgresses the pre-existing lines between prose and verse by predilecting the unusual novel-in-verse form for inscription of her life. According to Stewart Brown (1999), the author's crossing of boundaries, mixing of genres denote her desire to challenge established discourses on identity and to encapsulate her hybridity (p. 84). Giving herself the freedom to break out of traditional narrative boxes, Evaristo blends fact and fiction, poetry and prose, history and myth, the past and the present, which defies easy or singular definition, and manifests the complexities of her multi-ethnic identity. As the authors of autofiction take liberties with narrative forms in order to engage with the unknown and unconscious parts of the self, Bernardine employs poetic techniques in her narrative to go into the depths and to capture the essence of things (Payne, 2003, p. 5). She finds verse form more liberating than prose, leading her to grasp the meanings of things that she inquires, such as the multi-ethnic inheritances that comprise her subjectivity. However, like Doubrovsky, she recognises that the self cannot be known completely even after writing hundreds of pages about it, which can be inferred from her persistent urge to continue revising her book although she has already published a second version of it in 2009. She expresses her journey of self-discovery to be unfinished with the words,

> Nor is it over yet, I have to say, because I think there might be another version that I will feel moved to add to it in years to come. […]I think it's a book that may have – maybe there are a couple more additions to be made to the book in the future. (Evaristo, 2022, p. 7)

Bernardine Evaristo keeps returning to her autofictional self-narration, not being able to reach the moment of finalising her quest for the self. It seems as if there are always some parts of her life that remain unexplored. Along with the recognition that complete knowledge of one's subjectivity is not achievable, Doubrovsky deems autofiction with its transgressive tendencies as having potency to capture ambiguities of the self and to mirror the state of being split between two countries, two cultures, two languages, and so on. In a similar vein, Evaristo demonstrates autofiction's embodiment of seemingly opposite elements to be useful for representing the contrasting realities of one's life. She expresses her own sense of being surrounded by dualities, contrasts and contradictions as follows,

> I also grew up in a home of dualities: my mother was white English, my father was black Nigerian; my mother was a die-hard Catholic (until she fell out of love with the hypocrisy of the church), my father was a Communist, for a while; my mother was a white collar worker=school teacher, my father was a blue collar worker=welder; I was of mixed-race in London at a time when it was neither common, discussed or understood. Our family stood out in what was then a very white part of London and at school I was, for most of the time, the rare black child. Surely the effect of all this duality and difference, these contrasts, polarities and contradictions subconsciously fed a desire to work out these aspects creatively. (Evaristo, 2005, n. p.)

Bernardine's project of life writing, benefiting from the freedoms offered by autofiction is grounded on her wish to reflect on the assumed racial, cultural and social binaries that constitute who she is. By transgressing the boundaries between factual and fictional literary forms, the referential and the imaginative, and exploring the ambivalent third spaces between conventional categories, she attempts to delve into the intersections of her multiple identities. Through autoethnographic blurring of the dividing lines between self and others, the personal and the collective, past and present, she examines the ways in which both European and African cultural and racial heritages shape her sense of self and place in the world. Her investigation into the different cultural and historical narratives that make up her heritage yields the possibilities of hybrid identity and multiple belongings. Besides, her excavation of the ancestral pasts discloses the complex networks that connect cultures to each other, calling into question the homogeneity of nations. Transnational journeys which took place in the histories of not only her Nigerian but also English predecessors point to the idea of a British society that is racially hybrid and multicultural. The movements and intermarriages marking the pasts of her ancestry defy the myth of a pure, white Anglo-Saxon Britain and the perception of a homogeneous Africa. In this regard, situating fiction in dialogic relation with historicity, and examining personal memories in connection with collective pasts, Bernardine challenges and complicates dominant narratives of identity and belonging. Instead, she proposes a more fluid interpretation of cultural and national identity which can contain differences and multiplicities within, and enable diverse subjectivities.

History of the Self Knitted with "Untold" Stories of Ancestors

In her interview with Karen Hooper, Bernardine Evaristo explains her aims in writing *Lara* as "excavating my family history" and at the same time "exploring an area of British history that I felt hadn't been covered hardly at all in literature in this country" (Hooper, 2006, p. 4). Her story of the self hence becomes one that is interwoven with the transnational/transcultural memories of her predecessors which are neither passed on to her by family members nor represented in historical records. Accentuating the exclusionary tendencies of dominant historical and cultural narratives as well as the problematic nature of access to the realities of the past, Evaristo draws largely on the role of fiction in exploration of the past and creation of a space in history for multiethnic individuals like herself who are not addressed by the monolithic and homogenising discourses of Britain. By blurring the line between fact and fiction, she offers a fluid and subjective understanding of memory that encompasses the unheard voices and challenges the dominant accounts of the past. In this regard, Bernardine/Lara's first-person narration is often interrupted by the narrative voices of her ancestors who recount the past events from their own perspectives. Their testimonies are based on various sources such as myths, letters, diaries, photographs, stories, and significantly the author's imagination and unconscious connections with her forebears' pasts. Evaristo sets out to uncover the memories of her ancestors with consideration that they are deeply tied to her sense of subjectivity, and that the past has impacts on the present. As such, she concerns herself with grasping the significances of the lives of her ancestors for who she is today.

Evaristo's "obsession"[30] with the relationship between the past and the present can be discerned in the unchronological organisation of the chapters of her life story where the narration moves backwards and forwards to provide the past causes for the present occurrences. The constant shifts between the past and present point to inseparable links between the two temporal periods. In addition, the non-linearity of the narrative mirrors the process of recollection that is characterised by discontinuity and gaps between life moments. As autofiction promotes a free inhibited way of writing that allows language to unveil the mysteries and unconscious contents of mind, Evaristo experiments with language to profit from its revelatory power, in order "to capture the essence of things" (Payne, 2003, p. 5). Although Evaristo started writing *Lara* first in prose, she later switched to poetry which gives her the freedom that one finds in the patterns

---

30   In an interview with Toh Hsien Min, Bernardine Evaristo (2004) expresses to have an obsessive interest in the ways in which the past impacts on the present (n.p.).

of the act of remembering, the freedom to "hop and jump" (p. 5). She states the other reason for favouring verse to be imagery and the richness of poetic language, which recalls Doubrovsky's frequent employment of figures of speech such as pun with the conviction that they work to reveal meanings obscured from consciousness. In autofiction, language on its "adventure" reinvents meanings of life that escape the author. Similarly, Evaristo uses poetic language to create a dream-like state in which she is guided into meanings of the ancestral pasts for her selfhood.

In her reconstruction of family history, Evaristo resorts to imagination principally because the past is largely inaccessible to her. She reports her Nigerian father to have never spoken about his family or culture back home, and enunciates that "little of my father's Yoruba culture was passed on to me; not his language, his food or his traditions" (as cited in Kamali, 2016). Therefore, she grows up without the knowledge of her connections to the place of her paternal roots. In the interview with Karen Hooper (2006), she explains the various challenges that she faced during her research on her ancestral histories. For instance, she attempts to find out about the enslavement of her paternal grandparents in Brazil by interviewing her father; however, since her grandfather had died before her father was born, the information he had comes out to be hardly reliable (p. 4). When she visits Nigeria to meet her remaining relatives and to hear their stories of the past, she learns that people in Nigeria customarily do not like to talk of the dead. Moreover, she discovers that there is not a tradition of record-keeping in Nigeria to preserve information of the past events (p. 5). Bernardine indicates to have encountered restrictions on her trip to Brazil too. Her research into the history of slavery in Brazil was problematic fundamentally because she did not speak the Portuguese language (p. 5). Despite all these difficulties in attaining an access to the sources of historical occurrences, Bernardine finds stimulating the impressions that were left on her during her visits to these two countries, such as the sounds, smells, colours, textures and tastes. They have helped her visualise the settings for the past events which she is bent on exploring. Patricia Murray (1999) describes Evaristo's attempt of excavating the ancestral pasts as one which requires her to "piece together stories that have not always been passed on" (p. 38). Evaristo's reconstruction of her family history hence significantly depends on her imagination to fill in the gaps between the referential fragments of the past that she has been able to recover.

Bernardine Evaristo begins recounting the history of her origins in *Lara* (1997) with the mythical story of her paternal great-grandmother Tolulope who is violently raped by the white master of a sugar plantation in the nineteenth century Brazil where her ancestors were transported as slaves from Nigeria by the colonising forces. The silence over the rape is implicated by her transformation into a bird that later effectuates the growth of a baobab seed by the help of its droppings (p. 1). Similar to the African moringa tree in Jackie Kay's *Red Dust Road* (2010), baobab tree with African origins becomes the symbol of procreation of her ancestral lineage. Its seeds that are carried over the ocean represent her African relatives scattered across the world. They are tied to Nigeria by roots but disseminated over other lands. The mythical story of the beginning of her African ancestral family is understood to be intricately linked to the history of the Western world through colonialism and slavery. The violence emerging from the encounter of the coloniser and the colonised, which is exemplified with a particular incident involving her ancestral family, remains largely unheard and is omitted from the dominant historical narratives, yet it keeps haunting Lara through a sort of unconscious collective memory.

Next, the narration proceeds with the letters of Lara's father, Taiwo, who communicates to his mother in Nigeria his experiences of living in Britain where he moved for his university education in the 1950s. In *Manifesto* (2022), which Evaristo has published as a non-fiction chronical of her life, she notably writes that her father and her grandmother did never exchange letters when he moved to Britain: "[…] my father had migrated to England without telling her in case she tried to stop him, nor did he write when he arrived, or in fact at all. Perhaps he was ashamed of the way he'd left" (p. 4). Therefore, the letters exchanged by Taiwo and Zenobia in *Lara* (1997/2009) are understood to be inventions based on the author's imagination. Nevertheless, they capture effectively the reality of her father's experiences in Britain. Taiwo writes to her mother that similar to his enslaved ancestors' situation, his encounter with the English has not been without pains in that he gradually becomes alienated from himself in the face of persistent racist treatments in the British society. Taiwo marks the difference between the subject positions he acquires in Britain and Nigeria, saying that "Mama, in this country I am coloured. Back home I was just me" (Evaristo, 1997, p. 4). Taiwo is placed in a predefined social space and role within the British society where the Africans are commonly held to be outsiders. In compliance with the hegemonic definition of British nation as inherently white, the English assume the coloured people not to belong to their country. Accordingly, Taiwo is constantly reminded of his unbelonging and difference which he later feels compelled to make efforts to eliminate. In this respect, he changes his native name into Bill, after William the Great, having discovered that "an African name closes doors" (p. 5). Conceiving personal and social histories as intertwined, Bernardine/Lara points out the fact that Africans from the colonies fought together with the English in the World War II; however, the emperor's children are now disowned

(p. 6). The rejection and marginalisation which Taiwo becomes subject to in the public recur in the domestic sphere. His English wife's mother, Edith strongly disapproves her daughter of marrying "a native from colony!" (p. 29). She prejudges Taiwo with all the stereotypical images of Africans in the Western narrative of white supremacy, which he resents with the remark "She judges me but she does not know me [...] She does not see me [...] only a coloured" (p. 35-7). Taiwo's both private and social lives in Britain are afflicted with discriminatory and degrading forms of demeanour towards him, which instigates a process of disconnection from the land and culture of his roots.

When Taiwo marries Ellen, he decides to begin a new life in Britain and do all that is required to fit in the English society including cutting off his connections with Nigeria. Even when his twin sister Kehinde dies and her mother asks him in a letter to remember his roots and where he is from, Taiwo remains determined not to tell Ellen about his childhood, family, relatives and past in Nigeria, and to keep her mind "blank" about the history of his life in his native land (Evaristo, 1997, p. 28). Taiwo passes this "blankness" on to his children too. As a result, Lara grows up without being able to identify with her Nigerian heritage. As Taiwo comes to believe that he must erase the memory of his deceased family members, "Baba, Papa, Mama, Kehinde" (p. 57), in order to continue to live, Lara is severed from her ancestral past which is yet mysteriously revealed to her in the forms of strange dreams and visions, attesting to her unconscious connectedness to the ancestral memory and fatherland. The blankness provided to Lara through her deprivation of the knowledge of her Nigerian ancestry, is shown to be gradually replaced with flimsy images that appear in her mind and that she conceives as the "Daddy People". These imaginary figures or the spirits of her ancestors become the only means for Lara as a child to make sense of her origins, which she strives to do by establishing a connection between her self and the lives of her ancestors. Her visions of her ancestors and their past are seen to have influences on her identity in complex ways. On one occasion, Lara discloses to her mum to have seen "Daddy People in the garden singing [her]" (p. 48). While Ellen ridicules Lara for her childish dreams, Taiwo severely punishes her for talking of the ancestral spirits. He wants his children not to fantasy about their roots in some distance place but to assimilate into the English society. On the other hand, the harshness of his treatment of Lara is revealed to stem from his past in Nigeria. In addition to the cultural taboo of speaking of the dead, readers learn that Taiwo's father was harsh with him in an identical way when he was a child, which Taiwo now transfers to his own children. Besides, based partly on his personal experiences of living in Nigeria, Taiwo longs to prepare his children for the difficulties of life by being rough with them. Although Taiwo does not explicitly communicate to his children about the Nigerian ways of life, his experiences of the native land still impact on his relationships with his children and on the development of their sense of self.

When Lara grows into adolescence and becomes more conscious of her difference in Britain, she takes decisive steps to find out the "truths" about her origins. As a start, she persuades her father to tell her about Nigeria, his childhood and family and asks questions to make him speak about the relevant subjects that help her understand who she is. His answers, however, do not provide a whole picture of the places and people that she is connected to by her roots. His stories are meagre, loose, and patchy, which causes her to feel "cheated" yet "stirred" (Evaristo, 1997, p. 81). Taiwo does not want to impart to his daughter the painful stories of his family's and ancestors' histories, but Lara needs to hear these stories to be able to comprehend her position in the world. Next, Lara searches through the basement of their house in London that contains various objects belonging to her parents' pasts such as shovels, antique telephones, lamps, household bills, a tool bag, a record player, framed wedding photos and Yoruba carvings (p. 79). As the name of the house "Atlantico" signals to connections to the Middle Passage, the seemingly discarded relics in its basement prove to be of great value to Lara because they provide her with new possibilities for imagining her past and seeing herself in different ways that transcend the confines of race and nation. Lara unearths and invents memories out of lost stories and forgotten objects. These reconstructed memories become a part of her version of the reality and of the way she comes to perceive herself as tied to the pasts of her ancestors.

The memories of her ancestors are revealed to occupy a crucial place in Lara's life particularly during her trip to Nigeria. Her childhood visions of the ancestral past continue to haunt when she lands in Lagos in her 30s. As Lara sleeps in Yaba, in the old West Indian Quarter, the spirits of her ancestors again appear and talk to her: "She awakes to the singing, calling her. 'Daddy People!'/ [...] They are straight out of childhood, / there she was, back her bunk bed in Woolwich" (Evaristo, 1997, p. 109). Lara recognises her father's grandfather Baba Aguda, her father's grandmother Mama, her father's father Gregoria, her father's sister Kehinde and her father's mother Zenobia who utters: "My Omilara, now we take you into memory/ sleep now, sleep..." (p. 109). Lara's dream state opens up to the unspoken histories of her ancestors. As there is no clear distinction between reality and dreams in autofictional writing as a form of investigation into the unconscious part of mind, Lara is transported to Nigeria of her father's childhood and then to Brazil of her grandparent's enslavement in her sleep with the blurring of the lines between history and dreams, between past and present. The revelation of the pasts of her African ancestors helps Lara discover her Nigerian heritage in fresh ways that collide with the dominant views on black people and enables her to define her subjectivity outside the narrow categories of identification such as "black" and "English". Her ancestors' experiences of movement and displacement lead her to contemplate on the issues of home, belonging and identity in more fluid and pluralistic terms. Furthermore, her imagined reconnection with the unheard voices of the past permits expansion of the frontiers of dominant history and creation of a more inclusive historical memory.

"Family Is Like Water": Crossing the Waters

In Doubrovskian autofiction, the act of writing is considered to be a medium for journeying into the inner realities of the author's selfhood. The "adventure of language" initiated by a free-flowing writing process serves to unveil the unconscious contents of the mind. As a result, autofiction characteristically presents the author's internal quest for the hidden "truths" of the self. Similarly, authors of autoethnography employ the trope of journey to narrativize their travels back to places of origin and their discovery of the ways in which their subjectivities are inherently tied to these places. Along these lines, in her interview with Hooper, Bernardine Evaristo declares that "My books marry physical travel with inner journeys" (Hooper, 2006, p. 14). Thus, Evaristo's accounts of her physical journeys in *Lara* (1997/2009) are also narratives of her quests for the unknown aspects of herself, her connections to places, and her position in the world. In line with autoethnography's assumption of intricate relationships between individuals and societies, Evaristo illustrates Lara's sense of self to be reshaped and multiplied as she gets in contact with different communities in various locations. Moreover, while retracing physically the steps of her ancestors across continents, Lara is pictured as travelling into the ancestral pasts across generations. By means of unconscious connections to the memories of her ancestors, she discovers the impacts of their lives and experiences on her present self. While she explores the meanings of the legacies of traumatic historical events such as colonialism and slavery for her own individuality, she also significantly uncovers the interconnections between different nations and cultures, which yields fresh possibilities for defining the concepts of identity, belonging, nation and ethnicity beyond the limitations imposed by Western perspectives.

Growing up in London without the knowledge of her African heritage and being ostracised from English identity because of her skin colour, Lara feels an urge to cross the waters to other lands in search of a sense of home and belonging. She immerses herself in the cultures and ways of living in Belgium, Austria, France, Spain, Greece and Turkey. Getting darker with the Turkish sun and getting distanced from the Western obsession of defining Europeanness with whiteness, she is able to feel more British and less aware of race. She highlights that in Turkey, she is seen as coming from "simply İngiltere (England)" without being have to confront doubtful glances and answer uncomfortable questions in regard to her roots as she frequently experiences in Britain (Evaristo, 1997, p. 97). Therefore, her movement beyond the borders of "home" ironically brings her closer to the mother country, helping her to consider her relationship with Britain from new paradigms that exceed racial restrictions. Lara's travel to Turkey, in a sense, foreshadows the transformations in her understanding of the self and home that are to be enacted during her trips to the lands once inhabited by her forefathers.

As Lara keeps being haunted by the ancestral spirits, she is intrigued to know the meanings of her visions and dreams that she feels can decipher by delving into the histories of her ancestors. Thus, Lara responds to the call of Zenobia's spirit to bring her father home and travels with her parents first to Nigeria and then to Brazil, replicating the trajectory of her ancestors' transport for the transatlantic slavery. The idea of formation of the self by means of travels and her connectedness to the ancestral pasts are implicated in her name. "Omilara" in the Yoruba language means "the family is like water". As Şebnem Toplu (2011) argues, the image of water signifies both the family's and Lara's movements across the oceans (p. 4). Like the metaphor of baobab tree that suggests the dissemination of Lara's family over the world as a result of colonialism and slavery, the relationship established between family and water points to the historical events in which her ancestors were forced to leave their home and to cross the waters as slaves. In the way that Lara is connected to her ancestors' experience of the transatlantic slave trade through her name, her "being" or identity can be concluded to have ties with the legacies of slavery and colonialism. Her physical journeys that permit the discovery of the ways in which the ancestral pasts have influence on her subjectivity, reveal identity to be more complex than the neat categories defined by the Western discourses on race, nationality and ethnicity. As her enslaved ancestors who were carried to Brazil crossed the borders of nations and cultures, their African identity inevitably went through processes of transformation, which Paul Gilroy explains with his concept of the Black Atlantic. Gilroy's figure of ship moves across a vast stretch of water that touches the shores of various continents such as Africa, Americas and Europe. As people and goods are transported to and from many different communities, their cultures are mixed in unpredictable patterns. In this vein, Lara discovers her ancestral family to have been cross-fertilised culturally and racially along their movements across the waters. The fact that they were pushed to inhabit a de-centralised zone confounds the conventional definitions of nation. Besides, the fact that they were severed from their native traditions and ways of living, and forced to adapt to the colonial order shows cultural identity to be fluid and shifting, which is symbolised also by the image of water. As Gilroy shifts our attention on identity from "roots" to "routes", Lara's subjectivity is seen as being reshaped along her journeys in the pursuit of the past lives of her ancestors. Evaristo hints at the changing nature of one's sense of the self in relation to the histories of the places formerly inhabited by the predecessors when she expresses, "I was much more interested in exploring far-flung places like Brazil and Nigeria to make connections with the unknown side of my heritage" (Hooper, 2006, p. 6). Her journeys to these places are thus motived by her desire to find a viable history and identity for herself. She needs to investigate the roots of her family in order to grasp what her origins are truly like.

During her journeys to Nigeria and Brazil, Lara interacts with a diverse cast of characters, including the apparitions of her deceased relatives, who represent different aspects of her heritage and enable her to apprehend the complexities of her identity. They recount their "unheard" stories of slavery, transportations, displacement and labour on sugar plantations. As Evaristo has declared, "I am interested in the stories that haven't been told, to explore new ways of looking at our world" (Hooper, 2006, p. 11), the unrecorded stories of the individuals whom she has encountered guide her into reconsideration of her relationship to her African inheritance. The discovery of her ancestral family's hybridised and multicultural heritage helps her to realise that the Western historical and cultural narratives do not provide the only valid truths in respect to identity, ethnicity, culture and history. The subjective experiences and unknown stories of the past provide alternative approaches to established beliefs. Her quests therefore unveil that personal experiences can intervene in dominant narratives. By searching and collecting together transatlantic stories of her ancestors, Lara challenges the monolithic ways of perceiving the self and nation that are, in fact, structured by complex networks of relations. Lara's travels to Nigeria and Brazil are not only search for her multi-ethnic identity and her connections to multiple places, but also a way of understanding the ways in which histories and cultures of different continents are intertwined. Her quests awaken her to the idea of connection across diversities, helping her to reclaim her place in the British society. In this regard, Lara's journeys lead her through a number of transformative experiences that challenge her assumptions about herself and the world around her. She becomes more conscious of her mixed-race identity and finds a new sense of belonging that is not restricted to one particular place but based on the interconnectivity of histories and shared experiences of different communities.

"Where Are You from Originally?": Myth of "Purity"

Before Lara journeys physically to her places of origin and metaphorically into her inner world, her perceptions of belonging and identity are determined largely by the Western master narratives that identify people by fixed and homogenising categories of race, nation and ethnicity. Because being black and English at the same time is reckoned as a contradiction within the paradigms of the hegemonic conception of British nationality, Lara's realisation of her difference when growing up in London results in a sense of dislocation that starts first at a physical level. Having become conscious of "being the only child of discernible colour" in school (Evaristo, 1997, p. 35), she makes efforts desperately to disguise her African features; for instance, she sucks her lips in order to make sure that they do not seem so big as her father's (p. 60). Then, she makes comparisons between her physical appearance and that of her white friend Susie. She admires and envies the colour of Susie's lips, her long and lean legs, and her smooth hair. As Lara notices how different Susie's body is from hers, she starts to hate her own looks. She regrets having a stubborn and bouncy hair that she is able to put in a shape only with the help of abundance of pins and comb through its tangles with great difficulties (p. 62–63). She wishes she had white skin and blonde hair, feeling repulsive with her dark skin and wiry hair (p. 71). The process of Lara's self-alienation gains momentum as she is frequently confronted with remarks which imply that she does not belong to the English society because of her dark skin colour. Even her friend Susie directs her the poignant yet familiar question "where are you from originally?", by which she reiterates the prevalent conviction that Englishness is aligned with whiteness and that Lara's skin colour denies her of an "authentic" British identity. Susie's question hints that Lara does not belong to Britain, and "home" for her must be in another place; therefore, Susie proceeds to ask her out of curiosity if she comes from Jamaica or if his father lives in a jungle. Susie clearly repeats the Western stereotypes about black people that she has been taught by the dominant power in Britain. When Lara explains that her father is Nigerian and her mother is English, and that since she was born in Eltham, she identifies herself as English, Susie is still unable to place Lara with her dark skin within the conventional category of Englishness; therefore, she labels Lara as "half-cast", perceiving her as incomplete, "near-white", not fully belonging to the English nationality (p. 65).

Lara is alienated from her body, her African roots, and her sense of Englishness due to the racist treatments that she constantly experiences in London. To illustrate, Susie's boyfriend Daniel refers to Lara with derogatory terms like "nig nog" and overtly expresses how embarrassing it would be for him if he were seen with her. Moreover, Daniel intentionally makes Lara feel uncomfortable by aping a monkey that is offensively associated with African people in the Western discourse of white supremacy (Evaristo, 1997, p. 68). Hence, his gesture conveys the message to Lara that she does not belong to England. Lara becomes traumatised and disintegrated as a result of many other memories of racism that she has suffered. She recounts the racist attacks on the immigrant communities in her neighbourhood during her childhood by the skinheads with their "swastika tattoos", "crombies" and "Union Jack braces" who put the blame on Africans and Asians for England's economic and social problems. She remembers their targeting projectiles at the windows of her family's house and her fears for her father's safety in the streets of London. On the other hand, being persistently otherised and discriminated in the English society, she cannot help feeling ashamed of having a black father and hating her own black body (p. 70). Lara's alienation and self-loathing can be recognised in Franz Fanon's explanations of the pathological splitting of self-identification,

> As I begin to recognise that the Negro is the symbol of sin, I catch myself hating the Negro. But then I recognise that I am a Negro. There are two ways out of this conflict. Either I ask others to pay no attention to my skin, or else I want them to be aware of it. (Fanon, 1952/2008, p. 153)

Similarly, Lara articulates the split in her being with the conflictual statement "I wanted to be invisible. I wanted to be noticed" (Evaristo, 1997, p. 70). She both wishes to escape from the judgments of the white through self-denial and to be recognised by them for who she is. Her dilemma within herself emerges from her deprivation of the possibility that her black and English identities can coexist without excluding each other. In this regard, she is pictured as torn between her blackness and Englishness, which results from her internalisation of the Western binary of black/white. As such, she is positioned in a situation where she is unable to belong to either of her two sides. She expresses the feelings of disorientation and unbelonging that predominate her subjectivity with the words:

> Home. I searched but could not find myself,
> not on the screen, billboards, books, magazines,
> and first and last not in the mirror, my demon, my love
> which faded my brownness into a Bardot likeness.
> Seasons of youth stirred in my cooking pot, a spicy
> mix of marinated cultures, congealed into cold, disparate
> lumps, untended, festered […]. (p. 69)

Not being able to identify with any image in London, Lara finds it difficult to embrace her hybridity that she sees as constituted of incompatible elements, and that eventually leads her to question what home means for her. Because she is denied experience of Britain as a home, she longs for "an image, a story, to speak [her], describe [her], birth [her] whole" (Evaristo, 1997, p. 69). She wishes to belong to an identity and a place that can embrace her contrasts and define her subjectivity without forcing her to disregard certain parts of who she is. Lara's relative Beatrice, who is also a mixed-race girl like Lara, suggests her to learn how to behave like a Nigerian. Sharing her own experiences of racial intolerance in Britain, Beatrice reminds Lara of the prevalent attitude of the English to homogenise all black people as outsiders without exempting those who have English blood in that they consider black skin as going against the claims of Englishness. She proclaims, "They do not care whether/ your mother's white, green or orange with purple spots, / you are a nigger to them [...]" (p. 74). Having comprehended that she cannot belong to the English nationality while it is characterised as white by the dominant narratives of nation, Lara attempts to find a sense of belonging in her African inheritance by getting acquainted with Nigerian ways of life. She expects to learn how to be a Nigerian when she starts a relationship with Josh who comes from Nigeria. However, rather than providing her with some sense of rootedness in her life, he causes Lara to experience further racial alienation. Not only does he remind her constantly of her ignorance of Nigerian culture, but also, he leads her to face the reality of patriarchal oppression of women. In line with the patriarchal perception of female gender roles, Josh both sexually objectifies Lara and tries to assert dominance over her by making her adopt a submissive position in their relationship:

> You'll not marry a Nigerian if you can't obey me
> [...]
> Just as well, because you don't even know what
> Jollof rice is, let alone how to cook it. You're strictly
> a fish fingers and mash girl. You'll make a sorry wife. (p. 90)

The fact that Josh expects Lara to conform to the patriarchal norms shows London to be a place of both gender and racial oppression for her. She is led to experience double-marginalisation because of the hegemonic mechanisms of racial subordination and patriarchal regimes of power (Gendusa, 2010, p. 98). As the conventional definition of British identity that associates it with whiteness prevents Lara from identifying with the English people, the observance of patriarchal authority over women hinders identification with the members of the Nigerian community in London. As a black woman in Britain, she appears to be always forced into pre-defined roles and positions by the sources of power that carry out both racial and gender discriminations. In Britain, Lara is ascribed identities that are delineated in fixed terms of nationality, ethnicity and femininity, and that prove to be insufficient to define the complexity of the way she feels about her selfhood. Therefore, Lara sets out to search for a sense of belonging in her fatherland. However, in Nigeria too, she stands out as different and immediately gets labelled as "oyinbo" (whitey) because of her lighter complexion. The fact that she is considered to be black in Britain while perceived to be white in Nigeria shows identity to be a contingent concept dependent on value judgements of diverse communities. On the other hand, because Lara has been taught to understand the world in terms of binary oppositions, she hopes to belong to Nigeria seamlessly without taking into consideration influences of her English cultural heritage, which yet make themselves evident shortly after. Although Lars yearns to embrace Nigeria as home, she begins to become aware of her deep connections to England. To illustrate, on one occasion she cannot help missing her lifestyle back in Europe, which becomes clear from her statement "What I'd give for a cappuccino and croissant right now" (p. 107). Lara obtains a more affirmative sense of self only when she changes her monolithic perspective on identity and starts to consider it as emerging from reconnection with ancestral pasts as well as from acceptance of individual differences as Stuart Hall accentuates in his pluralistic reinterpretation of cultural identity.

Lara's inherent connectedness to the collective experiences of her family is revealed to her in Lagos through her dreams in which her ancestors recount their transcultural stories intertwined with the histories of slavery and colonialism. They give accounts of the life moments that involve the processes of their transportation to Brazil, their emancipation and their return to Nigeria. Lara's metaphorical journey through the memories of her ancestors begins with a culturally hybridised picture of Lagos in 1931 that bears traces of slavery and colonialism. The emancipated Nigerian slaves from Brazil have returned home with Portuguese surnames such as Salvador, Cardoso, Damazio, Carrena, Roberto, da Souza, da Silva, and da Costa, and they have settled in the Brazilian Quarter in Yaba (Evaristo, 1997, p. 111). Here it is possible to hear both the organist in the cathedral and the muezzin in the mosque, which shows the coexistence of different cultures (p. 119). Lara first identifies with her grandmother Zenobia's complaints of the patriarchal traditions in regard to marriage, of the fact that she was not allowed to choose the man she wanted to marry. Zenobia narrativizes the story of her giving birth to Taiwo and Kehinde (p. 113), but soon her voice is taken over by Taiwo's grandfather Baba Aguda. Lara overhears Baba when he tells his grandson his stories of slavery in Brazil. She imaginatively witnesses to her forebears' displacement from their native land to Brazil, enslavement in the sugar cane plantations and oppression by their masters. She learns about the murder of Baba Aguda's mother, Tolulope by the slaveowner Senhor Fernandes da Costa. Baba Aguda is ripped apart not only from the person who gives him life and plays a great role in shaping his sense of self, but also from the most crucial source of identification, his family name. The deprival of his original African surname and adoption of that of his master "da Costa" cause fragmentation and alienation in him and his family.

Lara next identifies with her ancestors' experiences of living in the oppressive and alienating environment situated in Brazil. Baba Aguda reports that as slaves, they were "the forgotten people" who were made to labour hard until late hours in the fields. The marginalisation and discrimination that Lara suffers in the British society make her feel in the same way, out of place like her enslaved ancestors who were disregarded and dehumanised. After being freed from slavery, Baba Aguda and his twin brother Gilberto move to the city of Salvador where they wish to begin a new life that requires them to struggle to fit in and to be accepted by the Brazilian society. Lara and her ancestors are thus united by similar strivings to find a sense of coherent identity and home. When Gilberto is killed by sailors, Baba Aguda undergoes a breakdown, yet he finds strength to go on living in the hybridised religion of Candomblé that combines elements from African cultures and with the ones belonging to Catholicism and indigenous beliefs of South Americas (Evaristo, 1997, p. 128). It helps him to reconnect with his own ancestors just like Lara who tries to establish a connection with the pasts of her ancestors. In both cases, sources of hybridity and reconstruction of the ancestral past provide affirmation of self and sense of rootedness.

Finally, Baba Aguda returns back to home in Nigeria with his son Gregoria; however, contrary to their anticipations, they do not immediately get the feeling that Yorubaland is their only and original home. They realise that they are now culturally hybridised and they are divided between Brazilian and Yoruba identities. Just as Lara wonders upon her arrival in Lagos if she could belong to his father's country, Baba Aguda asks himself "Was this, land of my grandmother, home? /This strange island of swirling cloth and colour clash? / I found these people so arrogant, quarrelsome, so proud" (Evaristo, 1997, p. 130). His sense of alienation and dislocation reminds of Lara's in-betweenness, her ambivalent position between England and Nigeria. As Lara gains consciousness of hybridised cultures through her journey to the fatherland and the reconstruction of the ancestral pasts, her perspectives on identity and belonging shift from fixed categories to the possibilities of multiplicity and interconnectivity of cultures, places and histories. Evaristo's use of autofictional/ autoethnographic strategies, by which she blurs the boundaries between life and dreams, between the self and history, enables her to depict the processes in which Lara comes to the realisation that border-crossings, in terms of nation, race, ethnicity and culture, have always been an essential part of her selfhood.

Transnational/Transcultural Reformulation of Cultural Identity

The Yoruba proverb "However far the stream flows, it never forgets its source", which Bernardine Evaristo uses as an epigraph for her self-narration, is resonant with Stuart Hall's conception of cultural identity that foregrounds "being" as well as "becoming", connectedness to a shared history and individual differences as a result of one's unique experiences of life. In the novel, the author depicts that Lara, Taiwo and Baba Aguda are displaced from Nigeria for very different reasons and they interact with other cultures in their own ways, yet they still remain connected to the culture and history of their ancestors. The metaphor of water that separates and unites Lara's family appears once again in the epilogue of the book as a medium of reconciliation with her racial and cultural hybridity. The quote from the lyrics of a song by the Brazilian contemporary singer Milton Nascimento suggests water as a symbol of renewal of the self[31], which foreshadows Lara's coming to terms with her multiethnicity. Her trip to Nigeria is understood to be only one step toward her self-discovery and the revelation of the truth of her identity and her connections to the ancestral past (Kamali, 2016, p. 234). Lara traces the memories of her ancestors to Brazil that she finds to be as much culturally diverse as Nigeria. She discovers a lot of Yoruba influences in the cities of Bahia and Salvador, which makes her hopeful about reaching further back to the origins of her African ancestors. It is during her visit to the Afro-Brasilero Museum in Salvador that she understands there is no "origin" to be found in a particular place. Although she enters in the museum, hoping that she finds "a clue, a photograph of a great grandfather or ancestor" who carries the surname "Da Costa", she learns that there are hundreds of thousands of Da Costas in the achieves who are predicted to be scattered all around the world (Evaristo, 1997, p. 138). This is a moment of great disappointment and realisation for her in that contrary to the conventional ideas of racial origins and national belonging for identification, Lara is awakened to the reality of scattered belongings of her ancestors which cannot be pinned down to a singular geographical

---

31 "Sing rainwater, sea water
River water, holy water
Wrap this child in mercy-heal her" (Evaristo, 1997, p. 135).

location. In addition, as Patricia Murray (1999) observes it, Lara is unable to recover a true identity in an essentialised past because her quests are consistently complicated by the facts of hybridity (p. 44). She constantly fails to uncover a culturally "pure" source of identification. In this regard, as Lara is "baptized" in the waters of Amazon and hears Catholic hymns hybridised by drums, witnessing to "one culture orchestrated by another" (Evaristo, 1997, p. 139), she experiences a cathartic moment of rebirth which allows her to recognise the self and place as inevitably pluralised with interactions between various people, cultures and histories. She becomes a transformed person with newly acquired consciousness of multiplicity and interconnectivity in respect to the issues of race, nation and ethnicity. As a result, while Lara begins to acknowledge the African part of herself, she also reclaims her ties to England which she refers comfortably as "my island" (p. 140).

As opposed to the traditional views of identity as a static and unchanging entity, Lara adopts a fluid understanding of subjectivity which leads her to continue with her quest for the realities of her self through an excavation of the histories of her maternal predecessors which she includes in the expanded version of *Lara* published in 2009. Her mother Ellen's family initially appears to be a typically white British family, yet once Lara starts digging in the histories of her English ancestors, she discovers them to be racially and culturally hybridised and to have gone through experiences of displacement, discrimination and alienation, which brings them into proximity with her African ancestors. Thus, her self-narration becomes also a contestation of the supposedly homogenous vision of English national identity. In her previous novel, *The Emperor's Babe* (2001), Bernardine Evaristo has already been concerned with exploring and exploding "the myth of Britain as monocultural and racially pure until 1948" (Niven, 2001, p. 20). Situating the black protagonist Zuleika in Roman London, Evaristo challenges the British history with its presumption that there was not a black presence until the Windrush in 1948, and by extension, she interrogates the notion of purity of Englishness. Evaristo's attempts in *The Emperor's Babe* are largely inspired by Peter Fryer's book *Staying in Power: The History of Black People in Britain* (1984/2018), in which he writes, "There were Africans in Britain before the English came here" (p. 1). In line with Fryer's assertion, Evaristo creates the tale of Roman London by merging past and present, history and fantasy, novel and verse, being driven by her wish to disrupt the idea that Britain was populated only with the white before the migrations, and to make people to consider the possibility of black presence in Britain long before them (Muñoz Valdivieso, 2004, p. 18). Her novel hence serves as a direct challenge to Britain's exclusionary narratives of history as well as of identity. Evaristo's critique of Englishness as a homogenous conception is strengthened further by her investigation into the histories of her maternal ancestors in *Lara* (2009).

As her African family was transported from Nigeria to Brazil as slaves who suffered the destructive outcomes of colonialism, Lara finds out her white ancestors to have immigrated from Ireland to Britain because of the ravaging impacts of the Great Hunger between 1845 and 1849. Catlin, Lara's great-grand mother from the seventh generation backwards, describes the dreadfulness of that time:

> [...] Its monster jaws had ravaged the island
> for four murderous years, masticated the emaciated
> bodies of a million poor souls, sucked the flesh
> off them and buried their bones in earth blighted
> with potatoes rotting with black and green mould. (Evaristo, 2009, p. 29)

Like Baba Aguda who was separated from his beloveds because of colonialism and slavery, Catlin reports to have lost five daughters to the Hunger, her husband to typhus, and his son to the exodus to find a job overseas. Therefore, she makes her granddaughter Emma swear to God that she would never leave their homeland, yet she is soon shown to be forced to abandon home due to the hardships of living in Ireland. Catlin resents bitterly at the fact that Britain did not take an action to help Ireland out of the famine because of their racist conceptions of the Irish. Catlin is convinced that the English consider Ireland as a place of "a human swinery, an abomination, a black howling Babel of superstitious savages" (Evaristo, 2009, p. 29). She accuses Oliver Cromwell for the devastations that the Irish faced. Catlin's accounts of the outcomes of Cromwell's reign in Ireland between 1649 and 1653, such as eradication of Gaelic language, persecution of Irish Catholics, Irish people's deprivation of their right to rule their country, and confiscations of their lands resemble in some ways to Lara's paternal ancestors' stories of colonisation of Africa.

Some historians like John Gibney, identify Ireland as an internal colony of Britain. According to Gibney (2008), Ireland must be viewed as colonised because of Britain's major plantation projects in the early modern period that involved significant levels of violence, expropriation, and cultural and sectarian conflict (p. 172). Although he recognises that there are crucial differences between Ireland and Britain's other overseas colonies, he accentuates them to be united by shared experiences (p. 175). He notes that British settlers radically and often brutally transformed the Irish society, which was carried on even more intensively with Cromwell's reconquest of Ireland when it became effectively subordinated to the government in London politically and economically (p. 176). As a result of the Britain's long tradition of hostile perspectives on the

Irish, along with the assumption that Ireland was uncapable of ruling itself, it was made a part of the United Kingdom with the Act of Union put into effect in 1801. Britons' perceptions of the Irish as their inferior can easily be compared to their views of Africans. Michael de Nie (2005) explicates that because the British held the Anglo-Saxon to be superior to the Irish Celt, they defined Irishness as their "other", representing everything that the British were not. Like Africans, the Irish were inherently "lazy, superstitious, violent, emotional, naive, improvident [...]" (p. 2). The Act of Union hence aimed to cure Ireland through anglicization by making the Irish adopt British morals and manners. Briton's negative conceptions of the Irish led the British government to evaluate the causes of the potato crop failure as arising from Ireland's rebelliousness and from the excess of its impoverished population (p. 3). Having seen the famine as a new opportunity for transformation of Ireland, Britain was delayed to take an action to help the Irish, which caused an extended period of starvation, diseases, deaths and immigration to other countries.

Because of the antagonistic political and cultural relationships between Ireland and England, Emma's marriage to an English solider Henry Robbins and her settlement in England are regarded as double cardinal sins from the perspective of her Irish relatives. Like Lara's grandmother Edith/Peggy who opposes to the interracial marriage of Ellen and Taiwo, Uncle Lorcan rejects Emma for marrying an Englishman. In the line of objection to interracial unions, having regretted her marriage with a non-Irish husband, Emma herself disapproves her daughter, Mary Jane, of wanting to marry a Briton. Mary Jane righteously stands up to show her mother's protestation to be irrational by pointing to her own choice of a husband: "Ma had a word, 'He [Sebastian]'s not Irish...'/ 'Neither is your husband', I [Mary Jane] retorted" (Evaristo, 2009, p. 47). Lara's investigation into the history of her maternal ancestors therefore reveals that the marriage of her own parents has not been the only interracial union which provoked resentment and resistance from the relatives. Racial discrimination and opposition to miscegenation are proven to have long been prevalent within her family and caused discontent even when both parties belonged to white ethnicities. Furthermore, Lara's engagement with the ancestral past of her mother's side suggests that when national identity is considered in monolithic terms, not only is Peggy with her Irish roots excluded from "authentic Englishness", but also Lara's grandfather Leslie cannot be considered as fully English in that his maternal ancestors, the Wilkenigs, immigrated from Germany in 1860.

The stories of Lara's grandfather, Leslie's German relatives who started a new life in Britain lay out the fact that despite being white, they were subject to similar racial discrimination and marginalisation as suffered by the Irish and the black. Leslie's grandfather Louis Wilkenig's accounts of his experiences of living in Britain unveil that he was constantly made to feel like an outsider, forced to fight against the British stereotypes of Germans which assumed them to have no morals and to drink excessively (Evaristo, 2009, p. 84). In the World War II when the hostility against Germans increased, Louis' bakery shop and other German businesses were attacked and burnt down by the locals and they were given clear messages to go back to their country (p. 88–89). As a result of increasing racist assaults and pressure, similar to Taiwo's attempts to assimilate into the English society, Louis's family changed their surname into Wilkins and strived to be English by adopting their cultural norms and manners. Although Louis considered himself as English towards the end of his life, when he died, he was buried in "a corner of Woolwich", which became an indication of him as eternally foreign (p. 91). Lara's discovery of the parallels between the histories of her African, Irish and German ancestors and of their shared experiences of dislocation, discrimination and marginalisation propounds a fresh way of thinking about cultural identity that transcends the established borders of nation, race and ethnicity. Contrary to singular and exclusivist configurations, she illustrates identity to be always crisscrossed by multiplicity of cultures and interconnected with histories of various geographical locations, eras and peoples all over the world. As a result, Lara casts doubts on the hegemonic claims of purity of English identity and encourages to consider Englishness in a broader context of transnationalism.

As autofiction helps authors to grasp unknown realities of the self through the act of narration, in *Manifesto* (2022), Bernardine Evaristo acknowledges that through the character of Lara as a fictionalised version of herself and narration of her story, she has come to a deeper understanding of her identity as a mixed-race and multi-ethnic person. Similar to the way that autofiction occupies plural spaces within the realm of literary classification, crossing the borders of conventional genres, Evaristo recognises her ethnic heritage to be composed of multitudes that enable her to feel part of more than a single cultural space (p. 96–97). She is awakened to the idea that borders delineating categories of identification are "artificial" and "man-made" which can be easily transgressed by means of intermarriages and other forms of transculturation as her ancestral histories have evidenced (p. 2). She concludes race not to be a biological fact but an outcome of lived experiences, and therefore, purely consequential (p. 2). In *Lara* (1997/2009), thus, Evaristo portrays the limitations of the conventional understanding of the term British for individuals whose ancestral pasts stretch beyond the borders of Britain. Within the global networks of interconnections between histories and cultures, monolithic definitions of race, nation and ethnicity lose their function and meaning. As Lara's autoethnographic investigation into her white roots unearths a transnational form of Britishness, in line with Hanif Kureishi's summon for new ways of being British, Evaristo underlines the urgency for reformulation of British identity in order to accommodate the incontestable facts of racial, cultural and ethnic hybridity.

Conclusion

This book has traced the development of autofiction and other directions it has led to, such as autoethnography and autotheory, and discussed how its hybrid form and in-between position within literary categorisation hold potential to advance critical thinking on multiethnicity. Because the scope of this work is limited to the context of Britain, its theoretical framework has been grounded on the anti-essentialist perspectives of cultural identity formulated by Black British authors and theorists, Stuart Hall, Hanif Kureishi and Paul Gilroy. In order to provide a comparative insight into male and female ways of experiencing multiethnicity, and to create a contrast with the white heterosexual male subject of traditional autobiography, autofiction of three Black British women authors, Charlotte Williams, Jackie Kay and Bernardine Evaristo, has been examined. The book has observed that these authors employ extensively autofictional/ autoethnographic strategies in their works to interrogate conventional boundaries that segregate people, nations and cultures, and that force them into rigid normative categories, conflicting with the multiplicity of the ways in which they experience the world. As transgressive tendencies and hybridity of autofiction/ autoethnography problematise preestablished literary forms, dominant discourses and homogenising categories created by the white man, these authors find spaces to explore and represent their racial and ethnic hybridity. Autofictional/ autoethnographic fusions of fact and fiction and of the subjective and the collective enable them to claim that their subjectivities are produced in the intersection and interaction of multiple cultures and places. As opposed to the limits and constraints of autobiography, autofiction provides these authors with the means to examine and to embrace complexities and contradictions of their multi-ethnic selves. Autoethnography allows them to recognise their connections and disconnections with various locations, and to reclaim legacies of their forebears from different ethnic backgrounds. Possibilities of borderline position between fact and fiction, between the personal and collective help them destabilise the essential categories of identity and counter the dominant ideas of fixed borders and rooted belonging, leading them to assert their multi-ethnic subjectivities into history. As a result, these authors offer notable insights on the issues of memory, belonging and the self that are relevant both to autofiction and multiethnicity which form the conceptual framework for the book.

Through autofictional/autoethnographic modes of narration, Charlotte Williams, Jackie Kay and Bernardine Evaristo delve into the complexities and contradictions of their subjectivities that emerge from the convergence of multiple cultural influences. Rather than seeking to inscribe the veracity of their lives, they investigate the ambiguities of the self fractured by different locations, discovering and inventing truths about themselves. When articulating their hybrid identities, they present their sense of fissured subjectivity in distinct manners and provide unique experiences that arise from being part of different and multiple cultures. Importantly, the way they use autofictional form varies too. Comparative analysis of these works enables us to have a glance at different formulations of autofiction. In *Sugar and Slate* and *Red Dust Road*, in line with Doubrovskian definition, the author, narrator and protagonist share a nominal identity. Williams employs autofiction to invent a collective heritage for herself whereas Kay resorts to it in order to imagine her beginning and other possibilities of her self and life. On the other hand, in compliance with Philippe Gasparini's definition, in *Lara*, an identitarian relationship is constructed through other shared aspects than the author's proper name. Moreover, consistent with Gasparini and Colonna's hybrid viewpoint on autofiction, in *Lara*, the first-person narration of autofictional "I" is constantly interrupted by narrative voices of her ancestors who tell their own stories. Compared to the works of Williams and Kay, Evaristo's narrative is evidently more fictionalised with multiple narrators and inclusion of the author's dreams and illusions that distort the sense of referentiality and create a surreal impression. All three authors' individual ways of making use of autofiction support the idea of its resistance to being defined with clear boundaries. Despite stylistic differences, these authors adopt a non-linear form of narration for the common purpose of depicting the impacts of multiethnicity on their lives. As the most distinctive feature of autofiction/ autoethnography, narrative discontinuities and nonlinearity of time frame in their works not only emulate workings of their imperfect memory but also capture their fragmented sense of identity, history and belonging. Non-chronological and chaotic representation of autobiographical reality mirror their dispersed subjectivities and lives across different locations. Through non-linear narrative strategies, they illustrate their back and forward movements between memories, places and cultures, which all contribute to formation of their multi-ethnic identity.

For Charlotte Williams, Jackie Kay and Bernardine Evaristo, the self and the past are largely inaccessible particularly for multi-ethnic individuals in that they are dispossessed of history in various ways. Williams grows up in a small Welsh town without the presence of her father or other members of an African community with whom she can identify. Kay's state of being as an adoptee, outcome partly of her interraciality, deprives her of the knowledge of her biological parents and ancestors. Evaristo's parents intentionally refrain from passing on their histories to the writer because of traumatic experiences in their pasts. As a result, all three authors are compelled to imagine ancestral pasts and lands, and to invent their connections to them. Their fantasies and inventions inescapably become an indispensable part of their reality and who they are. By blurring the lines between fact and fiction, these authors are able to show in their narratives that there are intricate relations between life and imagination. In agreement with Jonathan Sturgeon's reasoning, they maintain the self and the real to be composed of fiction. They do this by using indirectness of fiction to recover and reassemble events of the past and to make sense of the present. Their reconnection with ancestral pasts reveals that the self of multiple heritage is greatly influenced by collective memory. Their subjectivities are shaped by multi-generational histories as much as individual experiences. While they present their life stories as intertwined with those of family lineages, they provide evidence for autofiction's claims that fiction can enrich referentiality and allow a greater deal of truthness than factual literary forms.

In line with autofictional/autoethnographic trope of travel, all three authors portray their undertaking of both physical and symbolic journeys to uncover their connections to various locations and to discover hidden psychic and collectively shared truths about their selfhood. Their search is markedly a continuous activity that never reaches to an end point. Movement, place and subjectivity are represented as interconnected to one another. With each journey, the authors become conscious of new aspects and multiplicities of their being. Parts of the self are not only unveiled but also created during their movements, which evokes Paul Gilroy's concept of Black Atlantic that suggests travels across different places to result in cultural hybridity. Their subjectivities are shaped by complex relations between spaces, histories and cultures. As they picture their personal worlds as linked to collective worlds, they foreground the intricate ways in which histories and cultures of different continents are intertwined, which destabilises traditional demarcation of national boundaries. Their narratives positioned at the intersections between fact and fiction, the personal and the collective unfold towards a fluid understanding of identity and belonging, conveying that home and identity are not static and monolithic concepts.

In all three autofictional/autoethnographic narratives that have been examined, the authors depict themselves as positioned within dominant regimes of representation in Britain that impel them to perceive themselves as the Other. By digging into their past and history, however, they find out that they can identify only partly with Black identity that is never singular. In-betweenness of autofiction epitomises these authors' ambivalent position between essentialised conceptions of Europeanness and Africanness, both of which problematise their ethnic belonging based on skin colour. The authors' attempts to connect with their blackness by means of journeying to fatherlands result in realisation that despite their African heritage, they are equally products of British culture. The discovery of inherent connections with their African ancestors and their histories brings along recognition of their British heritage. This self-conscious identification with multiple cultures disrupts traditional perceptions of white ethnicity as well as the notion of an essential black identity. In line with Stuart Hall's formulation of cultural identity, while acknowledging their ties to a collective identity, they also foreground individualistic features of their own unique multi-ethnic identity. Autofiction allows these authors to explore the overlaps between the histories of their white and black heritages. They show that these histories are not completely separate from each other. By blurring the lines between the factual and the fictional, between the personal and the collective, Williams constructs historical and cultural connections between Wales and the West Indies, Kay between Scotland and Nigeria, Evaristo between England and Nigeria. With their individual stories of dual heritage, they intervene in traditional discourses on black and white identities and destabilise dominant ideas of national identities. By paying attention to racial, economic, political, cultural divides within each society, they illustrate the flawed nature of thinking about nations in monolithic terms. Autofictional/ autoethnographic strategies of recovering the pasts though fiction and interweaving individual and historical stories in the books work towards revelation of the constructedness of any narrative and identity. Rather than poststructuralist reduction to pure textuality, the state of hybridity produces new narratives that challenge dominant discourses of history and knowledge. Conventional narratives of national identity suppress differences, and yet autofiction/ autoethnography's blending of diverse genres help these authors to reason and express heterogeneities within nations. These authors' construction of parallels between the constituent countries of Britain and its ex-colonies through shared experiences of cultural dispossession, discrimination and marginalisation conveys Britain to have never been mono-national or monocultural. They accentuate that the Welsh, the Scottish and the Irish are disruptive of the imagined uniformity of Britishness. Interrogating thus singularity of nation, ethnicity and culture, these works attest to autofiction's presumptions of artificiality of borders and differences within normative categories.

Through hybridity of autofiction/autoethnography, all three authors illustrate that like boundaries, identities are not innate, but culturally and politically constructed. They show that border-crossings provide multiple points of identification. The plurality of autofictional subject, capable of embodying the referential self, the textual self, the unconscious self, the imagined selves, allows these authors to explore and reconcile multiple aspects of their subjectivities beyond the constraints of conventional categories. In contradistinction to the dominant presumptions that divide the white and black worlds, on the social level, the authors confront intricate connections between Britain and Africa. On the personal level, they reflect their feeling of being caught between different cultural communities, and the process of reconciling or embracing their diverse heritage. Williams demonstrates recognition of her multiethnicity in juxtaposition of "sugar" and "slate" in the title of her book. Kay concludes her identity to be constructed by multiple influences by the realisation that the self is produced in the intersection of the conventional question of "nature or nourish?", that is a combination of roots/genetic relations and culture/environment in which one grows up. Evaristo conceives her multi-ethnic identity as a product of inevitable interconnectivity between societies through interracial marriages, transnational movements and intercultural contacts. Individual experiences of multiethnicity of these mixed-descent authors problematise "purity" of national, ethnic and cultural identification, and challenge the monolithic definition of Britishness, pressurising it to be reconsidered in transnational terms to encompass individuals whose ancestral pasts transcend the borders of Britain. Complying with Hanif Kureishi's appeal for contemplation about new beings of British, these authors provide portrayals of distinct ways of being a part of Britain.

Autofictional/autoethnographic strategies of loosening the boundaries enable Charlotte Williams, Jackie Kay and Bernardine Evaristo to navigate the complexities of their identities and inquire into the interplay between personal and societal dynamics, inducing a broader understanding of multiculturalism and diversity. In addition to display of unique multi-ethnic subjectivities, the narratives of these authors express different ways of experiencing female gender. Williams depicts the process of alienation from her femaleness through internalisation of dominant discourses that idealise features of the white woman as beauty standards, leaving her with a sense of ambivalence in regard to her gender. Identical to constantly shifting nature of cultural identity, Kay calls attention to instability of her sexual identification that alternates between heterosexual and lesbian involvements and therefore upsets normative understandings of sexuality. Evaristo narrativizes her disidentification with Western stereotypes of black woman and patriarchal subordination of women within African societies, pushing her into a situation in which she is unable to recognise herself in dominant conceptions of black female gender. The works of all three authors point at the urgency for transformation of thinking systems that attempt to define their ethnicity and gender. Through strategies of fictionalisation and fragmentation, they defy the ways in which they are represented by men and give voice to their experiences of the self and the world. In addition to the influences of their diverse ethnic backgrounds, these authors' different ways of engaging with the ambivalence which they are brought into by masculine discourses on black womanhood indicate that the category of "black woman" cannot be reduced to a singular and homogeneous experience.

The authors use autofiction and autoethnography to challenge the ways in which multi-ethnic Black British women have traditionally been represented by dominant discourses on race, gender and cultural identity. By blurring the boundaries between literary genres and thus destabilising fixed truths, they create room for delivering the truth of a historically invisible experience which contradicts long-established assumptions of ethnicity, race, culture, nation and gender. They show that like hybridity of autofiction/ autoethnography, multi-ethnic identities intersect with multiple aspects of identification. Their emphasis on the idea of intersectionality serves to deconstruct assumed coherence of collective identities of "Black", "British" and "Woman". By laying bare the differences within these labels, they problematise the traditional views of homogeneity and stability of categories of identification. Autofiction/autoethnography enables these authors to negotiate their own sense of self. They are provided with an opportunity to re-imagine and re-assert their subjectivities in history. Engaging critically with the ways in which mixed-descent people are represented and represent themselves is a pressing issue in today's Britain. To this end, autofiction and autoethnography cater powerful tools to explore multiple layers of the self, to consider pasts from personal perspectives, and to create spaces of inclusion for individuals with multi-ethnic backgrounds.

The texts that have been examined in the book have been brought together by autofictional/autoethnographic tropes of memory, belonging and quest for the self, which have been argued to hold crucial significances for investigation and understanding of multi-ethnic subjectivities, particularly of female gender. The analysis of these works provides a number of critical insights into formulation of autofiction. First of all, they evidence that fiction plays an important role in shaping one's sense of self and life. Literary categories are constructs, and in effect, it is unrealistic and futile to assume clear divisions between them just as between normative categories of identification. Traditionally maintained boundaries are not stable or absolute. Third spaces between them, like the one autofiction occupies, are highly productive for systems of thinking and representation. Intersections provide new perspectives on issues in regard to various areas of life, and destabilise the idea of objective and unified realities. Next, the different ways in which these authors make use of autofictional strategies suggest that there is not one single way of narrating the self. There is a multitude of aspects of subjectivity to be told and retold. Instances of multifaceted self-narration in these works serve to problematise coherence of conceptions of fixed truth. Finally, the authors' diverse ways of unsettling boundaries and of blending distinct elements reveal autofiction's irreducibility to a set of rules to be its principal trait.

Lastly, these authors' narratives show that autofiction can impact substantially on thinking about the concept of multiethnicity. Autofiction's in-betweenness and hybridity permit mixed- descent authors to communicate their individual experiences of being caught between multiple cultural worlds and diverse realities of having a multi-ethnic identity, which can pose challenges to existing stereotypes and misconceptions. This representation and visibility can counteract marginalisation of multi-ethnic voices and foster a more inclusive understanding of multiethnicity. Drawing on autofictional playfulness, multi-ethnic authors can negotiate the subject positions ascribed to them by various communities, and subvert essentialist or fixed perceptions of identity. By embracing the multiplicity and contradictions inherent in the state of possessing dual heritage, they can break away from monolithic portrayals and offer alternative narratives that recognise the coexistence of distinct cultural elements in their subjectivities. Autofiction therefore provides multi-ethnic authors with a powerful vehicle to deconstruct and reconstruct ethnic identities, negate fixed categories, and reveal complex interplays between personal experiences and social dynamics. In this respect, autofiction's resistance to normative categories and discourses can be predicted to contribute to the production of new ethnicities that are constantly evolving and negotiated.

References

Ahmed, S. (1997). "It's a sun-tan, isn't it?": auto-biography as an identificatory practice. In H. S. Mirza (Ed.). *Black British feminism* (pp. 153–167). London and New York: Routledge.

Althusser, L. (1971). Ideology and ideological state apparatuses. *Lenin and philosophy and other essays* (B. Brester, Trans., pp. 127–193). New York and London: Monthly Review Press. (Original work published in 1970)

Anderson, B. (1983). *Imagined communities: reflections on the origins and spread of nationalism.* London: Verso.

Anderson, L. (2011). *Autobiography.* Abingdon and New York: Routledge.

Athanasiades, A. (2016). Tell me a story dad: (post)memory and the archaeology of subjectivity in Hanif Kureishi's my ear at his heart. *Journal of postcolonial writing,* 52(1), 26–37. https://doi.org/10.1080/17449855.2015.1125138

Backhouse, F. (2022, May 24). Nigerian civil war. *Britannica.* Retrieved January 19, 2023, from https://www.britannica.com/topic/Nigerian-civil-war

Barker C. & Jane. E. A. (2016). *Cultural studies: theory and practice* (5th ed.). London: Sage Publications.

Barthes, R. (1972). *Mythologies.* London: J. Cape. (Original work published in 1957).

Barthes, R. (1974). *S/Z* (R. Miller, Trans.). New York, NY: Hill and Wang. (Original work published in 1970)

Barthes, R. (1975). *The pleasure of text* (R. Miller, Trans.). New York, NY: Hill and Wang. (Original work published in 1973)

Barthes, R. (1977). Introduction to the structural analysis of narrative. *Image-music-text* (S. Heath, Trans., pp. 79–124). London: Fontana. (Original work published in 1966)

Barthes, R. (1977). The death of the author. *Image-music-text* (S. Heath, Trans., pp. 142–148). London: Fontana. (Original work published in 1967)

Barthes, R. (1977). From work to text. *Image-music-text* (S. Heath, Trans., pp. 155–164). London: Fontana. (Original work published in 1971)

Belsey, C. (2002). *Critical practice* (2nd ed.). London: Routledge.

Belsey, C. (2002). *Poststructuralism: a very short introduction.* New York: Oxford University Press.

Bertens, H. (2014). *Literary theory: the basics* (3rd ed.). Oxon: Routledge.

Bhabha, H. K. (1990). *Nation and narration.* London: Routledge.

Bhabha, H. K. (1994). *The location of culture*. London: Routledge.

Bloom, M. (2019). Sources of the self(ie): an introduction to the study of autofiction in English. *ESC: English studies in Canada*, 45(1–2), 1–18. https://doi.org/10.1353/esc.2019.0000

Baudrillard, J. (1994). *Simulacra and simulation* (S. Glaser, Trans.). Ann Arbor: University of Michigan Press. (Original work published in 1981)

Bentley, N. (2003). Black London: the politics of representation in Sam Selvon's the lonely Londoners. *Wasafiri*, 18(39), 41–45. https://doi.org/10.1080/02690050308589846

Bohata, K. (2004). *Postcolonialism revisited: writing Wales in English*. Cardiff: The University of Wales Press.

Boyle, C. (2007). *Consuming autobiographies: reading and writing the self in post-war France*. Oxford: Legenda.

Boyle, C. (2013). Je réel/je fictif: au-delà d'une confusion postmoderne. *French Studies*, 67(2), 287. https://doi.org/10.1093/fs/knt035

Brown, S. (1999). Lara, Bernardine Evaristo. *Reviews, Wasafiri*, 29, 83–4. https://doi.org/10.1080/02690059908589642

Burgelin, C. (2010). Pour l'autofiction. In Burgelin, C., Grell, I., & Roger-Yves, R. (Eds.). *Autofiction(s): colloque de cerisy* (pp. 5–21). Lyon: Presses Universitaires de Lyon. (Original work published in 2008)

Burten, P. (1976). Time in autobiography. *Comparative literature*, 28(4), 326–42.

Cairns C. (1996). *Out of history: narrative paradigms in Scottish and British culture*. Edinburgh: Polygon.

Carby, H. V. (1997). White woman listen! Black feminism and the boundaries of sisterhood. In H. S. Mirza (Ed.). *Black British feminism* (pp. 45–53). London and New York: Routledge. (Original work published in 1982)

Célestin, R. (1997). Interview with Serge Doubrovsky: autofiction and beyond. *Sites: the journal of twentieth-century/contemporary French studies/revue d'études français*, 1(2), 397–405.

Clifford, J. (1997). *Routes: travel and translation in the late twentieth century*. Cambridge, MA: Harvard University Press.

Colonna, V. (2004). *Autofiction et autres mythomanies littéraries*. Auch: Tristram.

Cole, T. (2011). *Open city*. New York: Random House.

Cooke, D. (2005). *Present pasts: Patrick Modiano's (auto)biographical fictions*. Amsterdam: Rodopi.

Connell, L. (2003). Modes of marginality: Scottish literature and the uses of post-colonial theory. *Comparative Studies of South Asia, Africa and the Middle East*, 23(1–2), 41–53. https://doi.org/10.1215/1089201X-23-1-2-41

Crump, E. (2013). Looking back at the Great Strike at Penrhyn Quarry. Retrieved from https://www.dailypost.co.uk/news/nostalgia/looking-back-great-strike-penrhyn-4698535

Currie, R. Jr. (2013). *Flimsy little plastic miracles: A true* story*. New York: Viking.

Cusk, R. (2014). *Outline*. London: Faber & Faber.

Cusk, R. (2017). *Transit*. New York: Farrar, Straus and Giroux.

Cusk, R. (2018). *Kudos*. New York: Farrar, Straus and Giroux.

Cussett, C. (2012). The limits of autofiction. Unpublished Conference Paper. Retrieved from http://www.catherinecusset.co.uk/wp-content/uploads/2013/02/THE-LIMITS-OF-AUTOFICTION.pdf.

Claasser, E. (2012). *Author representations in literary reading*. Amsterdam: John Benjamins Publishing Co.

Clare, R. (2020). Becoming autotheory. *Arizona quarterly: A journal of American literature, culture, and theory*, 76(1), 85–107. https://doi.org/10.1353/arq.2020.0003

Cominetti, E. A. (2018). *In-between wor(l)ds: Female autofiction and postcolonial identity in Marie Cardinal's Au pays de mes racines, Marguerite Duras's L'amant and Isabela Figueiredo's Caderno de memórias coloniais*. (Doctoral dissertation). Retrieved from https://run.unl.pt/bitstream/10362/50265/1/NOVA_Cominetti_Dissertation.pdf

Darrieussecq, M. (1996). L'autofiction, un genre pas sérieux. *Poétique*, 107, 368–380.

Darrieussecq, M. (2007). Je est un autre. In A. Oliver (Ed.), *Ecrire l'histoire d'une vie*. Rome: Spartaco.

Dawes, K (1998). Review: Lara by Bernardine Evaristo. *World literature today*, 72(2), 378–9.

de Bloois, J. (2007). Introduction: The artists formerly known as... or, the loose end of conceptual art and the possibilities of 'visual autofiction'. *Image & Narrative*, 8(19). Available: https://www.imageandnarrative.be/inarchive/autofiction/debloois.htm

de Man, P. (1973). Semiology and rhetoric. *Diacritics*, 3(3), 27–33. https://doi.org/10.2307/464524

de Nie, M. (2005). British conceptions of Ireland and Irishness in the nineteenth century. *History compass*, 3, 1–6. https://doi.org/10.1111/j.1478-0542.2005.00153.x

Derrida, J. (1976). *Of grammatology* (G. C. Spivak, Trans.). Baltimore, MD: Johns Hopkins University Press. (Original work published in 1967)

Derrida, J. (1989). Différance. In H. Adams & L. Searle (Eds.). *Critical theory since 1965* (pp. 120–146). Talahasse: Frorida State University. (Original work printed in 1972).

Derrida, J. (2002). Structure, sign, and play in the discourse of the human sciences. *Writing and difference* (A. Bass, Trans., pp. 278–294). London: Routledge. (Original work published in 1970)

Dix, H. (2017). Autofiction: the forgotten face of French theory. *A journal of literary studies and linguistics, 7*, 69–85.

Dix, H. (2017). *The late-career novelist: career construction theory, authors and autofiction.* London: Bloomsbury.

Dix, H. (Ed.). (2018). *Autofiction in English.* Cham: Palgrave Macmillan.

Donnell, A. J. (2008). Welsh and West Indian, "like nothing…seen before": unfolding diasporic lives in Charlotte Williams' Sugar and slate. *Anthurium: a Caribbean studies journal, 6*(2), 1–26. http://doi.org/10.33596/anth.120

Du Bois, W. E. B. (2007). The souls of Black folk (Edwards, B. H. Ed.). New York: Oxford University Press. (Original work published in 1903)

Dyker. R. (2004). Interview: Jackie Kay with Richard Dyer. In Nasta, S. (Ed.). *Writing across worlds: contemporary writers talk* (pp. 237–249). London: Routledge.

Edwards, J. D. (2010). "Imaginary hinterlands": travel and displacement in the writings of Denis Williams and Charlotte Williams. *Comparative American studies an international journal, 8*(2), 155–164. https://doi.org/10.1179/147757010X12677983681479

Edwards, N. (2015, February). *Jane Sautiere's autofictional explorations: Nullipare.* Paper presented at the "Non-Motherhood in Contemporary Women's Writing in French", Contemporary Women's Writing in French Seminar, University of London, Senate House.

Eguíbar-Holgado, M. (2018). Reading the body racial in black Canadian/ black Scottish nonfiction: Dorothy Mills Proctor and Jackie Kay. *African American review, 51*(3), 167–179. https://doi.org/10.1353/afa.2018.0030

Ellis, B. E. (2005). *Lunar park.* New York: Knopf.

Engels, F. (1949). Letter to F. Mehring. *Karl Marx and Friedrich Engels: selected works in two volumes*, vol. 2. Moscow: Foreign Languages Publishing House. (Original work published in 1893).

Evans, M. (2002). The cruel history of the Welsh Not which tried to shame children into abandoning their language. Retrieved from https://www.dailypost.co.uk/news/north-wales-news/cruel-history-welsh-not-tried-24916977

Evaristo, B (1997). *Lara* (1st ed.). London: Angela Royal Publishing.

Evaristo, B. (2001) *The emperor's babe*. London: Penguin.

Evaristo, B. (2005). Writers on writing. *Centre for transcultural writing and research* https://www.lancaster.ac.uk/transculturalwriting-archive/radiophonics/contents/writersonwriting/bernardineevaristo/index.html

Evaristo, B. (2009). *Lara* (2nd ed.). Northumberland: Bloodaxe Books.

Evaristo, B. (2022). *Manifesto: on never giving up*. New York: Grove Press.

Evaristo, B. (2022). Craft episode 6 transcript: Bernardine Evaristo. *Wasafiri: International Contemporary Writing*. Retrieved from https://www.wasafiri.org/content/craft-episode-6-transcript-bernardine-evaristo/

Fanon, F. (1963). *The wretched of the earth* (C. Farrington, Trans.). New York: Grove Press. (Original work published in 1961)

Fanon, F. (2008). *Black skin, white masks* (Trans. Z. Sardar). London: Pluto Press. (Original work published in 1952).

Fenton, S. (2010). *Ethnicity* (2nd ed.). Cambridge: Polity Press.

Ferreira-Meyers, K. (2015). Autobiography and autofiction: no need to fight for a place in the limelight, there is space enough for both of these concepts. In K. W. Shands, G. G. Mikrut, D. R. Pattanaik & K. Ferreira-Meyers (Eds.). *Writing the self: essays on autobiography and autofiction* (pp. 203–218). Sweden: Elanders.

Ferreira-Meyers, K. (2018). Does autofiction belong to French or Francophone authors and readers only? In H. Dix (Ed.). *Autofiction in English* (pp. 27–48). Cham: Palgrave Macmillan.

Folarin, T. (2019). *A particular kind of black*. New York: Simon & Schuster.

Folarin, T. (2020). Can a black novelist write autofiction? *The new republic*. Retrieved from https://newrepublic.com/article/159951/can-black-novelist-write-autofiction

Forest, P. (2007). La vie est un roman. In J. Jeannelle & C. Viollet (Eds.). *Genèse et autofiction* (pp. 211–217). Louvain-la-Neuve: Éditions Academia-Bruylant.

Forna, A. (2010). Red dust road: an autobiographical journey by Jackie Kay. Retrieved from https://www.theguardian.com/books/2010/jun/26/red-dust-road-jackie-kay

Foucault, M. (1978–2021). *The history of sexuality*. New York: Pantheon Books. (Original work published in 1976–2018).

Foucault, M. (1984). What is an author? In P. Rabinow (Ed.). *The Foucault: reader* (pp. 101–120). New York: Pantheon Books. (Original work published in 1969).

Foucault, M. (1984). Truth and power. In P. Rabinow (Ed.). *The Foucault: reader* (pp. 51–75). New York: Pantheon Books. (Original work published in 1980).

Foucault, M. (2012). *Discipline and punish: the birth of the prison* (A. Sheridan, Trans.). New York: Vintage Books. (Original work published in 1975)

Fournier, L. (2021). *Autotheory as feminist practice in art, writing, and criticism*. Massachusetts: The Mit Press.

Fox, P. (2015). The "telling part": reimagining racial recognition in Jackie Kay's adoptee search narratives. *Contemporary women's writing*, 9(2), 277–296. https://doi.org/10.1093/cwwrit/vpu041

Fraser, M. (2015). *Genres instables: Ludic performances of autofiction in the works of Catherine Cusset, Philippe Vilain, Chloé Delaume and Éric Chevillard*. (Doctoral dissertation). Retrieved from https://research-repository.st-andrews.ac.uk/bitstream/handle/10023/7325/MorvenFraserPhDThesis.pdf;jsessionid=9F7A8A3B438713FA752B316D46172518?sequence=3

Friedman, S. S. (1988). Women's autobiographical selves: theory and practice. In S. Smith & J. Watson (Eds.). *Women, autobiography, theory: a reader* (pp. 72–82). Wisconsin: The University of Wisconsin Press.

Freud, S. (1999). *The interpretations of dreams* (J. Crick, Trans.). New York: Oxford University Press. (Original work published in 1899)

Freud, S. (1953). Screen memories. In Strachey, J., Freud, A., & Rothgeb, C. L. (Eds.). *The standard edition of the complete psychological works of Sigmund Freud* (Vol. 3, pp. 303–322). London: Hogarth Press and the Institute of Psycho-Analysis. (Original work published in 1899)

Freud, S. (1953). A note upon the "mystic writing pad". In Strachey, J., Freud, A., & Rothgeb, C. L. (Eds.). *The standard edition of the complete psychological works of Sigmund Freud* (Vol. 19, pp. 227–232). London: Hogarth Press and the Institute of Psycho-Analysis. (Original work published in 1925)

Fryer, P. (2018). *Staying in power: the history of Black people in Britain*. London: Pluto Press. (Original work published in 1984).

Gagiano, A. (2019). Recovering and recovering from an African past: four women's quest narratives. *Journal of transatlantic studies*, 17, 269–289. https://doi.org/10.1057/s42738-019-00025-x

Gasparini, P. (2004). *Est-il je? Roman autobiographique et autofiction*. Paris: Seuil.

Gendusa, E. M. E. (2010). Transnational axes of identity articulation in Bernardine Evaristo's Lara. In S. Schultermand & S. Toplu (Eds.). *A fluid sense of self: the politics of transnational identity* (pp. 95–111). New Brunswick and London: Transaction Publishers.

Genette, G. (1993). *Fiction & diction* (C. Porter, Trans.). New York: Cornell University. (Original work published in 1991)

Genon, A. (2013). *Autofiction: pratiques et théories*. Paris: Mon Petit Éditeur.

Gibney, J. (2008). Early modern Ireland: a British Atlantic colony? *History compass*, 6(1), 172–183. https://doi.org/10.1111/j.1478-0542.2007.00505.x

Gilmore, L. (1994). *Autobiographics: a feminist theory of women's representation*. New York: Cornell University.

Gilroy, P. (1987). *There ain't no Black in the Union Jack: the cultural politics of race and nation*. London: Hutchinson.

Gilroy, P. (1993). *The black Atlantic: modernity and double consciousness*. London: Verso.

Gilroy, P. (2000). *Against race: imagining political culture beyond the color line*. Cambridge, MA: Belknap Press of Harvard University Press.

Gish, N. K. (2004). Adoption, identity and voice: interview with Jackie Kay. In M. Novy (Ed.). *Imagining adoption: essays in literature and culture* (pp. 171–80). Ann Arbor: The University of Michigan Press.

Gratton, J. (2001). Autofiction. In M. Jolly (Ed.). *Encyclopedia of life writing: autobiographical and biographical forms*. London: Routledge.

Grell, I. (2014). *L'Autofiction*. Paris: Armand Colin.

Grell, I. (2018). Foreword. In H. Dix (Ed.). *Autofiction in English*. Cham: Palgrave Macmillan.

Gronemann, C. (2019). Autofiction. In M. Wagner-Egelhaaf (Ed.). *Handbook of autobiography/autofiction: volume I theory and concepts* (pp. 241–246). Berlin: de Gruyter.

Gronemann, C. (2019). Serge Doubrovsky: le livre brisé (1989) [the broken book]. In M. Wagner-Egelhaaf (Ed.). *Handbook of autobiography/autofiction: volume I theory and concepts* (pp. 1977–1988). Berlin: de Gruyter.

Hall, S. (1990). Cultural identity and diaspora. In. J. Rutherford (Ed.). *Identity: community, culture, difference* (pp. 222–237). London: Lawrence & Wishart.

Hall, S. (1996). New ethnicities. In D. Morley & K. H. Chen (Eds.). *Stuart Hall: critical dialogues in cultural studies* (pp. 442–451). London: Routledge. (Original work published 1988).

Hall, S. (2017). *Familiar stranger: a life between two islands*. Durham: Duke University Press.

Hamburger, K. (1973). *The logic of literature*. Bloomington: Indiana University Press.

Heti, S. (2007). An interview with Dave Hickey. *Believer*. Retrieved from https://believermag.com/an-interview-with-dave-hickey/

Heti, S. (2010). *How should a person be?*. Toronto: House of Anansi Press.

Heti, S. (2018). *Motherhood*. London: Harvill Secker.

Hooper, K. (2006). On the road: Bernardine Evaristo interviewed by Karen Hooper. *Journal of commonwealth literature*, 41(1), 3–17. https://doi.org/10.1177/0021989406062824

Hubier, S. (2003). *Littératures intimes. Les expressions du moi, de l'autobiographie à l'autofiction*. Paris: Armand Colin.

Hughes, A. (1999). *Heterographies*. Oxford: Berg Publishers.

Hughes, A. (2002). Recycling and repetition in recent French autofiction: Marc Weitzmann's Doubrovskian borrowings. *The modern language review*, 97(3), 566–576. https://doi.org/10.2307/3737492

Hunt, C. (2018). Autofiction as a reflexive mode of thought: implications for personal development. In H. Dix (Ed.). *Autofiction in English* (pp. 179–196). Cham: Palgrave Macmillan.

Hunt, E. (2017). Chris Kraus: I love Dick was written "in a delirium". *The guardian*. Retrieved from https://www.theguardian.com/books/2017/may/30/chris-kraus-i-love-dick-was-written-in-a-delirium

Hutcheon, L. (2006). *A theory of adaptation*. Abingdon, Oxon: Routledge.

Jacobson, R. (2002). The metaphoric and metonymic poles. In Dirven, R. and Pörings, R. (Eds.). *Metaphor and metonymy in comparison and contrast* (pp. 41–48). Berlin; New York: Mouton de Gruyter. (Original Work Published in 1956)

Jacques, J. (2016). The best books on autofiction. Retrieved from https://fivebooks.com/best-books/autobiographical-fiction-juliet-jacques/

Jameson, F. (1984). Postmodernism, or the cultural logic of late capitalism. *New left review*, 146, 53–92.

Jenkins, R. (1997). *Rethinking ethnicity: arguments and explorations* (2nd ed.). London: Sage Publications.

Jensen, M. (2018). How art constitutes the human: aesthetics, empathy and the interesting in autofiction. In H. Dix (Ed.). *Autofiction in English* (pp. 65–83). Cham: Palgrave Macmillan.

Jones, E. H. (2007). *Spaces of belonging: home, culture, and identity in 20th century French autobiography. Spatial practices*, 3. New York: Editions Rodopi.

Jones, E. H. (2009). Serge Doubrovsky: life, writing, legacy. *L'esprit créateur*, 49(3), 1–7. http://www.jstor.org/stable/26289554

Jones, E. H. (2010). Autofiction: a brief history of a neologism. In R. Bradford (Ed.). *Life writing: essays on autobiography, biography and literature* (pp. 174–184). London: Palgrave Macmillan.

Jouve, N. W. (1991). *White woman speaks with forked tongue: criticism as autobiography*. London: Routledge.

Kamali, L. (2016). "Awakening to the singing": Bernardine Evaristo's Lara. *The cultural memory of Africa in African American and Black British fiction, 1970–2000* (pp. 213–241). New York: Palgrave Macmillan. https://doi.org/10.1057/978-1-137-58171-6_8

Kay, J. (1998). *Trumpet*. London: Picador.

Kay, J. (2007). Missing faces. *The guardian*. Retrieved from https://www.theguardian.com/books/2007/mar/24/featuresreviews.guardianreview25

Kay, J. (2010). *Red Dust Roads: an autobiographical journey*. London: Picador.

Kay, J. (2021). I felt a strange grief when I found my birth mother: Jackie Kay on The adoption papers. *The guardian*. Retrieved from https://www.theguardian.com/books/2021/feb/27/i-felt-a-strange-grief-when-i-found-my-birth-mother-jackie-kay-on-the-adoption-papers

Kellaway, K. (2014). Rachel Cusk: "Aftermath was creative death. I was heading into total silence". *The guardian*. Retrieved from https://www.theguardian.com/books/2014/aug/24/rachel-cusk-interview-aftermath-outline

Khair, T. (2017). Ethnicity. In M. R. Thomsen, L. H. Kjaeldgaard, L. Moller, D. Ringggard, L. M. Rösing & P. Simonsen (Eds.). *Literature: an introduction to theory and analysis* (pp. 213–223). London: Bloomsbury Publishing.

Knausgaard, K. O. (2013). *My struggle* (D. Bartlett, Trans.). New York: Farrar Straus & Giroux. (Original work published in 2009)

Kraus, C. (2006). *I love Dick*. Los Angels: Semiotext(e). (First Published in 1997)

Kundera, M. (1981). *The book of laughter and forgetting* (M. H. Heim, Trans.). New York, NY: Penguin Books. (Original work published 1979).

Kunzru, H. (2014, March 7). Karl Ove Knausgaard: the latest literary sensation. *The guardian*. https://www.theguardian.com/books/2014/mar/07/karl-ove-knausgaard-my-struggle-hari-kunzru

Kureishi, H. (1986). The rainbow sign. *My beautiful launderette and the rainbow sign* (pp. 7–38). London: Faber and Faber.

Kureishi, H. (1995). *The black album*. London: Faber and Faber.

Kureishi, H. (2004). *My ear at his heart: reading my father*. London: Faber and Faber.

Kureishi, H. (2009). *The Buddha of suburbia*. London: Faber and Faber. (Original work published 1990)

Lacan, J. (1998). *The four fundamental concepts of psychoanalysis: seminar of Jacques Lacan book XI* (A. Sheridan, Trans.; J. A. Miller, Ed.). New York: W. W. Norton & Company. (Original work published in 1973).

Lacan, J. (2006). The situation of psychoanalysis and the training of psychoanalysts in 1956. *Ecrits* (B. Fink, Trans., pp. 384–411). New York: W. W. Norton & Company. (Original work published in 1956).

Lacan, J. (2006). The instance of the letter in the unconscious, or reason since Freud. *Ecrits* (B. Fink, Trans., pp. 412–441). New York: W. W. Norton & Company. (Original work published in 1957).

Lara, Bernardine Evaristo (n.d.). Retrieved from https://mixedmuseum.org.uk/amri-exhibition/lara-bernadine-evaristo/

Lecarme, J. (1993). L'autofiction: un mauvais genre? In S. Doubrovsky, J. Lecarme & P. Lejeune (Eds.). *Autofictions & Cie* (pp. 227–249). Nanterre: Université Paris X.

Lerner, B. (2014). *10:04*. New York: Faber & Faber.

Lejeune, P. (1989). The autobiographical pact. In Eakin, P. J. (Ed.). *On autobiography* (K. M. Leary, Trans., pp. 3–30). Minneapolis: University of Minnesota Press. (Original work published in 1975)

Lejeune, P. (1989). *On autobiography*. Minneapolis: University of Minnesota Press. (Original work published in 1975)

Lin, T. (2013). *Taipei*. New York: Vintage.

Lin, T. (2014). An interview with Ben Lerner. *Believer*. Retrieved from https://believermag.com/an-interview-with-ben-lerner/

Lin, T. (2018). *Trip: psychedelics, alienation, and change*. New York: Vintage.

Lorentzen, C. (2018). Sheila Heti, Ben Lerner, Tao Lin: how "auto" is autofiction? *New york vulture*. Retrieved from https://www.vulture.com/2018/05/how-auto-is-autofiction.html

Lyotard, J. F. (1984). *The postmodern condition: a report on knowledge* (G. Bennington & B. Maussumi, Trans.). Minneapolis: University of Minnesota Press. (Original work published in 1979).

Marcus, L. (2018). *Autobiography: very short introduction*. Oxford: Oxford University Press.

Menn, R. (2018). Unpicked and remade: creative imperatives in John Burnside's autofictions. In H. Dix (Ed.). *Autofiction in English* (pp. 163–78). Cham: Palgrave Macmillan.

Min, T. H. (2004). Never forgetting the source: Bernardine Evaristo makes productive use of history. *Quarterly literary review Singapore*, 3(2). Retrieved from http://www.qlrs.com/issues/jan2004/interviews/bevaristo.html

Mirza, H. S. (1997). Introduction: mapping a genealogy of black British feminism. In H. S. Mirza (Ed.). *Black British feminism* (pp. 1–28). London and New York: Routledge.

Mormons (2021). In *History*. Retrieved January 15, 2023, from https://www.history.com/topics/religion/Mormons

Muñoz-Valdivieso, S. (2004). Interview with Bernardine Evaristo. *Obsidian III literature in African diaspora*, 5(2), 9-20. https://www.jstor.org/stable/44479690

Murray, P. (1999). Stories told and untold: post-colonial London in Bernardine Evaristo's Lara. *Kunapipi*, 21(2), 38-46. https://ro.uow.edu.au/kunapipi/vol21/iss2/9

Nalbantian, S. (2003). *Memory in literature: from Rousseau to neuroscience.* Hampshire: Palgrave Macmillan.

Nasta, S. (Ed.). (2004). Jackie Kay with Richard Dyer. In *Writing across worlds: contemporary writers talk* (pp. 237-249). London: Routledge.

Nelson, M. (2015). *The argonauts*. Minneapolis, Minnesota: Graywolf Press.

Niven, A. (2001). Alastair Niven in conversation with Bernardine Evaristo, *Wasafiri*, 16(34), 15-20. https://doi.org/10.1080/02690050108589749

O'Brien, T. (2009). *The things they carried*. New York: Houghton Mifflin Harcourt. (Original work published in 1990).

O'Byrne, C. (2019). 'Betwixt and between': rereading Poppy as autofiction. *Philament*, 25,7-28. Retrieved from http://www.philamentjournal.com/articles/betwixt-and-between-rereading-poppy-as-autofiction/

Offill, J. (2014). *Dept. of Speculation*. New York: Knopf.

Ouellette-Michalska, M. (2007). *Autofiction et dévoilement de soi: Essai*. Montréal, Québec: Les Éditions XYZ.

Page, B. (2010). Jackie Kay: relative strangers. Retrieved from https://www.thebookseller.com/author-interviews/relative-strangers

Parks, T. (2018). How best to read auto-fiction. *The New York review*. Retrieved from https://www.nybooks.com/daily/2018/05/25/how-best-to-read-auto-fiction/

Payne, T. (2003, Mar 15). A writer's life Bernadine Evaristo. *The daily telegraph*. Retrieved from http://lproxy.yeditepe.edu.tr/login?url=https://www.proquest.com/newspapers/writers-life-bernadine-evaristo/docview/317707838/se-2

Phillips, A. (2011). *Tragedy of Arthur*. New York: Random House.

Pitcher McDonough, S. (2011). *How to read autofiction* (Honors thesis), Wesleyan University, Middletown, Connecticut. Retrieved from https://citeseerx.ist.psu.edu/viewdoc/download?doi=10.1.1.648.2641&rep=rep1&type=pdf

Powers, R. (1995). *Galatea 2.2*. New York: HarperCollins.

Power, C. (2018). After autofiction. *The new statesman*. Retrieved from https://www.newstatesman.com/uncategorized/2018/08/after-autofiction

Pratt, M. L. (1992). *Imperial eyes: travel writing and transculturation*. London and New York: Routledge.

Pratt, M. L. (1994). Transculturation and autoethnography: Peru 1615/1980. In F. Barker, P. Holme, & M. Iverson (Eds.) *Colonial discourse/postcolonial theory* (pp. 24–46). Manchester and New York: Manchester University Press.

Proust, M. (1992). *In search of lost time* (Trans. C.K. Scott-Moncrieff & T. Kilmartin, Rev. D. J. Enright). London: Chatto & Windus. (Original work published in 1913)

Rankine, C. (2014). *Citizen*. Minneapolis, Minnesota: Graywolf Press.

Reed-Danahay, D. E. (Ed.). (1997). *Auto/Ethnography: rewriting the self and the social*. New York: Berg.

Rhydderch, F. (2003). How black is noir? *New welsh review*, 61, 2–5. Retrieved from https://newwelshreview.com/product/new-welsh-review-61-autumn-2003

Robin, R. (1997). L'autofiction: Le sujet toujours en défaut. In S. Doubrovsky, J. Lecarme & P. Lejeune (Eds.). *Autofictions & Cie* (pp. 73–86). Nanterre: Université Paris X.

Roth, P. (1994). *Operation shylock: a confession*. New York: Vintage.

Rousseau, J. J. (1953). *The confessions* (J. M. Cohen, Trans.). London: Penguin Books. (Original work published in 1782–1789).

Said, E. W. (1978). *Orientalism*. New York: Random House.

Said, E. E. (1994). *Culture and Imperialism*. New York: Vintage Books.

Said, E. W. (1999). *Out of place*. New York: Alfred A. Knopf, Inc.

Saunders, M. (2008). Life-writing, cultural memory, and literary studies. In A. Erll & A. Nünning (Eds.). *A companion to cultural memory studies: an international and interdisciplinary handbook* (pp. 321–332). Berlin: De Grutyer.

Saussure, F. de (1959). *Course in general linguistics*. New York: McGraw-Hill. (Original work published in 1916).

Schacter, D. (1995). *Memory distortion: how minds, brains, and societies reconstruct the past*. Cambridge, MA: Harvard University Press.

Schmitt, A. (2010). Making the case for self-narration against autofiction. *a/b: auto/biography studies*, 25(1), 122–137. https://doi.org/10.1080/08989575.2010.10815365

Schmitt, A. & Kjerkegaard, S. (2016). Karl Ove Knausgaard's my struggle: a real life in a novel. *a/b: auto/biography studies*, 31(3), 553–579. https://doi.org/10.1080/08989575.2016.1184543

Schmitt, A. (2020). Avatars as the raison d'être of autofiction. *Life writing*, 19(1), 1–12. https://doi.org/10.1080/14484528.2020.1753486

Schoene, B. (1998). Emerging as the others of our selves: Scottish multiculturalism and the challenge of body in postcolonial representation. *Scottish studies review*, 25(1), pp. 54–72. ISSN 1475-7737

Schwartz, A. (2018). "I don't think character exists anymore": a conversation with Rachel Cusk. *The New Yorker*. Retrieved from https://www.newyorker.com/culture/the-new-yorker-interview/i-dont-think-character-exists-anymore-a-conversation-with-rachel-cusk

Sheppard, L. (2018). Autoethnography in post-British literatures: a comparative reading of Charlotte Williams and Jackie Kay. In H. Dix (Ed.). *Autofiction in English*. Cham: Palgrave Macmillan.

Shields, D. (2010). *Reality hunger: a manifesto*. New York: Vintage.

Smith, S. (1987). *A poetics of women's autobiography*. Indiana: Indiana University Press.

Smith, S. & Watson, J. (2002). *Reading autobiography: A guide for interpreting life narratives*. Minneapolis: University of Minnesota Press.

Snauwaert, E. (2020). Autofiction and its fantastic modalities in César Aira's cómo me hice monja. *Alambique. Revista académica de ciencia ficción y fantasía/ Jornal acadêmico de ficção científica e fantasia*, 7(2), 1–19. https://doi.org/10.5038/2167-6577.7.2.3

Somerville-Arjat, G. & Wilson, R. E. (Eds.). Jackie Kay. *Sleeping with monsters: conversations with Scottish and Irish women poets* (pp. 120–130). Edinburgh: Polygon.

Spear, T. C. (1998). Autofiction and national identity. *Sites*, 2(1), 89–105. https://doi.org/10.1080/10260219808455928

Stanley, L. (1992). *The auto/biographical I: theory and practice of feminist autobiography*. Manchester: Manchester University Press

Stumm, B. (2019). The phenomenology of autobiography: making it real by Arnaud Schmitt (review). *Biography*, 40(2), 451–455.

Sturgeon, J. (2014). The death of the postmodern novel and the rise of autofiction. Retrieved from https://www.flavorwire.com/496570/2014-the-death-of-the-postmodern-novel-and-the-rise-of-autofiction

Sturgeon, N. (2010). Introduction. In Kay, *Red dust road* (pp. ix–xiv). London: Picador.

Sukenick, R. (1999). *Up: a novel*. Normal, IL: First Collective 2. (First published in 1968)

The Welsh slave owner and anti-abolitionist MP Richard Pennant. (2015). Retrieved from https://www.blackhistorymonth.org.uk/article/section/history-of-slavery/the-welsh-slave-owner-and-anti-abolitionist-mp-richard-pennant/

Tomson, G. (2018). More life: on contemporary autofiction and the scourge of "relatability". *Mrq online*. Retrieved from https://sites.lsa.umich.edu/mqr/2018/08/more-life-on-contemporary-autofiction-and-the-scourge-of-relatability/

Toplu, Ş. (2011). *Fiction unbound: Bernardine Evaristo*. Newcastle: Cambridge Scholars Publishing.

Tournay-Theodotou, P. (2014). Some connection with the place. *Wasafiri*, 29(1), 15–20. https://doi.org/10.1080/02690055.2014.861254

Upstone, S. (2011). Hanif Kureishi. *British Asian Fiction: Twenty-first-century voices* (pp. 37–61). Manchester: Manchester University Press.

Upstone, S. (2015). Postcolonial and diasporic voices – bringing Black to the Union Jack: ethnic fictions and the politics of possibility. In N. Hubble, P. Tew, & L. Wilson (Eds.). *The 1990s: a decade of contemporary British fiction* (pp. 123–148). London: Bloomsbury Academic.

Vinson, S. F. (2018). Lives in story: Tim O'Brian's the things they carried. In H. Dix (Ed.). *Autofiction in English* (pp. 145–159). Cham: Palgrave Macmillan.

Vonnegut, K. (1973). *Breakfast of champions, or goodbye blue monday*. New York: Random House.

Wagner-Egelhaaf, M. (2019). Introduction: autobiography/autofiction across disciplines. In M. Wagner-Egelhaaf (Ed.). *Handbook of autobiography /autofiction: volume I theory and concepts* (pp. 1–7). Berlin: de Gruyter.

Wallace, D. F. (2011). *The pale king*. New York: Little, Brown.

Watson, J. (2001). Autoethnography. In M. Jolly (Ed.). *Encyclopedia of autobiographical and biographical forms volume I A-K* (pp. 83–85). London and Chicago: Fitzroy Dearborn Publishers.

Weber, M. (1978). *Economy and society*. In G. Roth & C. Wittich (Eds.). Berkeley: University of California Press. (Original work published in 1922)

Weedon, C. (2004). *Identity and culture: narratives of difference and belonging*. Berkshire: Open University Press.

Weedon, C. (2004). Identity and belonging in contemporary Black British writing. In V. Arana & L. Ramey (Eds.). *Black British writing* (pp. 73–97). Basingstoke: Palgrave Macmillan.

Weedon, C. (2008). Migration, identity, and belonging in British Black and South Asian women's writing. *Contemporary women's writing*, 2(1), 17–35. https://doi.org/10.1093/cww/vpn003

White, H. (1985). *Tropics of discourse: essays on cultural criticism*. Baltimore: The Johns Hopkins University Press.

Williams, C. (2002). *Sugar and slate*. Kingston, Jamaica: Ian Randle Publishers.

Williams, C. (2003). From Llandudno to Llanrumney: inscribing the nation. *New welsh review*, 62, 27–34. Retrieved from https://newwelshreview.com/interview-with-charlotte-williams

Williams, C. & Johnson, M. R. D. (2010). *Race and ethnicity in a welfare society*. Berkshire: Open University Press.

Woolf, K. M. (2010). In conversation: Bernardine Evaristo on updating Lara. http://opennotebooks.co.uk/2010/09/bernardine-evaristo-on-updating-lara/

Worthington, M. (2017). Fiction in the "post-truth" era: The ironic effects of autofiction. *Critique: studies in contemporary fiction*, 58(5), 471–483. https://doi.org/10.1080/00111619.2017.1331999

Worthington, M. (2018). *The story of "me": contemporary American autofiction*. Lincoln: University of Nebraska Press.

Young, S. (1997). *Changing the wor(l)d: discourse, politics, and the feminist movement*. New York: Routledge.

Zipfel, F. (2005). Autofiction. In D. Herman, M. Jahn & M. L. Ryan (Eds.). *Routledge encyclopaedia of narrative theory* (pp. 36–37). London and New York: Routledge.

www.ingramcontent.com/pod-product-compliance
Lightning Source LLC
Chambersburg PA
CBHW052021290426
44112CB00014B/2321